# The Book of the Dead

# WORKS ON EGYPTOLOGY

AND

# KINDRED SUBJECTS.

## BY THE TRANSLATOR OF "THE BOOK OF THE DEAD."

**An Egyptian Reading Book for Beginners:** Being a Series of Historical, Funereal, Moral, Religious, and Mythological Texts, printed in Hieroglyphic Characters, together with a Transliteration and a complete Vocabulary. By E. A. WALLIS BUDGE, Litt. D. (Cantab.), Keeper of the Egyptian and Assyrian Antiquities in the British Museum. Demy 8vo. Price 15s. net.

*Uniform with the above.*

**First Steps in Egyptian.** By E. A. WALLIS BUDGE. Price 9s. net.

**TYLOR, J. J., Wall Drawings and Monuments of El Kab.** Part I.: Paheri. 18 Plates. With Notes by SOMERS CLARKE. £2 2s. [Other Parts in preparation].

**BUDGE, E. A. WALLIS, The Book of the Dead.** The Papyrus of Ani, in the British Museum. With Translation and Transliteration. 4to, half-morocco, £1 10s.

**Archaic Classics, Assyrian Texts.** Being Extracts from the Annals of Shalmaneser II., Sennacherib, and Assur-Bani-Pal, with Philological Notes. Small 4to, 7s. 6d.

**History of Esarhaddon.** (Son of Sennacherib), King of Assyria, B.C. 681-668. Translated from the Cuneiform Inscriptions in the British Museum. Post 8vo, 10s. 6d. *(Trübners Oriental Series.)*

**Inscriptions in the Hieratic and Demotic Character.** Folio, £1 7s. 6d.

**Egyptian Texts of the Earliest Period.** From the Coffin of Amamu. 32 Coloured Plates. Folio, £2 2s.

**Fac-simile of an Egyptian Hieratic Papyrus of the Reign of Rameses III.,** now in the British Museum. Folio, £3.

**Photographs of the Papyrus of Nebseni,** in the British Museum. Unmounted, £2 2s.; or, mounted and in portfolio, on special terms.

# A VOCABULARY

IN HIEROGLYPHIC
TO THE THEBAN RECENSION
OF THE

# BOOK OF THE DEAD

BY

E. A. WALLIS BUDGE
LITT. D., D. LIT., F. S. A.
KEEPER OF THE EGYPTIAN AND ASSYRIAN ANTIQUITIES
IN THE BRITISH MUSEUM



LONDON
KEGAN PAUL, TRENCH, TRÜBNER & CO., LTD.
PATERNOSTER HOUSE, CHARING CROSS ROAD
1898.

Printed by Adolphus Holzhausen, Vienna.

# PREFACE.

THE following pages contain a Vocabulary to all the hieroglyphic texts of the Chapters in the edition of the Theban Recension of the Book of the Dead which is issued simultaneously with the English translation of that work, and also to the supplementary Chapters from the Saïte Recension which are given therewith. To have made a concordance would have entailed needless labour, but wherever possible a large number of references have been given in order that the reader may have abundant examples of the various uses of words for purposes of comparison and identification of passages. In the case of words of unfrequent occurrence I have given all the examples found in the book. The arrangement of the words and their various forms is usually alphabetical, and it is hoped that the exceptions to this rule will cause the reader no difficulty.

The order of the letters and syllables is that adopted by the late Dr. Brugsch and M. Pierret; for the values of the latter the reader is referred to the grammars and sign-lists.

My thanks are due to Mr. Holzhausen of Vienna for the care which he has taken in printing the long series of hieroglyphic texts and this Vocabulary.

E. A. WALLIS BUDGE.

# ALPHABETIC EGYPTIAN CHARACTERS.

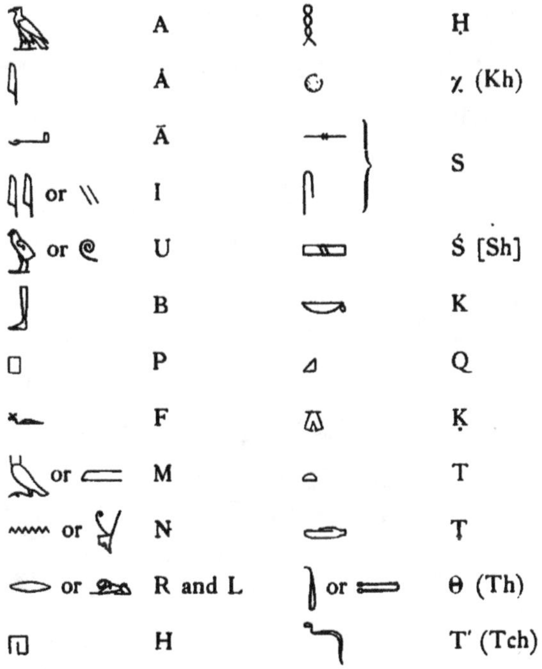

A
Á
Ā
or I
or U
B
P
F
or M
or N
or R and L
H
Ḥ
χ (Kh)
S
Ś [Sh]
K
Q
Ḳ
T
Ṭ
or θ (Th)
T′ (Tch)

# A.

**aata** or **atita** ministrant 449. 2

**aȧr** to put in restraint, to tie together 307. 4; 493. 9

**au** the young 280. 8; var. *šeriu* children.

**ausek** sceptre 340. 2

**ait** cakes or bread for offerings 507. 14

**apṭ**
**apṭu** feathered fowl, birds offered as sacrifices 229. 9; 251. 8; 292. 11; 294. 8; 332. 16; 366. 6; 400. 5, 10; 454. 1; 510. 3

**af** offerings (?) 449. 13

**afu** to injure 165. 15

***Amu*** the Fire City 203. 5

**am**
**amem** to grasp 113. 7; 190. 7; 482. 10; 487. 5

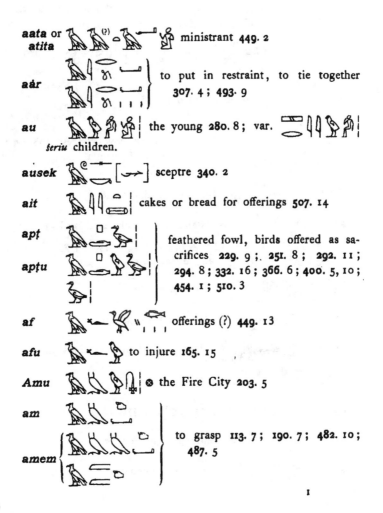

**ames** sceptre **335.** 2, 12; **336.** 8; **337.** 4, 15; **338.** 12; **339.** 7; **340.** 15; **341.** 11

***Ani*** name of a scribe **1.** 4, 11; **25.** 15; **58.** 16; **72.** 16; **73.** 8, 16; **130.** 15; **176.** 8; **189.** 4; **197.** 16; **246.** 6; **247.** 3; **248.** 9, 16; **288.** 1; **359.** 5; **457.** 10

***Areθi-ka-sa-θika*** proper name **418.** 14

**ah** to be troubled **149.** 6

**ahat** name of a cow-goddess **408.** 15; **409.** 3, 13; **410.** 1

***Ahit*** name of a goddess **326.** 6

**aḥet** fields, estates, farm, cultivated land **23.** 9; **27.** 17; **124.** 9; **198.** 11; **203.** 14; **209.** 14; **243.** 12; **251.** 3; **268.** 5; **398.** 7; **417.** 15; **493.** 3; **495.** 14

**aχ** to blossom **229.** 8

**aχab** to give to drink **397.** 9

**aχabiu** a class of divine beings **391.** 13

**aχaχ** stars **153.** 10

**aχi** reeds, water-plants **378.** 13

**asu** running water **251.** 11

***Aseb*** name of a fire-god **152.** 15; **153.** 1

**asbiu** 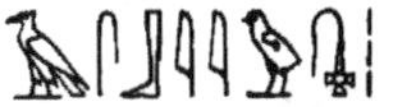 flame, fire 134. 3

**aseχ**  to reap 209. 15; 222. 4; 224. 2; 225. 10; 227. 8; 229. 15; 368. 4; 369. 5; 454. 11; 496. 3

**asta åb** (?) 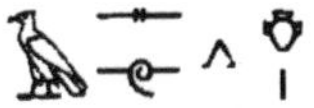 to judge hastily 256. 14; 257. 5

**Aśu**  name of a god 200. 9

**Aśbu**  the warder of the fifth Ārit 328. 10

**Aśer**  name of a city or god 325. 4

**aśer**, **aśert**  roasted joints of animals, or birds 294. 8; 300. 1; 317. 8; 318. 3

**Aker**  a proper name 199. 11; 205. 14

**Akeru**  name of two gods 140. 4; 391. 13

 a proper name 391. 13

 a proper name 393. 9

**akriu** 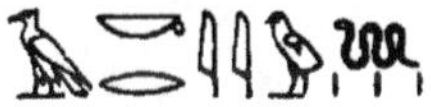 divine serpents 220. 8; 370. 15

**aḳab**  flood, flowing stream, a mass of water or the god thereof 27. 16; 132. 5; 456. 13; 464. 1; 465. 16; 493. 14

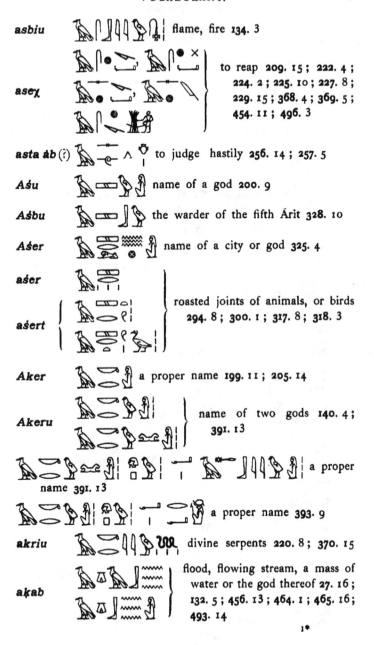

1*

**aḳbȧ** watery abyss 136. 5

**at**
**atu** injury 237. 3; 401. 13

**at** standard 486. 16

**at** back 413. 16

**at** moment 115. 2; 126. 10; 157. 9, 10; 210. 12; 251. 11; 280. 2; 281. 12; 283. 14; 295. 2, 12; 299. 14; 310. 12, 13; 356. 6; 482. 14; 483. 7

**āt**
**atet** moment 2. 16; 34. 12; 38. 16; 42. 4; 359. 8

**at** = *at* standard 359. 16

**at** = *ȧt* not 462. 7

**atui** fiends 416. 15

**atutu** a kind of wood 337. 5

***Ati***
***Atet*** the ninth nome of Lower Egypt, the capital of which was Per-Ȧusȧr (Busiris) 321. 4; 323. 9

**atep** load 139. 2; 144. 2

**atef** name of a crown 276. 13; 477. 3; 482. 9; 487. 7

**atfu** name of a crown 262. 3

***Atef-ur*** a proper name **321**. 14 ; **324**. 7

**aṭ** to be wounded **94**. 2

**aṭȧu** name of a garment **438**. 2

**aṭu** crocodile **299**. 4 ; **310**. 13 ; plur. **160**. 2 ; **283**. 16

***Aṭes-ḥrȧ-śe*** a proper name **361**. 8

***aṭet*** back **414**. 2

# A.

**ȧ** I, me, my 2. 14; 3. 5; 3. 6; 4. 13; 5. 5; 15. 13; 417. 1

**ȧ** O 307. 12, 13, 14

**ȧ** O! Hail! 1. 12; 10. 13; 20. 12; 21. 1; 25. 16; 26. 1, 10; 27. 3; 29. 7; 39. 15, 16; 61. 7; 64. 1; 66. 5; 71. 3, 14; 72. 7, 15; 73. 7; 74. 5, 13; 75. 8; 81. 3; 83. 2; 84. 1; 87. 11; 90. 9; 91. 15; 92. 1, 2; 98. 1; 100. 11; 101. 11; 105. 14; 107. 5, 13; 110. 12, 15; 111. 7; 115. 13; 120. 14; 130. 15; 147. 7; 169. 1; 189. 4, 5; 196. 12; 197. 16; 203. 8; 244. 7; 252. 13; 253. 12; 254. 11; 255. 5; 256. 8; 262. 2; 272. 2; 274. 12; 275. 4; 289. 10; 301. 8; 358. 12; 364. 9, 10, 11, 12; 365. 5, 6, 12, 13, 14, 15; 367. 4; 369. 7; 370. 1; 371. 3; 372. 8; 373. 5; 384. 6, 11; 390. 4; 396. 1; 410. 6; 418. 9; 445. 4, 5, 13; 446. 16; 447. 9; 448. 4, 13; 450. 5, 16; 451. 9; 457. 10; 458. 7; 460. 3; 468. 5; 496. 4; 502. 7; 503. 4

**ȧ** acclamation 11. 5

**ȧa** boat 50. 7

**ȧa** standard 483. 16

**ȧaa** plants, growing crops 203. 12

**áaau** doubly plumed 456. 7

**áaat** standard 277. 16

**áau** aged one, old age 177. 2; 182. 14; 199. 7; 325. 6; 361. 3; 488. 5; plur. 243. 6

**áaut** aged one 183. 13

**áait** divine aged ones 133. 8; 134. 2

**áau**, **áaut** praise, acclamation, rejoicings 2. 2; 46. 2, 9; 49. 15; 108. 1; 164. 15; 175. 16; 223. 3; 230. 12; 246. 8; 281. 10; 282. 13, 15; 289. 13; 388. 12; 389. 6, 14; 392. 8; 484. 3; 489. 9

**áau** praise 484. 7; 486. 13

**áau** praise 305. 14

**áaiu** praise 7. 5, 10; 452. 7

**áaui** praise 22. 15; 316. 8; 342. 15; 416. 5

**áait** tombs under the care of priests 309. 16

**áaiti** the gods of the Áats 319. 12

see 30. 13

***Áaru*** the city of reeds 465. 16

**áaru** plants, reeds 301. 9

**åareret** eyes (?) **356.** 4

**åaret** vine **185.** 6; **287.** 5

***Aaheṭ*** name of a god (?) **168.** 16; **169.** 2

**åaχu** the god of light **244.** 10

***Åaχabit*** name of a goddess **343.** 6; **344.** 13

***Åaku*** a class of beings in Re-stau **240.** 6

**åakebi**, **åakebit** mourners, wailing women, those who weep **19.** 8; **177.** 11; **352.** 14

**åakebu** wailings **243.** 1; **432.** 3

**åaqet** flowers **101.** 15

***Åaqeṭqeṭ*** name of a god **59.** 8

**åat** dignity, rank **13.** 11; **482.** 16; **485.** 8; plur. **250.** 5

**åaat** odorous things **469.** 13

**åat** girdle **239.** 5

**åat** back **112.** 16; **117.** 15; **169.** 6

**åat** to cleave **212.** 6

**ȧat** standard, perch, pedestal **101.** 6 *(bis)*; **112.** 1; **166.** 11; **175.** 9; **184.** 14; **262.** 3; **358.** 16; **360.** 2

**ȧat ent Ȧp-uat** name of the lower deck **206.** 1

**ȧat** domain, district in the underworld **55.** 6; **64.** 8; **179.** 11; **367.** 4; **369.** 7, 10; **370.** 2; **371.** 3, 6; **377.** 6, 10, 14; **378.** 4; **379.** 1, 3, 11; **381.** 14; plur. **369.** 11; **185.** 16; **367.** 3;— **367.** 11;— **369.** 6;— **369.** 15;— **371.** 2;— **371.** 13;— **372.** 7;— **373.** 4;— **374.** 1;— **375.** 1;— **375.** 15;— **377.** 4;— **378.** 2;— **379.** 11

**ȧat χu** **369.** 6; **381.** 7

**ȧat en χet** **64.** 9

**ȧati** the two *Ȧats* of Osiris **240.** 7, 8; **477.** 8

**Ȧat-urt** a proper name **324.** 12

**Ȧat ent χer-āba** the Ȧat of Kher-āba **379.** 11, 13; **382.** 1

**ȧatu** praise **24.** 16

**ȧati** shambles **66.** 9, 12

**ȧaṭ** child, young man **185.** 10

**ȧaṭet**
**ȧaṭeti** — net 390. 3, 10; 394. 1; 396. 3; 436. 10
**ȧaṭet**

**ȧaṭet** rain storm, dew 202. 15; 356. 10

**ȧaṭeti** oppressor 408. 14

**ȧā** to wash 218. 2; 439. 6; 449. 5; 450. 12; 483. 7; washing, cleansing 19. 13

**ȧā neter** to curse the god (?) 257. 8; 257. 14

**ȧāāu** apes 28. 6

**ȧāb** to come towards, to meet, to present something 133. 10; 479. 3; one opposite 229. 13; for, on behalf of 309. 10; offering 407. 1 *(bis)*

**ȧāb** offering of a libation 389. 2

**ȧāb** a vessel 333. 8, 11; 422. 5, 7, 9, 10, 13, 15; 423. 2, 12, 15; 425. 4, 6, 9, 12, 15; 425. 4, 8, 10, 13, 16; 426. 3, 6, 8, 11, 14; 427. 1, 4, 7, 10, 13, 16; 428. 3, 6, 9, 12; 428. 2, 4, 8, 10, 13; 430. 1, 4, 7, 10, 13, 15; 431. 3, 6, 9, 12, 15; 432. 2, 4, 7, 10, 13, 16; 433. 2, 5, 8, 11; 434. 3, 7, 10, 12, 15; 435. 2, 5, 8

**ȧābet** offerings 336. 1, 2; 433. 13

**ȧānu** praise 33. 3; 34. 11; 215. 1; plur. 180. 10; 280. 5

**àār** — uraeus 46. 5; 181. 8; 456. 12; 326. 10; plur. *āāretu*
**àāret** — uraei goddesses 244. 7; 265. 8;
**àāretu** — uraei 377. 9

**àārti** *i. e.*, Isis and Nephthys 169. 8

**àārtu ānχu** the living uraei 267. 7

**àāḥ** — moon 294. 15; 397. 6
**àāḥu**

***Àāḥ*** Moon-god 26. 1 *(bis)*; 26. 10, 11; 177. 3; 391. 16; 445. 15

**àātu ent χert** lower deck 206. 1

**àu** praises 416. 3

**àu** = *àa* old man 128. 18

**àu** = *er* from, to, into, for, at, in 509. 2, 5, 11; 510. 2, 11; 511. 4, 8, 16; 513. 3

**àu** , limbs, members, flesh 128. 16; 417. 13

**àu** to be:— *àu-à* I am 14. 12; 120. 1; 122. 4; *àu-k* thou art 6. 7; 11. 4; 13. 13; *àu-f* he is 23. 5; *àu-n* we are 32. 7; 301. 9; *àu-s* 304. 5, 7, 8, 9, *etc.* As an auxiliary *àu ufā* 16. 1; 16. 2; and see *passim.*

**àua** ox (of Seb) 264. 13; 265. 10

*Àuu-ba* a proper name **435.** 6

*àuf* limbs, members, flesh **23.** 8; **46.** 7; **118.** 14; **130.** 8; **140.** 6; **195.** 4; **317.** 7; **411.** 3; **441.** 1; **478.** 10

*Àuf-ānχ* a proper name **34.** 6; **77.** 10; **78.** 4, 8, 14; **80.** 2, 12; **98.** 8; **131.** 7; **245.** 15; **276.** 9; **294.** 16; **295.** 4, 6; **314.** 14; **316.** 9; **334.** 8; **335.** 3, 14; **336.** 10; **337.** 6; **338.** 1, 14; **339.** 8; **340.** 4; **341.** 1, 13; **342.** 4, 11; **343.** 2, 10; **344.** 1, 9, 15; **345.** 7, 15; **346.** 6; **349.** 7; **404.** 4; **405.** 1, 10; **411.** 7; **412.** 7, 10; **413.** 8; **419.** 4; **412.** 6; **413** 2; **501.** 4, 12

*àumes* entreaty (?) **151.** 6

*àun* . . . . . . **257.** 13

*àuhet* to utter words **263.** 15

*àuχemu* stars (?) **231.** 3

*àuχemu urṭu* stars which rest **35.** 16; **171.** 4; **203.** 1; **214.** 10

*àuχemu seku* stars which diminish **36.** 1; **119.** 12; **308.** 7; **377.** 12

*àuχemu-pen-*. . . . (?) . . . . . . . **494.** 8, 15; **495.** 3, 7, 15

*àuχeχ* night **256.** 16

*àuχeχu* darkness **354.** 13

*Àusàr* the god Osiris **1.** 12; **3.** 9, 10; **132.** 10; **137.** 14; **153.** 1; **198.**

10; 271. 3; 273. 16; 315. 11; 443. 9; and the eight gods of his company 294. 4

***Ȧusȧr*** a name given to the deceased, who is generally identified with the god, see *passim.*

***Ȧusȧr*** Osiris 39. 7; 214. 1

***Ȧusȧr-Ȧnpu*** 428. 10

***Ȧusȧr-ānχti*** 320. 9

***Ȧusȧr-Un-nefer*** 276. 10; 285. 8; 484. 4, 6

***Ȧusȧr-bati-Erpit*** 321. 2

***Ȧusȧr-Ptaḥ-neb-ānχ*** 321. 2

***Ȧusȧr-nub-ḥeḥ*** 321. 2

***Ȧusȧr-neb-ānχ*** 320. 9

***Ȧusȧr-neb-er-ṭer*** 24. 5; 320. 10

***Ȧusȧr-neṭesti*** 321. 14

***Ȧusȧr-Ḥenti*** Osiris of two crocodiles 324. 3

***Ȧusȧr-Ḥeru*** 513. 6

***Ȧusȧr-Ḥeru-χuti-Tem*** 325. 13

***Ȧusȧr-ḥer-ȧb-set*** Osiris in the mountain 321. 3

***Ȧusȧr-ḥer-šāi-f*** Osiris on his sand 322. 3

***Ȧusȧr-χent-Ȧbṭu*** Osiris in Abydos 489. 8

**Ausår-χent-Åmentet**  Osiris, governor of Åmentet 77. 13; 78. 5, 7, 9; 326. 12; 347. 14; 501. 9

**Ausår-χent-Åmentiu**  Osiris, governor of those in Åmentet 479. 14; 512. 1; 514. 5, 12

**Ausår-χenti-Åmenti**  common name of Osiris 271. 13, 16; 274. 16; 275. 1; 303. 15; 304. 3, 6, 10; 305. 2; 306. 1, 5, 7, 10; 307. 8; 308. 10; 318. 4

**Ausår-χenti-per** 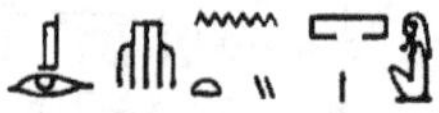 320. 12

**Ausår-χenti-Nefer** (?) 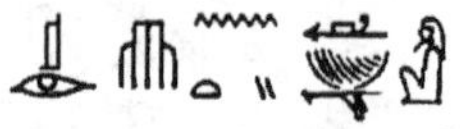 320. 10

**Ausår-χenti-nut-f** 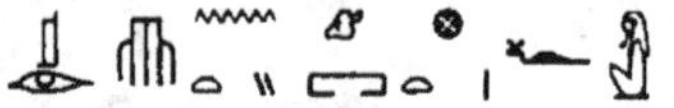 321. 11

**Ausår-χenti-Re-stau**  321. 3

**Ausår-χenti-Seḥ-ḥemt** 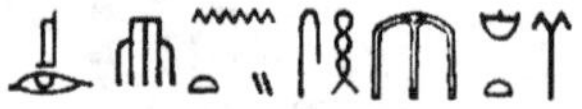 322. 4

**Ausår sa Nut**  477. 3

**Ausår-Saa**  320. 11

**Ausår-Seb**  153. 7

**Ausår-Saḥ**  320. 11

**Ausår-Sekri**  321. 10, 15

**Ausår-Tua (Uta)**  321. 15

**Ausår-Taiti**  322. 2

***Ȧusȧr-Ṭem-ur*** 321. 14

***Ȧusȧrti*** beings like Osiris 189. 9

***Ȧuset*** the goddess Isis 67. 2; 68. 4; 69. 7; 73. 5; 153. 1, 2; 192. 3, 10; 232. 10; 276. 16; 277. 3; 382. 12; 454. 16; 486. 13; 37. 14; 46. 14; 79. 13; 81. 13; 83. 9; 112. 12; 117. 7; 166. 11; 208. 13; 210. 15; 233. 9; 293. 8; 294. 4; 301. 15; 315. 13; 318. 9; 339. 4; 375. 11; 403. 4, 5, 11; 404. 4; 405. 2; 407. 11; 443. 9; 464. 10; 478. 17; 479. 13; 12. 14; 15. 6; 53. 12; 65. 9; 72. 4; 73. 11, 13; 74. 5; 76. 8; 394. 14; = 326. 4

***ȧuset*** seat, place, habitation, abode, shrine 3. 8; 22. 16; 58. 5; 65. 9; 70. 15; 79. 10; 80. 6; 92. 8; 100. 6; 103. 2, 4; 114. 2; 111. 8; 119. 13; 121. 3; 127. 10; 161. 11; 162. 17; 246. 11; 315. 7; 320. 16; 326. 13; 348. 15; 385. 12; 394. 10; 406. 10; 415. 7; 426. 5; 429. 3, 14; 441. 11; 442. 6, 12; 443. 13; 446. 15; 447. 8; 456. 6, 9, 11; 457. 14; 459. 14; 471. 9; 473. 9; 476. 9, 10; 486. 2; 493. 12; plur. , 195. 15; 279. 6; 280. 12; 321. 12, 13

***ȧuset ȧb-f*** the heart's chosen place 226. 3

***ȧuset āāui*** place of the hands 234. 8

***ȧuset urt*** great place, heaven 2. 9; 218. 1; 485. 10

***ȧuset uṭat*** seat of the Eye of the sun 38. 15

***ȧuset maāt*** place where right is done 250. 3

***ȧuset ḥert*** heaven 135. 3

**àuset ḥeḥ** everlasting abode 416. 8

**àuset ḥetep** place of repose 416. 6; 490. 12

**àuset ḥetep àb** place of rest for the heart 430. 13

**àuset śetau en Ḥeru** secret places of Horus 404. 5

**àuset qebḥ** place of coolness or refreshment 430. 5

**àuset taa** abode of fire 430. 6

**àuset ṭesert** holy place, shrine 433. 4

**Àuḳer**, **Àuḳert** the underworld 11. 12; 138. 2; 183. 1; 259. 3; 262. 2; 471. 8; 474. 10

**Àuḳert** goddess of the underworld 143. 13 *(bis)*

**Àuḳert-χentet-àuset-s** a proper name 318. 11

**àu-t** thou art 415. 11

**àu-ten**, **àu-θen** ye are 114. 14; 121. 7

**àb** word (?) 186. 14

**àb** pegs (?), stakes (?) 390. 14

**àb** thirst 463. 12, 14

**àb** thirsty man 261. 2; 516. 7

**Ȧb** = *Ābu* Elephantine 247. 9; 512. 2

**Ȧb** = *Ȧbṭu* name of a fish 5. 7

**ȧb** , left side 19. 15; 152. 5, 7; 266. 3; 284. 14; 389. 12; 395. 14; 420. 8; 436. 2

**ȧbi**

**ȧb** , heart 4. 5; 7. 9; 70. 2; 89. 3, 4, 5; 90. 11, 17; 91. 2, 4, 5, 7; 92. 3; 93. 3, 12, 13; 94. 1, 8, 17; 100. 5; 150. 13; 151. 14; 298. 2; 333. 7; 376. 10; 385. 11; 436. 3; 447. 13; 454. 5; 475. 2; 479. 15; 483. 2; 485. 16 *(bis)*; 490. 5; 496. 9; 501. 9; 502. 4; 510. 13; 512. 12; 513. 16; will, desire 106. 1; self 10. 7; plur. , 28. 6; 50. 1; 89. 4; 90. 10; 93. 14; 93. 16; 116. 2; 158. 8; 244. 15; 262. 14; 367. 8; 378. 12; 456. 16; 487. 10; 490. 1; 477. 6; 446. 11; *asta ȧb* to judge hastily 256. 14; 257. 5; *ȧri ȧb* to do as a man pleases 330. 12; *āāa ȧb* 380. 11; *ȧb neṭem* joyful heart 76. 8; 173. 3; *ȧb āu* joyful heart 76. 9; 173.4; *ām ȧb* to eat the heart, *i. e.*, to lose the temper 231. 14; 257. 11; *ur ȧb* valiant 332. 12; *uṭa ȧb* brave 154. 13; *meḥ ȧb* to satisfy 268. 8; *ḥer ȧb* in the heart of, within 291. 11; with heart's desire 153. 12; with 77. 2; 82. 17; *ȧb en sehert* the amulet of the carnelian heart 94. 8

**ȧbu** drink 437. 7

**Ȧbu-ur** a proper name 112. 2

**ȧbu** to cease 3. 6

**ȧbu (ābu)** cessation 42. 2

**àbi** panther skin 337. 15; 345. 3

**àber** a kind of unguent 337. 14

**àbeḥu** teeth 97. 16; 112. 11; 117. 6; 446. 11

**àbeχ** to make a way among 40. 6

**àbsit** hull of a boat 207. 5

**àbku** grief, wailing 79. 13; 83. 9

**àbet** thirst 201. 6; 378. 8, 11; 466. 4

**Àb-ka**
**Àbet-ka** a proper name 147. 3, 5

**Abṭet** the nome or city of Abydos 5. 14; 13. 7; 21. 4; 37. 6

**àbt** left hand side 264. 10; 382. 8; 386. 8; 387. 12

**àbet** east wind 155. 8; 407. 12; 129. 7

**Àbet** Abydos 326. 7

**àbet** net? 289. 3

**àbtu** slaughters 357. 3

**àbt** east 218. 13; 287. 2; 105. 15

**àbti** east, eastern 52. 2; 368. 7; 503. 7, 14; 507. 11

**åbti**, **åbti** east, eastern 88. 13; 134. 12; 142. 12; 164. 13; 460. 14; 61. 5

**åbti** east 219. 1

**åbti** eastern (plur.), beings in the east 12. 16; 46. 12; 106. 5; 114. 15; 221. 3; 222. 5; 319. 9

**åbtet** east, eastern 1. 3; 2. 2; 3. 13; 6. 13; 8. 12; 12. 13; 29. 2; 36. 11; 80. 6; 99. 2, 4; 160. 9; 190. 11; 196. 12; 197. 1, 9, 16; 198. 4, 15; 199. 2; 210. 9; 245. 11; 278. 14; 288. 11; 310. 9, 11; 311. 2; 319. 3; 334. 16; 347. 16; 364. 12; 384. 10; 398. 4, 5, 6; 412. 16; 418. 11; 483. 16; 319. 15; 514. 12

**Åbṭ** a mythological fish 44. 11

**åbeṭ** , month 234. 6, 10; 236. 3; 237. 4; 238. 13; 288. 8; 294. 15; 366. 2; 496. 16; monthly festival 330. 1; 371. 9; plur. , 88. 12; 158. 15, 16; 177. 6; 458. 2

**åbet sen pert** the second month of the season *pert* 252. 5; 314. 13, 14; 315. 8; 316. 13

**åbṭu** a mythological fish 3. 1; 211. 5

**Åbṭu** , Abydos, an ancient shrine of Osiris 14. 11; 39. 3; 70. 2; 78. 13; 79. 8; 245. 14; 276. 12; 326. 11; 336. 3; 348. 7, 13; 440. 1; 489. 8; 13. 14; 55. 7; 74. 1,

4; **81.** 14; **136.** 9; **176.** 13; **239.** 6; **241.** 1; **304.** 4; **313.** 8, 10; **350.** 16; **358.** 11; **360.** 1; **452.** 5; **477.** 10; the god of Abydos **325.** 8, 10

**áp** to count, to number, to reckon, to consider **30.** 9; **228.** 13; **229.** 11; **289,** 5, 14; reckoner **280.** 10; counting **195.** 9; **88.** 11; counted **195.** 8; reckoner **111.** 10

**áp** to judge, to be judged, to decree, be decreed **82.** 7; **113.** 13; **154.** 4; **160.** 1; **187.** 1; **227.** 13; **236.** 1; **303.** 6; judged **28.** 12; **384.** 6, 11; judgment **158.** 7; judge **235.** 14; judged **437.** 12; **28.** 14; **180.** 11; **384.** 6, 11; , **236.** 1; **238.** 12; , adjudged **13.** 3; **184.** 15; great judgment **260.** 12

**áp**, **ápu** to judge between, to dispute with, to be awarded, judged **27.** 16; **111.** 12; **203.** 13; **337.** 1; **461.** 14; judge **359.** 14; **465.** 3; decree **474.** 1; to bring a message **102.** 12; message **191.** 14; judge of words **481.** 2

**ápt** decree, judgment **24.** 14; **181.** 10; sentence of death **74.** 8, 10; *áp Maāt* **15.** 16

**áp, ápu** to open **21.** 7; **114.** 10, 11; **116.** 3; **137.** 10; **143.** 9; **144.** 12; **239.** 6; **272.** 9; **275.** 10; **277.** 13; **360.** 1; **450.** 15; **484.** 2; **510.** 16; opened **139.** 13; *áp* open!

**áp re** the ceremony of opening the mouth **309.** 11; **312.** 2; **427.** 14; **502.** 2; **86.** 12; **86.** 14

***Ȧp-uat*** "opener of ways", a name of the god Anubis **74**. 5; **119**. 11; **206**. 2; **277**. 14; **347**. 1; **450**. 15; **465**. 5; **484**. 3; **510**. 16; **112**. 10; **117**. 4

***Ȧp-uat-meḥt-χerp*** (or ***seχem***)-***pet*** a name of Osiris **325**. 14

***Ȧp-uat resu χerp*** (or ***seχem***)-***taiu*** a name of Osiris **325**. 13

***ȧp-ḥer*** except **10**. 3; **308**. 12; **366**. 10; **374**. 4, 10, 12; **376**. 5; **497**. 8; except thyself **408**. 1

***Ȧpu*** Panopolis **245**. 15

***ȧpu***, ***ȧpiu*** those **75**. 6; **58**. 3; **59**. 7; **95**. 8; **98**. 11; **158**. 6; **165**. 2; **181**. 8; **201**. 7; **269**. 5; **313**. 10; **334**. 15; **335**. 9; **336**. 16; **375**. 13; **398**. 5; **435**. 14; **438**. 4; **501**. 10; **506**. 15; those in **259**. 9; those gods **47**. 12

***ȧpui*** openers **21**. 5; **422**. 4

***ȧputi*** messenger **93**. 5; **279**. 7; plur. **262**. 5; two envoys **97**. 12

***ȧpepiu*** judges **269**. 7

***ȧpepet*** reckoning, account **106**. 16

***ȧpen*** these **88**. 2; **191**. 10; **201**. 4; **215**. 3; **309**. 1; **333**. 2; **336**. 5; **337**. 12; **338**. 9; **339**. 3, 15; **340**. 12; **341**. 8; **390**. 7; **497**. 15; **107**. 14

**Ȧp-si** a proper name (?) 238. 6

**ȧpt** shrine 412. 15

**Ȧptet** a district of Thebes, the modern Karnak 489. 12

**ȧpt** to open 126. 7; 142. 3

**ȧpt** message 102. 7; 186. 9, 16; 299. 13; 401. 2; envoy 137. 13; 235. 12

**ȧpt** messengers 414. 11

**ȧpt** brow 8. 7; 30. 6; 40. 13; 68. 5; 148. 12; 195. 2, 10; 219. 2; 304. 8, 10; 369. 13; 386. 10; 387. 13; 441. 13; 487. 7; 505. 11; 381. 5; 381. 15; 381. 12

**ȧpt** sceptre 502. 14

**ȧptu** these 309. 3; 329. 5

**Ȧp-śāṭ-taui** a name of Osiris 323. 3

**ȧpten** these 29. 12; 214. 9; 221. 10; 368. 12

**ȧf** flesh, members 112. 15; 113. 5; 128. 16; 187. 4; 209. 4; 242. 6; 268. 10; 300. 1; 366. 6; 399. 2; 400. 1; 407. 4; 440. 15

**ȧftu** four 180. 6; 181. 7

**ȧfti** a kind of cloth or garment 449. 3

**ȧm** (?) a standard 445. 14

**ȧm** to arrive happily 424. 7

**ȧm** a kind of cloth **340.** 3

**ȧm** not, do not **98.** 2; **143.** 12; **149.** 6, 16; **166.** 13; **202.** 3; **217.** 4; **291.** 9; **308.** 11; **400.** 12, 13; **403.** 13; **407.** 15; **410.** 9

**ȧm** to eat **65.** 3; **100.** 13; **101.** 10; **103.** 5; **104.** 15; **110.** 5; **111.** 1; **123.** 13; **124.** 2, 7, 17; **132.** 14; **141.** 16; **146.** 1; **179.** 7; **238.** 5; **300.** 7; **393.** 11 *(bis)*; **414.** 7; **418.** 3; **449.** 2, 7, 8; **470.** 3; **492.** 8; eater **175.** 8; **312.** 4

**ȧmu**, **ȧmi** to eat **89.** 5; **109.** 7; **510.** 6; eating, eater **155.** 13; eaters, devourers **146.** 8; **375.** 4; **99.** 2

**ȧmt** food, something eaten **125.** 11; **136.** 7; **254.** 2; **256.** 15

**ȧmti** eater **101.** 13; eater of souls **411.** 1

**Ȧm-beseku** "Eater of guts", one of the 42 assessors **254.** 7

**Ȧm-snef** "Eater of blood", one of the 42 assessors **254.** 5

**ȧm** (?) to eat **31.** 13; **123.** 6, 7, 15, 16; **124.** 6; **125.** 5; **151.** 8; **165.** 4; **179.** 12, 13, 16; **180.** 1; **214.** 10, 11; **224.** 2; **225.** 8; **226.** 5; **227.** 7; **243.** 13, 14; **244.** 16; **295.** 10; **305.** 13; **376.** 14; **379.** 15; **380.** 10; **397.** 9; **398.** 8; **465.** 12; **466.** 4; **492.** 9, 10, 16; **493.** 1, 10, 16; **494.** 1, 15; **495.** 1, 9; food **465.** 12; **357.** 12

**Åm-ḥauatu-ent-peḥui-f** a proper name 328. 1 (doorkeeper of Ārit 3); 359. 11

**åm** there, therein 9. 3; 15. 13; 23. 10; 29. 3; 58. 5; 59. 15; 60. 2, 3; 87. 9; 89. 5; 103. 6; 111. 4; 124. 4; 143. 5; 161. 1; 162. 17; 165. 15; 166. 7, 10; 196. 15, 16; 198. 2, 3; 202. 14; 224. 1, 2, 3; 245. 3; 333. 7; 336. 2; 346. 16; 347. 1, 2; 360. 11; 384. 8, 14; 438. 13; 441. 3; 454. 11; 465. 13, 14, 15; 480. 11; 491. 11, 12; 505. 6; 517. 1

**åm**, **åmt** in, with, among, through, upon, by, around, at 4. 15; 9. 14; 10. 4; 14. 14. 18. 9; 22. 6; 52. 6; 66. 15; 67. 7; 87. 9; 94. 2; 133. 13; 150. 9; 182. 13; 204. 15; 229. 6; 364. 15; 426. 16; 450. 16; 462. 1, 2; 492. 14; 512. 11; 123. 8; 296. 6, 15; 297. 13; 455. 3; 415. 13

**åm** dweller in 9. 8; 15. 12; 30. 7; 138. 2; 490. 10; 491. 11

**åmi** dweller in 13. 14; 14. 8; 19. 5; 39. 6; 48. 6; 126. 5, 11, 12; 157. 8, 14; 191. 9; 192. 2; 224. 8; 364. 8; 374. 5, 8, 10; 375. 6; 380. 2; 389. 1; 465. 4; 508. 7; plur. those in 22. 6; 24. 7; 26. 3, 13; 40. 15; 46. 11; 87. 7, 8; 146. 8; 148. 16; 149. 1, 14; 162. 10; 164. 14; 167. 3; 174. 11, 13; 175. 15, 16; 192. 1; 259. 9, 16; 260. 7; 321. 13; 331. 4, 6; 374. 8; 375. 6; 398. 6; 436. 14; 496. 2; 163. 3; 174. 13; 175. 3; 275. 2; 342. 16; *åm ā* 505. 12; *åm åuset ā* title of an office 34. 10; *åm* *ut neb Ta-ṭesert* a title of Anubis 431. 12; 482. 14; 472. 3; 497. 8; 52. 1; 274. 13; 271. 7, 12; 302. 13; a title of Sebek 58. 12; 266. 7, 15; 144. 13; 433. 4; (var. , ) 237. 3, 4, 6; 219. 6; 415. 12; , 61. 7; 374. 5, 10, 13; 459. 2, 13; 289. 1; 301. 8; 138. 6; 375. 6; 313. 10; 180. 13; 103. 9; 275. 16; 104. 9; 27. 5; 55. 15; 135. 9; 290. 1; 66. 3; 266. 13; 267. 4; 234. 15; 216. 3; 455. 16; 12. 1; 17. 7; 51. 15; 365. 16; 39. 15; 56. 4; 57. 11, 16; 58. 11; 62. 14; 73. 6; 210. 7; 232. 5; 374. 9; 405. 14; 452. 11; 480. 7; 184. 12; 159. 4; 217. 1; 240. 5; 136. 3;

104. 8 ; 58. 3 ; 103. 10 ; 184. 14 ; 138. 11

**ȧm-tu** among, between 29. 15 ; 456. 3 ; 221. 11 ; 314. 17 ; 368. 13

**ȧmi-tu**
**ȧmi-θu** among, between 64. 9 ; 165. 2 ; 181. 10, 12 ; 142. 16 ; 361. 3 ; 387. 11 ; 372. 3

**ȧm-θ** , in, between, with, among 25. 8 ; 88. 12 ; 372. 1

**ȧmt-f ḥāt** . . . . 482. 15 ; 357. 10

**ȧm-ȧb** prayer (?) 457. 4

**ȧm χent** a title of a priest who performed certain funeral ceremonies 128. 15 ; 149. 12 ; 407. 2 ; 435. 13 ; 503. 4, 13

**ȧmam** date palm 151. 11 ; 180. 2

**ȧmaχ** veneration one to whom veneration is paid 28. 11 ; 81. 4 ; 103. 1 ; 139. 12 ; 156. 4 ; 201. 2 ; 222. 10 ; 223. 5, 13 ; 248. 16 ; 421. 16 ; 444. 13 ; 452. 6 ; 460. 10 ; 461. 9 ; 463. 8, 13 ; 464. 10 ; 466. 13 ; 468. 6, 8 ; 488. 6 ; 110. 10 ; 464. 11 ; 468. 8

**ȧmaχi** , blessed one 5. 14 ; 44. 2 ; 47. 4 ; 357. 3 ; plur. 326. 12 ; 345. 4 ; 155. 13 ; 513. 11

**ȧmu** divine beings **360.** 9

**ȧmu** plants **504.** 8

**ȧmu** flames, fire **68.** 16; **69.** 8; **20.** 1

**ȧmu** (?) colour **366.** 5

**Ȧm-urt** a proper name **335.** 10

**ȧmi** shrine, chamber **145.** 12

**ȧmiḥetetut** apes **210.** 14

**ȧmem** palm tree **312.** 1

**ȧmem** to putrefy **401.** 7, 9

**ȧmem** skin **419.** 9, 11

**ȧmmā** , , , grant, let, give **2.** 2; **55.** 15; **126.** 4; **156.** 7, 12; **157.** 2, 6, 7, 12, 13, 16; **158.** 1, 4; **234.** 14; **389.** 6; **452.** 10; **16.** 10; **17.** 2; **17.** 7; **69.** 15; **70.** 9; **186.** 8; **186.** 16; **410.** 7

**ȧmmu** beams **41.** 14

**ȧmmu** boats **203.** 9

**ȧmmeḥet** a part of the underworld or tomb **30.** 13; **159.** 12; **213.** 5; **236.** 9; **269.** 15; **371.** 14, 16; **381.** 8

**Ȧmen** the great god of Thebes **34**. 11; **413**. 6; **418**. 10; **509**. 9; **510**. 1, 15

**Ȧmen-Rā** **9**. 15

**Ȧmen-Rā-Ḥeru-χuti** **513**. 5

"Ȧmen which art in heaven" **410**. 6, 7

**Ȧmen-pa-ka-χeprer** **413**. 1

**Ȧmen-naθek-re-θi-Ȧmen** **418**. 11

**Ȧmen-na-ȧn-ka-entek-śare** **418**. 15, 16

**Ȧmen-neb-nest-taui** **443**. 11

**Ȧmen-rereθi** **418**. 16

**ȧmen**, **ȧment** to hide, be hidden, hidden one, something hidden **41**. 10; **119**. 11; **157**. 4; **166**. 1; **225**. 15; **248**. 2; **272**. 13; **346**. 3; **348**. 5, 11; **383**. 12; **391**. 1; **406**. 16; **412**. 12; **418**. 12; **425**. 11; **433**. 6; **471**. 9; **489**. 12; plur. , **103**. 3; **169**. 16; **174**. 9; **177**. 11; **185**. 7; **142**. 11; **363**. 10; hider **138**. 16; **357**. 11, 16; secrecy, in secret **309**. 16; **458**. 6

**ȧment** hidden place **311**. 4; plur. **143**. 15; **288**. 11; **341**. 10; **355**. 10

**ȧmenu-ā** **429**. 9

***Åmen-ren-f*** title of a god 275. 3; 419. 10; 473. 3

***åmen-ḥāu*** 427. 11

***åmen seśetau*** 430. 8

***åmenḥiu*** knives of slaughter 62. 13

***Åmen-ḥetep*** father of the scribe Nu 26. 9; 88. 9; 95. 1; 97. 9; 100. 11; 101. 4; 104. 6; 142. 9; 178. 4; 191. 7; 269. 4; 363. 5; 443. 16; 444. 1; 468. 16; 491. 9; 492. 9

***Åmentet*** the "hidden" land or underworld, the abode of departed spirits, the west 2. 2; 12. 13; 15. 6; 24. 7; 30. 7; 37. 15; 50. 10, 11, 12; 58. 7; 59. 16; 63. 13, 14; 65. 2; 70. 2; 78. 5, 7, 9, 15; 90. 4; 95. 6, 12; 98. 13, 15; 100. 3; 103. 3; 111. 1; 160. 10; 173. 5; 190. 13; 194. 9; 239. 15; 254. 3; 270. 1, 9; 271. 1, 11, 14; 272. 1; 214. 3; 275. 1; 281. 15; 300. 6; 307. 12; 308. 13; 317. 12; 367. 4; 377. 5; 384. 10; 422. 6, 9; 423. 13; 426. 14, 15; 430. 11; 433. 12; 435. 7; 438. 9; 467. 9; 470. 9; 471. 15; 479. 8, 10; 481. 9; 482. 5; 483. 16; 489. 8; 501. 8, 9, 14

***Åmentet nefert*** the beautiful Åmentet 50. 20; 91. 10; 130. 11; 242. 10; 287. 7; 371. 7; 382. 4; 424. 1, 10; 473. 2; 474. 1; 320. 8

***Åment*** the hidden land 430. 11; 431. 4; 435. 8; 471. 1; 475. 16; 476. 12

***Åment, Åmentet*** the hidden land, the west 25. 9; 129. 8; 278. 14; 310. 8; 311. 3; 319. 2; 364. 11; 462. 9

***Åmenti*** the hidden land, the west 142. 11; 457. 1, 3

**ȧmentiu** beings in the hidden land or west **13.** 1; **36.** 11; **47.** 13; **106.** 4; **114.** 15; **169.** 13; **218.** 11; **220.** 13; **319.** 9; **364.** 16; **470.** 15; **514.** 5, 12; **517.** 2; **319.** 16

**ȧmenti** west wind **129.** 6; **155.** 10; **407.** 11

***Ȧmsu*** the god of generation **53.** 8, 10; **243.** 13; **255.** 7; **442.** 3; **462.** 16

***Ȧmsu-Ḥeru*** **347.** 3

***Ȧmsu-suten-Ḥeru-neχt*** a name of Osiris **327.** 1

***Ȧmsu-qeṭ*** a proper name **367.** 10

***Ȧmseθ*** one of the four children of Horus **326.** 9

**ȧmkaḥ** to be feeble **138.** 14

**ȧmt** possession **61.** 1

**ȧmt** tree (?) **469.** 3

**ȧmt** light **50.** 2

**ȧmt** abode **504.** 5

**ȧmt** (?) ***en mu*** . . . . . . **422.** 11

**ȧmt** book-chamber, library **485.** 9

**ȧmt** in, what is in **27.** 12; **36.** 13; **38.** 5; **46.** 5; **125.** 6; **149.** 5, 13, 16; **360.** 16; **455.** 9; **463.**

12; 471. 6; 502. 7; 506. 6, 7; great inner place 95. 11

**Åmt-ṭehen-f** a proper name 245. 8

**åmtiu** . . . . . . . 49. 12

**ån** columns, pillars 73. 2, 5, 7

**ån** , a mark of emphasis or interrogation, used sometimes as a preposition, behold! lo! 1. 4; 3. 14; 10. 16; 27. 9; 34. 13; 101. 12; 121. 7; 145. 13; 150. 8; 156. 8; 157. 3, 7, 13; 158. 1, 5; 169. 2; 205. 6, 8, 10, 12, 14; 206. 1, 3, 5, 6, 9, 14; 207. 3, 5, 7, 9, 12, 13; 208. 1, 3, 5; 214. 15; 215. 17; 216. 2; 231. 6; 238. 6, 7; 237. 6; 244. 4; 279. 13; 281. 6; 292. 7; 358. 6; 392. 10; 400. 7; 452. 6, 8; 506. 4; 93. 5; 231. 4; 396. 2, 5, 6, 8, 10, 12, 14, 16; 397. 2, 4, 6

**ån ḳert** 56. 12

**ånmā** who 504. 14; 50. 6, 10, 11; 507. 5

**ån** , no, not 2. 8; 10. 2; 36. 14; 56. 1; 66. 10, 11, 12, 13; 70. 3, 4, 6; 80. 8; 89. 5, 7; 92. 13; 98. 16; 99. 5; 110. 1, 2, 3; 113. 4, 6, 7; 114. 8; 119. 2, 3; 147. 13, 14; 183. 3, 4, 5; 307. 11, 12; 309. 6; 311. 12, 13; 312. 4; 331. 12; 337. 10; 358. 14; 362. 9; 372. 4, 5, 15; 373. 11; 375. 7; 377. 12; 390. 9, 11; 393. 16; 394. 1; 414. 10, 12, 13; 419. 7; 426. 7; 430. 2; 436. 13, 14; 437. 12, 13, 14, 16; 439. 1; 443. 4; 458. 1; 460. 14, 15; 469. 8; 470. 1; 473. 7, 8; 476. 15; 477. 1; 486. 13; 488. 3, 8; 490. 5; 491. 3; 492. 9, 10, 11, 12; 493. 9, 10, 16; 494. 1, 2, 3; 495. 1, 2; 496. 9; 503. 13. 17; 504. 7; 507. 10; 508. 7; 513. 15; 515. 12; 516. 2, 8;

most certainly there cannot be done **458.** 11; = of **155.** 6; **161.** 2; I am not **266.** 13; **267.** 4

**ȧnȧs** except, unless **264.** 4, 7, 10, 12; **265.** 4, 10

**ȧn-ȧbu** ceaselessly **3.** 5

**ȧn-urṭ** unresting **221.** 9

**ȧn-petrȧ** unobserved **141.** 15; **145.** 15

**ȧn-maa** unseen **24.** 11; **141.** 14; **145.** 15; **63.** 7, 9; **68.** 3; **185.** 13

**ȧn-mu** waterless **458.** 8

**ȧn-meḥ**, **ȧn-meḥ-f** undrowned **139.** 7; **142.** 1; **144.** 7

**ȧn-nifu** airless **458.** 9

**ȧn nefet** not to be gainsaid **340.** 9

**ȧn-reχ** unknown **41.** 13; **160.** 1; **408.** 1; **489.** 11; **497.** 4; **10.** 2; **338.** 4, 6

**ȧn-χeper** never **13.** 15

**ȧn-sep** at no time, never **146.** 11

**ȧn-smȧ** untold **41.** 13

**ȧn-sek** incorruptible **185.** 11

**ȧn-seṭ** unsplit **185.** 13

**ȧn-śenār-tu** unturnable 14. 11

**Ȧn-ȧr-f** the place where nothing grows 83. 8

**Ȧn-ȧarer-f** the place where nothing grows 248. 3

**Ȧn-erṭā-nef-bes-f-χenti-heh-f** a proper name 59. 8

**Ȧn-ḥeri-ertit-sa** a proper name 152. 2, 5

**ȧn** to bring, to bear, to carry 39. 5; 57. 1; 66. 15; 69. 13; 87. 11; 111. 7; 141. 12; 174. 16; 302. 2; 360. 10; 361. 1; 367. 8; 373. 11; 385. 11; 388. 12; 389. 1, 9, 10; 393. 11; 402. 9; 421. 10; 437. 8; 438. 5; 452. 9; 453. 4, 5; 454. 4. 5; 455. 2; 456. 5; 461. 13; 466. 8; 471. 5; 472. 5; 478. 11; 479. 16; 483. 16; 484. 12; 494. 15; 503. 4, 5; 504. 3, 16; 505. 3, 8; to bring 450. 1; *ȧnnu* brought 435. 16; , brought 189. 7; 233. 10; 469. 16; 494. 6; 502. 11; 503. 3; the bringing of 421. 10; bringing 124. 4; 492. 14, 15; those who bring 146. 9; 190. 5; 204. 4; something brought 124. 5

**ȧnu** what is brought in, increase 485. 13

**ȧntu** offerings 462. 8

**Ȧneniu** a proper name 189. 4

**ȧnit ḥetepu** peace-offerings 446. 9

**Ȧn** name of a god 14. 7; 38. 6

**Ȧn-ṭemt** name of a god 38. 6

***ȧnit*** a dwelling (?) **439. 9**

***ȧnuk*** I **103. 1 ; 104. 7**

***Ȧnnu*** Heliopolis, On **4. 12 ; 7. 4 ; 9. 12 ; 19. 5 ; 27. 12 ; 37. 12 ; 38. 4, 5 ; 53. 2 ; 60. 12 ; 61. 3 ; 68. 13 ; 71. 7, 11 ; 78. 11 ; 81. 6 ; 83. 4 ; 86. 16 ; 92. 1 ; 124. 10 ; 129. 2 ; 138. 1 ; 151. 12 ; 162. 17 ; 179. 9 ; 180. 3 ; 185. 15 ; 189. 11 ; 236. 10, 14 ; 237. 10, 12, 14 ; 252. 5, 7, 13 ; 255. 1 ; 296. 2 ; 297. 7 ; 323. 4 ; 324. 8 ; 325. 6 ; 347. 6 ; 361. 1 ; 365. 4 ; 387. 2 ; 388. 4, 15 ; 391. 15 ; 406. 8 ; 409. 5 ; 439. 13 ; 449. 12 ; 450. 10 ; 455. 17 ; 463. 11 ; 477. 7 ; 490. 4 ; 493. 4, 11 ; 511. 5 ; 515. 2**

***ȧnnu*** skin **418. 12**

***ȧnnuit*** hair **318. 13**

***Ȧn-ȧtef-f*** "bringer of his father", a proper name **195. 5**

***Ȧn-ā-f*** "bringer of his hand" **61. 15**

***Ȧn-ā-f*** one of the forty-two assessors **259. 3**

***Ȧn-urt-emχet-uas*** name of the mast **205. 16**

***ȧnh*** to dance, to rejoice **84. 3**

***ȧneb*** wall **139. 4 ; 144. 3 ; 145. 13 ; 358. 15 ; 435. 1 ; 436. 14** ; plur. , **115. 9** *(bis)* ; **221. 14 ; 267. 6 ; 367. 14 ; 436. 13**

***ȧnep*** . . . . . . **491. 9**

***Ȧnp*** the god Anubis **315. 14 ; 326. 3 ; 339. 15**

347. 2; 361. 10; 510. 8; 327. 4; 327. 5

**Ånpu** , Anubis 58. 4; 59. 5; 62. 16; 67. 4; 89. 14; 130. 9; 153. 13; 154. 2; 201. 3; 205. 11; 242. 7; 247. 16; 248. 8, 11; 310. 15; 382. 9; 383. 15; 447. 3, 10; 450. 7; 479. 6; 506. 13; *tep tu-f* 441. 7

**Ånpu** Anubis 74. 11; 76. 4; 112. 11; 117. 5; 331. 4; 385. 15; 386. 5, 10; 466. 16

**Ån-mut-f** a proper name 195. 5

**Ån-mut-f** a proper name 69. 12; 313. 5; 326. 1; 450. 15

**ånem** skin 129. 8; 408. 9; 419. 2

**Ånenit** a proper name 428. 7

**Ån-ruṭ-f** the place where nothing grows 323. 14; 348. 6, 12

**åner** , stone 109. 11; 450. 12; a proper name 509. 3

**Åner** , a proper name 293. 1; 346. 2

**Ånerti** "double stone" (?) 293. 1

**ånhetet** ape 7. 5

**ånḥui** eyebrows 61. 13; 64. 4; 183. 12; 382. 9; 386. 8; 387. 12; 402. 1; 446. 4

**ȧnḥu-tu** surrounded **410**. 3

***Ȧn-ḥeru*** name of a god **326**. 3

***Ȧn-ḥrȧ*** warder of the sixth Ārit **328**. 14; **361**. 7

***Ȧn-ḥetep-f*** one of the forty-two assessors **257**. 3

**ȧnes** name of a garment or bandlet **59**. 10; **204**. 8; **415**. 4; **417**. 8; **457**. 4

**ȧneq** fastened **440**. 15

**ȧnqet** to embrace **442**. 8

***Ȧnqet*** "Clincher" **396**. 4

**ȧnt** name of a mythological fish **3**. 1; **5**. 8; **44**. 9

**ȧnt** name of a boat of the sun **3**. 1; **17**. 5, 9

**ȧnt** the funeral valley, land of the tomb **80**. 8; **176**. 13

**ȧntet** **239**. 8; **272**. 1; **279**. 15; **359**. 1; **371**. 1; **437**. 4; plur. **497**. 4

***Ȧnti*** a people of *Ta-kensel* or Nubia **416**. 3

**ȧnti** hindrance **411**. 6

**ȧntet** to go back **105**. 4

**ȧntet** cord **147**. 4; fetter **186**. 13; **220**. 10

***Ȧn-ṭebu*** name of a god **205**. 1

**ȧnef** Hail! Homage! 23. 14; 38. 4, 6, 8, 10, 13, 16; 39. 3, 5, 7; 242. 15; 249. 6; 477. 2; 482. 12; 489. 13; with 1. 5; 4. 1; 5. 15; 6. 15; 8. 14; 9. 15; 11. 4; 70. 1, 2; 85. 4; 95. 6, 7, 8; 358. 9; 363. 5; 374. 13; 379. 3; 386. 3; 387. 8; 398. 16; 401. 4; 408. 6; 455. 10; 476. 2; with 334. 9; 335. 4, 14; 336. 10; 337. 6; 338. 1, 14; 339. 9; with 340. 5; 341. 1, 13; 342. 4, 12; 343. 2, 11; 344. 1, 9, 16; 345. 8, 15; 346. 6; with 57. 14; 90. 10; 236. 2; 271. 1, 2; 501. 10; with 102. 11; 174. 7, 8, 10, 11, 12, 13; 236. 5; 259. 9; 260. 7; 491. 1

**ȧr** to tie together 306. 11

**ȧr** . . . . . . 177. 12

**ȧr** if, now 28. 13, 14; 29. 11; 52. 3, 4; 53. 5, 7, 10, 11; 55. 4; 58. 6, 8, 10; 59. 12; 65. 10; 67. 1, 4, 6, 8, 10, 11; 69. 4, 6, 9; 71. 11, 12; 72. 3, 5, 11; 73. 4, 5, 13; 74. 4, 10. 12; 75. 3, 13, 14; 87. 1; 88. 13; 120. 9; 129. 3, 5, 6, 7; 147. 11; 190. 1; 196. 16; 197. 2; 198. 3; 211. 3; 212. 13; 218. 12; 219. 6; 226. 6; 232. 8; 244. 13; 248. 8, 11; 246. 10; 268. 6; 286. 5; 295. 10; 296. 11; 308. 7; 317. 2; 362. 11; 366. 11; 371. 11; 384. 6, 11, 12; 394. 11, 13; 402. 13; 403. 10; 407. 8; 414. 10; 461. 4; 477. 13; 493. 15; 497. 11; 504. 12; 505. 10, 11

**ȧr sa** now as for 69. 4

**ȧr ḳert** if, moreover; however 55. 2, 6, 11; 58. 15; 59. 2, 13; 60. 6; 61. 2, 4, 15; 64. 9; 141. 3; 145. 9; 421. 13

**ȧr, ȧri**
**ȧri**
**ȧru**
**ȧrit**

to do, to make, to be made, done, wrought, maker, creator, making 1. 7; 2. 1; 4. 3; 8. 16; 33. 13; 45. 14; 51. 4; 66. 8; 70. 4; 90. 2; 108. 1; 134. 12; 142. 10; 147. 7; 284. 16; 303. 10; 314. 6; 317. 11; 354. 12; 379. 6; 395. 2; 419. 10; 435. 15; 457.

15; 482. 2; 488. 10; 506. 4; 511. 4; 516. 2, 5; made, begotten 26. 9; 28. 12; 222. 11; 223. 12; 386. 1; 387. 7; 444. 11; 501. 5; made, done 3. 8; 52. 11; 66. 13; 197. 2; 198. 8; 199. 1; 317. 1; 333. 14; 380. 12; 441. 3, 4; 507. 13; made 120. 8; 244. 9; 444. 5; 479. 5; make ye 468. 6

**ȧrit** work, something done 1. 8; 457. 16; 491. 4; plur. actions, deeds, works, things done or to be done 16. 4; 28. 14; 110. 9; 111. 16; 140. 11; 162. 9; 226. 7, 12; 334. 3; 383. 2; 384. 12; 395. 2; 421. 2; 404. 9; 445. 9

**ȧriu** doers, makers, workers 47. 7; 96. 7; 153. 3; 158. 8; 171. 4; 185. 6; 196. 1; 215. 4; 299. 14; 329. 5; 331. 2, 3; 359. 10; 361. 12; 400. 1; 445. 8, 9; 448. 13

**ȧriu** workmen 151. 4; 152. 3

**ȧrit** workwomen 151. 4; 152. 3

**ȧri šāt** to write or recite a book 34. 5; 314. 13; 414. 10; 496. 16; done in writing 23. 6

[illegible] to make a way 334. 10; 335. 5; [illegible] 337. 7; 338. 2, 15; 339. 10; 340. 5; 341. 14; [illegible] 343. 2, 12; 344. 2; 345. 1; 346. 7; 347. 2; 349. [illegible] 351. 3; to prepare food 372. [illegible] a festival 347. 8; [illegible] 108. 4; to protect 404. 10; [illegible] *ȧri ȧb* 106. 1; [illegible]mation 75. 5

**ȧr, ȧri** as an auxiliary verb see *passim.*

**Ȧri-Maāt** a title of Osiris **397.** 14; a title of Hathor **490.** 12

**Ȧri-em-ȧb-f** one of the forty-two assessors **258.** 3

**Ȧri-en-ȧb-f** a proper name **230.** 2

**Ȧri-nef-ṫesef** name of a plank or peg **207.** 1

**ȧri** name of leather straps **206.** 6

**Ȧri-ḥeṫ-f** a proper name **443.** 3

**Ȧri-si** a proper name **479.** 16

**ȧru** to make **510.** 2; **511.** 3; **514.** 11; **515.** 12; **516.** 8; **517.** 1

**ȧru** form, attribute **2.** 4; plur. **9.** 12; **37.** 11; **61.** 13; **62.** 13; **69.** 1; **70.** 14; **72.** 12, 15; **114.** 6; **115.** 1; **138.** 3; **145.** 1; **147.** 6; **159.** 15; **166.** 6; **167.** 4; **171.** 1, 10, 12; **174.** 9; **175.** 6; **243.** 12; **295.** 2; **308.** 2, 15; **374.** 12; **425.** 1; **491.** 12, 14; **510.** 5

**ȧri** belonging to **63.** 5; **233.** 12; **363.** 9; **363.** 16; **369.** 5

**ȧri**, **ȧri**, **ȧru**, **ȧrit** that which belongs, the things which belong, those who belong, watcher, guardian, things laid up **20.** 8; **54.** 8; **58.** 2, 16; **66.** 1; **76.** 16; **91.** 2; **168.** 5, 9; **169.** 1;

175. 4; 214. 9; 269. 14; 270. 6; 386. 3; 407. 5; 443. 17; 444. 2; 453. 2; 461. 14; 464. 1; 478. 9; 496. 1; 504. 14; 187. 4; 121. 16; 172. 16; 190. 1; 86. 9; 165. 6; 301. 3; 484. 16; 216. 15; 31. 2; 221. 8; 368. 10; 172. 16

**åri āa** porter, doorkeeper, guardian 110. 16; 124. 12; 154. 4; 265. 4, 9; 266. 4; 350. 4, 10; 351. 1, 15; 352. 8, 15; 353. 7, 16; 354. 7; 358. 3; 359. 2, 11; 360. 4, 12; 361. 6, 14; 469. 6; 493. 6; 64. 12; plur. 187. 4; 244. 8; 271. 2; 272. 2; 274. 3; 275. 4; 320. 2

**åru ārertu** warders of Ārits 299. 9; 327. 12, 15; 328. 2, 6, 10, 14; 329. 2; 331. 12

**åri māχait** warder of the Scales 15. 12; 96. 4

**Åru-hut** a proper name 428. 1

**åri ḥemit** steersman 3. 2; 5. 6

**åri ḥenbiu** warden of the cultivated lands 474. 8

**åru χeχut** denizens of light 428. 15

**åri såpu** keeper of sentences 53. 3; plur. 66. 7; 67. 2

**Åri sebχet-f** "keeper of his pylon" 474. 5; plur. 475. 15

**åri qeb en śe en χet** keeper of the Bight of the Lake of Fire 64. 5

**årp** wine 223. 9; 264. 11; 466. 2; 514. 13

**årpu** . . . . . 435. 15

**åref** an emphatic particle 21. 6, 7; 57. 3; 86. 9; 124. 2; 166. 3; 179. 14; 201. 7; 203. 6; 261. 5, 6; 263. 13; 307. 5; 394. 6, 16; 473. 4, 11, 13; 492. 13; 494. 9; 495. 4, 11; 505. 3, 7, 8, 12, 13, 15; 507. 11

**åremā** with 413. 11

**årek** a particle 11. 7; 30. 10; 49. 16; 58. 5; 59. 15; 165. 11; 166. 4; 241. 1; 248. 15; 266. 1; 270. 4; 289. 1; 296. 2; 297. 6; 335. 3, 13; 336. 9; 337. 5, 16; 338. 13; 339. 7; 340. 3, 16; 341. 12; 342. 3, 10; 343. 1, 9, 16; 344. 8, 14; 345. 6, 13; 346. 5; 399. 5; 409. 11; 457. 16; 462. 12; 476. 11; 486. 9; 506. 5, 13; 507. 8; 508. 12; 512. 15

**årt** to flow from 314. 15

**årt** . . . . . . 122. 9

**årtet** milk 130. 7; 223. 9; 242. 5; 251. 5; 303. 12; 333. 11; 437. 1; 450. 11

**åh** calamity, sorrow 280. 12, 13

**åhabu** joy 74. 3

**åhen** a kind of wood 336. 9

**åhehi** rejoicings **109. 1**; **263. 6**; **354. 13**

***Åḥ*** the Moon-god **3. 5**; **70. 6**

**åh** . . . . . . . **514. 9**

**åh** , collar **311. 4**; embrace **103. 9**; **to** ward off **225. 3**

**åḥ** ox 333. 7

**åḥu** oxen **154. 15**; **229. 1**; **480. 2**; **506. 8**; **510. 3**; **514. 13**

**åḥu** fields **197. 5**

**åḥu** cords **393. 7**; **505. 11**

***Åḥi*** a proper name **215. 12**; one of the **forty-**two assessors **258. 4, 11**; *Åḥi* . . . **367. 8**

***Åḥiu*** the two *Åḥu* gods 245. 4; var.

***Åḥibit*** a proper name **356. 14**

**åḥemu** (?) those who belong to **196. 8**

***Åḥeti*** a name of Osiris **325. 12**

**åḥeti** throat **100. 2**

**åχ** O! **165. 12**, **167. 6**, **172. 11**, **232. 4**; **O,** would that **244. 6**; O, tell me **186. 10**

**åχabu** grain **397. 11**

**åχib** to speak **7. 11**

**áχemu urṭu** a class of stars **40**. 6; **99**. 14

**áχeχu** darkness **134**. 15; **142**. 13

**Áχsesef** a proper name **163**. 5

**Ás** a proper name **215**. 12

**ás** intestines **401**. 13

**ás** behold, to wit **41**. 6; **80**. 11; **131**. 1; **151**. 7; **184**. 14; **187**. 5; **197**. 4; **198**. 10; **241**. 3; **252**. 3; **288**. 14; **289**. 8; **291**. 4; **302**. 2; **337**. 10; **367**. 6; **372**. 3; **416**. 2; **448**. 15; **460**. 16; **462**. 2; **464**. 5; **474**. 3; **491**. 10; **492**. 10; **496**. 6; **502**. 10; **31**. 12, 14; **25**. 7; **43**. 2; behold me **224**. 9; behold, am I not? **217**. 5, 6; with **128**. 11

**ás** , to pass quickly **105**. 5; **196**. 2; **313**. 2; **335**. 5, 13; **336**. 9; **337**. 5, 16; **338**. 13; **339**. 7; **340**. 3, 16; **341**. 12; **342**. 3, 10; **343**. 1, 9, 16; **344**. 8, 14; **345**. 6, 13; **346**. 5

**ás** ,
**ási** tomb, sepulchre **194**. 12; **415**. 9; **448**. 3; **460**. 5

**ásu** . . . . . . **275**. 13

**ásu** recompense **231**. 6; or in return for, in place of **458**. 12, 13

**ȧsu** (?) } to decay, to rot, destruction **201**. 12; **398**. 15; **399**. 3, 8, 15; **400**. 4;
**ȧsi** (?) } **401**. 10; **399**. 13;

incorruptible **399**. 3

**ȧsi** who?, what? **267**. 8; **506**. 2, 3; **507**. 7

**ȧsti** (?) . . . . . **505**. 16

**ȧsp** grief (?) **172**. 10

**ȧsfet** } faults, sins, evil deeds, evil ones, sinners **34**. 14; **44**.
**ȧsfeti** } 1; **57**. 15; **58**. 11; **62**. 7, 8; **65**. 12; **110**. 1, 2; **159**. 14; **175**. 3; **183**. 10; **184**. 4; **187**. 3; **249**. 16 *(bis)*; **252**. 13; **259**. 14; **260**. 13; **269**. 12; **270**. 5; **397**. 14; **414**. 15; **422**. 4; **456**. 11; **457**. 13; **458**. 1; **480**. 6; **488**. 10, 13; **496**. 5; **508**. 7; **515**. 3, 14; **516**. 3, 10

**ȧsfeti** fiends **43**. 13

**ȧsentu** cords, ropes **147**. 3

**ȧser** tamarisk **112**. 5, 7; plur. herbs, plants, grass **246**. 10

**Ȧsert** name of a city **465**. 6

**ȧsha** linen **420**. 9

**Ȧses** } a city in the seventh Ȧat **372**. 8, 13; **381**. 10
**Ȧsset** }

**ȧssu** to rope in **390**. 11, 12

**ȧsstu** (?) a rope **390**. 12; those whose heads are tied **398**. 11

**ȧsk** behold! 26. 4; 95. 4; 268. 3; 303. 11; 362. 3; 395. 13; 501. 12

**ȧseśet** (?) persea tree 60. 11; 61. 2; 261. 13; 496. 5; 511. 4

**ȧst** behold 26. 13; 28. 15; 87. 8; 142. 1; 201. 15; 227. 10, 12; 229. 4; 234. 13; 275. 10; 280. 8; 284. 9, 12; 293. 12; 312. 4, 5; 471. 10; 479. 4; 190. 9; 272. 10

**ȧsθ** behold 90. 18; 167. 12, 16; 168. 7; 298. 8; 304. 4; 469. 10

**ȧsṭ** to tremble 456. 1

**Ȧsṭennu** name of a god 74. 11

**ȧsteḥ** to beat down 384. 14

**ȧsṭeḥet** to beat down 384. 7

**Ȧsṭes** name of a god 58. 7; 341. 8; 348. 8; 349. 5

**Ȧsṭeṭet** name of a district 377. 5

**ȧśāt** knife 394. 7, 15; 396. 13

**ȧśeset** see *ȧqeset*

**ȧśeś** to be carried 235. 8

**ȧśet** subsistence 465. 2; oppression, oppressor 488. 16

**àk** injury **309**. 9

**àkebu** hair **225**. 2

**àkeb**

**àkebet** lamentation, wailing, weeping **81**. 13; **431**. 15

**àkebit** wailers **471**. 11

**Àkeniu** a proper name (?) **275**. 7

**Àken-tau-k-ha-χeru** the porter of the sixth Ārit **328**. 13

**Àkenti** a proper name **352**. 15

**Àqesi** a city in the ninth Àat **374**. 1, 2, 15; **382**. 3

**Àqen** name of a god **432**. 7

**Àqeh** name of a god **431**. 10

**àqer** perfect, strong **5**. 10; **20**. 13; **30**. 5; **42**. 15; **145**. 4; **194**. 5; **212**. 1, 11, 15; **295**. 9; **364**. 8; **404**. 12; **413**. 11; **431**. 9; **438**. 8, 9; **443**. 16; **461**. 4; **470**. 11; **488**. 11; plur. **516**. 13; a skilful scribe **480**. 14

**àqes** bad, wicked evil **17**. 5; **70**. 3

**àqeset** (or **àśeset**) who? what? where? **124**. 3; **220**. 4; **457**. 10; **459**. 4; **494**. 9; **495**. 4; **503**. 15; **504**. 3; **505**. 7, 10; **506**. 4; **507**. 11; **370**. 11

**àqet** a kind of beer or wine **514**. 13

**àqeṭu** builders **145**. 13

**Åḳau** name of a god 136. 12

**åḳap**
**åḳep** } rain storm 204. 9; 338. 16

**Åḳeru** gods of the underworld 224. 9

**Åḳert** a name of the underworld 14. 6; 38. 9; 70. 13; 272. 6; 275. 7, 13; 419. 6

**Åḳert-χent-Åuset-s** name of a cow 364. 2

**åḳeḳit** robe 352. 13

**åt** father 47. 1; 456. 1

**åt**
**åti**
**åtet** } no, none, not, cannot, without 5. 10; 8. 3; 43. 4; 115. 13; 134. 3; 150. 1; 184. 6; 259. 14; 298. 6; 313. 14; 369. 8; 373. 6; 374. 4; 375. 5; 376. 2; 378. 4; 415. 13; 494. 6; powerlessness 176. 16; plur. , things which are not, evil beings 79. 3; 99. 15; 507. 13; *åtu*, *åtet* without, destitute, abjects 250. 3; 260. 8; 262. 6; 269. 11; 392. 7; unquenchable 340. 8; immutable 173. 8; painless 42. 12; invisible 392. 7; unknown 174. 10; 175. 7; irresistible 51. 15; 107. 13; 497. 14; incorruptible 399. 3; undecaying 399. 9; impassable 340. 9; 371. 3

**åt** emanation (for ) 436. 8

***Ȧta-re-ȧm-ṫer-qemtu-ren-par-śeta*** a proper name 416. 10

**ȧtef** father 4. 7; 5. 13; 13. 4; 24. 16; 30. 6; 52. 9; 53. 10, 16; 54. 4; 55. 8; 59. 4; 94. 3; 102. 14; 121. 7; 128. 19; 153. 7, 15, 16; 232. 9; 286. 11; 293. 6; 301. 15; 306. 5, 9, 10; 308. 12; 313. 12; 317. 11; 347. 4; 360. 8; 385. 7; 395. 6; 401. 5; 405. 1; 407. 16; 443. 4; 451. 7, 14, 15; 460. 3, 4, 8; 473. 11; 486. 11; 487. 2; 493. 6; 31. 3; 30. 16; 31. 1; two fathers 449. 8; plur. 13. 11; 104. 14; 302. 12; 388. 12; 390. 7; 393. 15; 365. 6; 399. 1; 399. 3

***Ȧtem*** the god Tem 78. 2

**ȧten** the sun's disk 7. 15; 10. 14; 11. 6; 38. 2; 41. 2; 45. 9; 61. 8; 274. 8; 435. 4; 476. 5 *(bis)*; 511. 10

**ȧten ābui** two-horned disk 413. 13

**ȧtennut** appellations 412. 8

**ȧter**, **ȧtru** river, water-flood, stream, league 132. 6; 151. 3; 152. 1; 208. 1; 247. 6; 321. 16; 378. 13. 382. 2; 417. 15; 420. 12; 436. 10; 444. 9; plur. 10. 9; 42. 3

**ȧtert** the northern or southern half of the

heavens; 278. 14; 278. 15; 319. 6; 319. 7; 11. 8; 46. 8; 76. 9; 82. 3; 78. 5; 326. 12

**Åthabu** name of a city 411. 8

**åtḫu** to draw 127. 1; 129. 8; 383. 11

**Åtek-tau-kehaq-χeru** a proper name 361. 6

**åṭ** oppressed one 488. 16

**åṭ** (?) to be deaf 293. 1; 401. 14; 497. 6

**Åṭu** a city of the eleventh Åat 376. 7; 381. 13

**åṭu** children 398. 6

**åṭeb** domain, region 376. 16; plur. 162. 13

**åṭmå** a kind of cloth 308. 3

**åṭmå** a garment 340. 2

**åṭen** deputy, vicar, chief (?) 302. 2

**åṭḫu** Papyrus swamp 404. 6

**åṭerit** misfortunes, calamities 262. 6

**åṭeṭiu** those who injure 262. 5

**àθi** 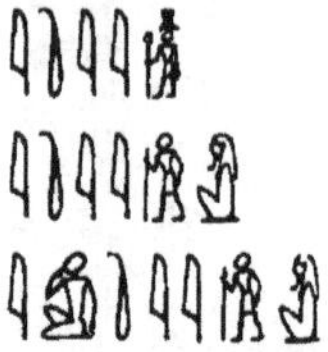 prince, sovereign **2.** 3; **12.** 3; **13.** 10; **110.** 6; **314.** 3; **322.** 1; **325.** 9, 10; 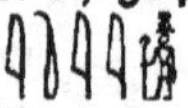 **64.** 2;   **478.** 3

**àθen** 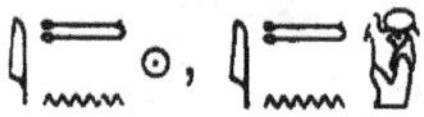 disk **3.** 4; **43.** 8; **70.** 6; **112.** 9; **138.** 5; **151.** 12; **182.** 6; **205.** 2; **210.** 11, 13; **245.** 5; **260.** 10; **301.** 12; **363.** 6; **406.** 16; **289.** 9

**àθeθ** 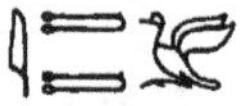 to alight **202.** 13

**àfa**  violent one **467.** 6

# Ā.

**ā** hand, power 11. 6; 80. 14; 86. 1; 99. 8; 136. 10; 139. 13; 158. 13; 306. 8; 308. 4; 311. 5; 330. 3; 331. 3; 344. 5; 371. 10; 406. 4; 441. 2, 9; 455. 9; 482. 9; 491. 3; side, place 212. 9; plur. 1. 8; 2. 7; 5. 7; 55. 16; 68. 8; 76. 5; 85. 6; 89. 10; 90. 1; 107. 10; 112. 12; 113. 6; 117. 8; 123. 9; 124. 1; 137. 4; 143. 4; 139. 16; 150. 14; 151. 16; 153. 4; 170. 12; 214. 13; 244. 2; 355. 9; 385. 16; 448. 10; 449. 1; 462. 11; 471. 12; 472. 8, 10; 478. 15; 479. 3, 8; 488. 7; 494. 3; 495. 2; 448. 5; 342. 15; 343. 7; sides 3. 3; 45. 1; 107. 9; paws of an ape 116. 5

**āāi** power 78. 3

**ā** let me take a flight to you 390. 16; with 32. 4; 2. 13; with 271. 3; 61. 6; 408. 8; 485. 16; 196. 7; 201. 15

**āāiu** etc. the name of the posts of the net 391. 14

**āa** house 431. 5

**āa** to advance, to journey onwards **246.** 7, 9; **247.** 4; **261.** 14; **266.** 10; **267.** 1; **480.** 1

**āa** door **136.** 14; **139.** 3; **391.** 4; **405.** 15; plur. gates, doors **278.** 15; **374.** 15; **160.** 13; **320.** 1, 3; **187.** 4; **445.** 16; **475.** 15; **271.** 9; the two leaves of the door **279.** 1; **341.** 4; **438.** 7; **462.** 13; **55.** 13; **89.** 11; **131.** 8; **376.** 16; **377.** 1; **131.** 8

**āa**, **āai** great, to be great **5.** 1; **13.** 7; **18.** 9; **82.** 3; **107.** 15, 16; **149.** 7; **150.** 2; **282.** 8; **283.** 6; **298.** 6; **374.** 12; **379.** 6; **386.** 15; **387.** 2, 16; **456.** 2; great against the weak **457.** 15; mighty one **489.** 14, 15; **490.** 1; majesty **476.** 7 *(bis)*; most mighty one **510.** 9; twice great **370.** 1; Great god **397.** 9, 10; fem. **6.** 1; **15.** 17; **48.** 5; **126.** 7; **140.** 13; **141.** 5; **350.** 15; **352.** 3; **386.** 15; **388.** 3; **145.** 11; a proper name **326.** 7; plur. great, mighty **122.** 5; **195.** 3; **215.** 16; **216.** 1, 3; **318.** 6

**āa** to be proud **380.** 11; great one of forms, *i. e.*, abundant of forms **37.** 11; **295.** 2; most exceedingly great **410.** 1;

276. 14; 442. 7, 10; 47. 8; 43. 12; 91. 3; 43. 14; 489. 15; 290. 14; 477. 7; 14. 2; 47. 7; 381. 15; 487. 16; 30. 14; 46. 15; 68. 13; 112. 16; 118. 14; 171. 5; 194. 1; 276. 12

***Āa-χeru*** the warder of the seventh Ārit 329. 2; 361. 16

***Āat-em-χut*** a proper name 344. 12

**āat** amulet (?) 299. 7; plur. 191. 1; 331. 11; 333. 9

**āt** members, limbs 419. 16; 315. 5; 419. 5

***āātu-pu-ent-Neter-χert*** name of oar-rests 205. 12

**āāu** ass 2. 15; 261. 16

**āān**
**āānāu** } ape 163. 2; 269. 5

**āu** to make an offering, to be offered 450. 10

**āut** offerings of meat and drink, sacrificial food 160. 4; 209. 5, 6, 7, 8; 217. 13; 272. 11; 422. 6, 8, 9; 423. 12; 424. 5, 10; 466. 15; 472. 14; 474. 16; 475. 4

**āu** the shipwrecked man 149. 6; 150. 1; 169. 11; 205. 3; 261. 4; 281. 5; 281. 3

**āu** long, length, the opposite of breadth 125. 4; 218. 14; 218. 17; 219. 3; 226. 2; 287. 9; 370. 4; height of a *khu* 222. 4; length of a boat 291. 1; lavish hand 483. 12; length of a backbone 368. 4; 369. 5; 372. 11; 188. 4; 456. 5; 180. 6; 100. 2

**āu** exceedingly 14. 2; 43. 14

**āu** to expand, to dilate (of the heart) 4. 5; 7. 9; joy, gladness, pleasure 9. 6; 11. 8; 12. 9; 13. 2; 35. 14; 44. 4; 49. 6; 65. 4, 5; 76. 9; 82. 4; 96. 8; 228. 2, 7; 230. 6; 286. 7; 365. 3; 485. 16; 479. 1; 204. 8

**Āu-ā** a proper name 208. 4

**āu** crime, sin, iniquity 54. 4; 342. 2; 343. 15; 356. 1; ill luck 351. 7

**āui** evil 336. 15

**āuit** defects, evil, deceit 135. 14; 250. 2; 257. 11, 15

**āut** to do harm to 123. 2

**āu** (or **uḫa** [?]) to unloose, to be delivered from, to strengthen, to return 86. 8, 10; 116. 3; 140. 4; 156. 6, 11; 157. 1, 6, 12, 16; 158. 3

**āu** cord (?) 147. 5

**āu** to fish, to snare, snarer 390. 5; 391. 1; 393. 14

**āu** fisherman, fowler 392. 11; plur. 390. 6; 391. 12; 393. 8; 396. 1; 397. 3

**āu** to speak, to cry out 183. 7; 202. 2

**āuāu** dogs, jackals 215. 2

**āu** pregnant, conceived 19. 6

**āu** body 447. 15

**āuā**, **āuāu** flesh and bone, joint of meat, haunch, carcase 9. 11; 11. 11; 132. 15; 215. 5, 6; 449. 4

**āu**, **āuāā**, **āuāu** to inherit 25. 5; flesh and bone, inheritance, heir 77. 15; 79. 6; 133. 1, 11; 180. 11; 341. 11; 347. 3; 419. 3; 476. 10, 11

**āu**, **āu** heir 443. 2; 460. 5; heir 459. 2, 13; heir 472. 16; 473. 10

**āuāt** heir, inheritance 73. 3; 81. 11; 83. 7; 128. 19; 237. 1, 5, 12

**āuāu** heirs, kinsfolk, people of one's own flesh and blood 153. 6; 203. 15

**āuiu** those who lacerate or cut 158. 7

**āuur** one who has conceived **68.** 6; **148.** 9; **153.** 11; **456.** 3; **466.** 6; a pregnant goddess **139.** 2; **144.** 2; heir **443.** 1

**āu** animals **7.** 6

**āut** animals, quadrupeds **75.** 5; **141.** 16; **146.** 1; **251.** 7; **268.** 5; **312.** 5; **389.** 9; **399.** 13; **400.** 7, 10; **453.** 12

**āut** companies **138.** 9

**āua**

**āuat** to be strong, to act with vigour or violence, to rob, to plunder, to vanquish, violence **29.** 8; **110.** 3; **113.** 10; **119.** 15; **128.** 4; **188.** 13, **191.** 14; **253.** 1; **254.** 10; **313.** 16; **314.** 1; **469.** 13; **61.** 14; **62.** 2; wrong, evil **159.** 4; , violent act **220.** 7; **334.** 13; **370.** 15; **515.** 5; ill treated **198.** 15; *āut* plundered (?) **226.** 15

**āuai** violence **110.** 1

**āun** to be strong **254.** 15

**āun-ȧb** (?) to do violence **253.** 1, 14

**āunt** dressed **226.** 14

**Āurȧu-ȧaqer-sa-ȧnq-re-baθi** a proper name **409.** 1

**āuḥ-θȧ** steeped in something **403.** 7

**āusu** scales 251. 4

**āusu** balance 262. 1

**āuq** pool, watery ground 10. 10

**āuț** to travel through 10. 7

**āb** (with ), opposite, before, in front of 154. 4; 292. 16; 464. 16; 505. 1; 472. 4; 461. 14; 466. 14

**āb** altar 223. 8; 449. 10

**āb** to offer up a sacrifice, to make offerings, offering 218. 3; 309. 4; 440. 5; 505. 5; plur. 63. 10; 466. 1; 230. 10

**ābetet** to make an offering 54. 11; offerings, sacrifices 20. 3; 125. 13; 180. 2; 333. 16; 350. 15; 483. 11

**ābai** sacrifice 173. 9

**āb**, **ābu**, **ābet** clean, holy, purity, to be pure, to purify, to sprinkle or pour out water ceremonially 54. 9; 66. 14; 77. 1; 82. 15; 108. 16; 109. 7; 151. 10; 161. 3; 163. 3; 174. 15; 178. 6; 182. 1; 187. 2; 211. 7; 215. 12; 217. 10; 240. 13; 252. 1; 262. 8, 12; 265. 14; 266. 11; 267. 14; 284. 12; 293. 3; 312. 4; 316. 12; 334. 15; 335. 8, 9; 336. 5, 16; 337. 1, 12; 338. 9; 339. 1, 15;

340. 12; 341. 8; 345. 3; 357. 2; 358. 8; 362. 2; 437. 1; 441. 3; 444. 7, 8, 10; 448. 4; 450. 9, 16; 460. 16; 479. 7, 16; 480. 4, 5; 488. 12; 488. 13; 496. 16; 508. 5, 7; 174. 7; pure one, libationer 141. 15; 145. 16; 156. 3; 178. 6; 331. 16; pure 335. 3, 13; 336. 10; 337. 5, 16; 338. 13; 339. 8; 340. 4, 16; 341. 12; 342. 3, 10; 343. 1, 10, 16; 344. 8, 15; 345. 7, 14; 346. 5; 85. 6; 299. 16

**āb** libation, purification 330. 15; 361. 4; 456. 15; plur. 240. 6; 279. 6; 280. 9; 468. 10; 436. 16; 252. 1, 2; 262. 9

**āb**, **āb** libationer, pure man 20. 4; 329. 12; 489. 11

a pool of clean water 512. 2

**ābu** a holy garment, clean raiment 443. 8, 15, 17; 448. 14

**ābet** water house, clean place 59. 6; 67. 4; 208. 4; 339. 5; 441. 6; 449. 5; 452. 1; plur. 251. 1

**ābti** the double holy place 490. 4

**āb** clean-handed 261. 8; 480. 14 pure-mouthed 261. 7; 465. 6, 8; clean faces 496. 5

**ābu** transgressions (?) 216. 14

**Āb-ur** the great god of the holy place, *i. e.*, Osiris 326. 2

**āb, āba** to open, to make a way through 30. 3, 13; 129. 9; 156. 9; 159. 12; 159. 15; 160. 8; 172. 15; 208. 11, 16; 236. 9; 269. 15; 273. 5; 280. 10, 14; 332. 3; 390. 6; 406. 16; 407. 9; 438. 9, 16; 473. 1; 497. 4; 111. 7

**āba**, **ābet**, **ābata** entrance 406. 15; 407. 9, 13

**āba** opposition 376. 3

**ābuaa** to bring before 155. 1

**ābat** courts 137. 7 . 143. 7

**ābet** (or *ḥemet*) artificer 449. 6

**ābet** (or *ḥemet*) work, handicraft 318. 14

***Āba-ta*** a proper name 393. 14

**ābui** two-horned 137. 11; 229. 14; 413. 14; 418. 13; 427. 10; 462. 3; 480. 15

**ābu** horns 183. 5; *useχt ābui* broad-horned 227. 12; *neb ābui* Dhu 'l-Ḳarnen 477. 3

**āba** (or **aḥā**) to fight, to do battle, battle 19. 2; 52. 9, 14; 56. 8, 10; 165. 14; 166. 8; 167. 1, 7; 168. 15; 243. 1; 362. 14; 504. 15; 404. 8

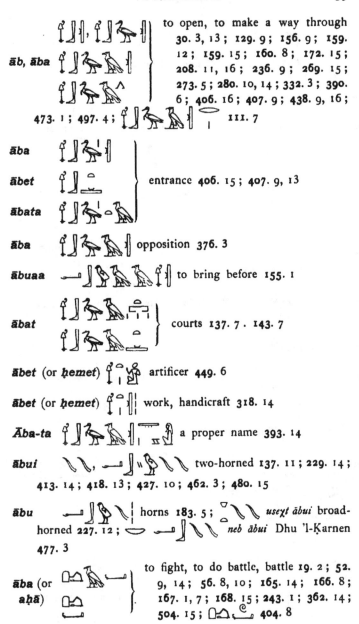

**ābai** fighter 18. 10

**āba-tu** fight, struggle 308. 11

**ābau**
**ābui**
**ābati**
the two combatant gods, *i. e.*, Horus and Set, 92. 1; 163. 12; 224. 15; 225. 1, 2

**āba** *āba-ā* 61. 5, 6; 71. 8; 78. 2; 81. 7; 83. 4

**ābau** fighting implements, weapons 47. 14; 438. 2

**Āba-āāui** "Fighting Hands", a proper name 430. 5

**Ābau-ḥrȧu** "fighting faces" 140. 6

**ābiu** divine slaughterers 196. 6

**ābit** the *mantis* 164. 1; 216. 16; var.

**ābtu** figures, persons of 124. 11; 493. 5

**Ābt-ṭesi-ruṭ-en-neter** a proper name 392. 4

**ābet** (or **ḥemet**) a mineral 211. 7

**ābu** overseer, inspector (a name of Anubis) 450. 8

**Ābu** Elephantine 380. 3; 454. 4

**ābu** cessation 42. 2

**āp** to bring to naught 314. 5

**Āpep** the enemy of Rā 2. 16; 29. 6; 49. 9; 62. 5; 105. 14; 106. 3, 7; 108. 7; 204. 10; 210. 16; 271. 10; 281. 15; 282. 3; 292. 7; 302. 8; 316. 4; 332. 2; 361. 2; 369. 15

**Āapef** a fiend 105. 5

**āper** to be equipped or provided with 31. 5, 12; 70. 14; 86. 10; 99. 16; 112. 3; 131. 14; 134. 1; 170. 10; 171. 16; 177. 3; 194. 4; 199. 10; 230. 5; 245. 11, 13; 282. 6; 330. 14; 389. 5; 491. 14; 507. 6; 507. 6

**Āper**, **Āpert** name of a city 321. 9; 323. 16; 324. 12

**āpeś** tortoise (or turtle) 406. 16; 407. 2, 4, 6

**āpśait** a kind of beetle 102. 3

**āfa** filth 99. 2

**āfnet** wig, headdress 101. 12; 506. 16; plur. 367. 6; 372. 2; 247. 16

**āftet**, **āfṭet** place, abode, chest 67. 5; 164. 12; 303. 1

**ām** — to eat, to devour, to consume 32. 4; 64. 6, 8; 137. 15; 143. 12; 192. 8; 197. 3; 198. 6, 9; 289. 2 *(bis)*; 393. 12; 397. 11; 398. 8; 463. 10

**āmam** — to eat, to comprehend, to understand 98. 14; 419. 9, 16

**āmi** — eaters, devourers 272. 3

**āmt** — what is eaten, food 219. 12; 393. 12

**ām ȧb** — to eat the heart, *i. e.*, to become angry and rage 231. 14; 256. 11

**Ām āā** — "Eater of the Ass", a proper name 108. 10; 109. 2, 6

**Ām ȧsfetti** — "Eater of sinners" 109. 15

**Ām-baiu** — "Eater of sinners" 412. 11

**Āmam-maat** — "Eater of the Eye" 515. 8

**Ām-ḥeḥ** — "Devourer of Eternity" 64. 8

**Ām-χebitu** — "Eater of shades", one of the forty-two assessors 253. 2

**Āmām** — the "Devourer" 346. 11

**Āmemet** — the "Devourer" 16. 10

**Āmemet** — a proper name 430. 9

**āa-meḥt** — a kind of stone 502. 1

**ān** — a proper name 413. 10

**ān** to turn back **92.** 2; **438.** 3

**āniu** those who turn back **490.** 4

**ān** , to write, **2.** 5; to copy **199.** 14; **213.** 8; written **211.** 6; to be written in a list **155.** 6; drawn, painted **284.** 11, 13; inscribed **140.** 14; **294.** 5; palette **110.** 2; writting **97.** 2; **211.** 6; and see **332.** 14; **333.** 5, 6; **389.** 1; **420.** 4

**ānu** writings, decrees, descriptions, books, copies, documents, archives **17.** 1; **25.** 3; **41.** 15; **63.** 12; **118.** 8; **151.** 13; **183.** 7; **199.** 10; **268.** 4; **282.** 5; **309.** 11, 12, 13; **345.** 12; **357.** 8; **386.** 12; **409.** 15; **485.** 8; **511.** 11; **510.** 10

**ān** scribe **1.** 4; **28.** 12; **71.** 4; **72.** 16; **73.** 8, 15; **74.** 6, 15; **85.** 12; **138.** 4; **194.** 13; **199.** 13; **312.** 13; **348.** 2; **360.** 7; **385.** 16; **387.** 5; **405.** 4, 16; **421.** 1, 10; **429.** 15; **450.** 2; **461.** 9; **463.** 11; **465.** 1, 2, 7, 9, 11, 15, 16; **466.** 2, 5; **467.** 3, 7, 12, 16; **468.** 4, 6, 8; **469.** 13; **480.** 14; **154.** 4; a skilful scribe **480.** 14; **488.** 11; **480.** 15; **488** 12; plur. **489.** 12; scribe of the offerings to the god **95.** 16; **54.** 1; **58.** 16; , **110.** 10; **386.** 1; **387.** 7; **452.** 6 *(bis)*; **444.** 10; **445.** 3; with **451.** 4; **461.** 9; **462.** 2; **463.** 7, 14; **464.** 1, 8; **465.** 6; **466.** 12, 14; **468.** 8

***āni*** a board **366.** 5

***Ānpet*** a name of the city of Mendes **231.** 2

**ānχ** a kind of unguent **340.** 15

**ānχ**, **ānχu** to live, living, to live upon, to feed upon, life, living one **6.** 8; **7.** 2; **11.** 14; **35.** 10; **64.** 4, 16; **66.** 1; **68.** 15; **77.** 12, 13; **93.** 15; **97.** 11; **98.** 3, 12; **99.** 6, 10; **102.** 17; **103.** 15; **104.** 5, 15, 16; **111.** 1; **114.** 2; **119.** 16; **120.** 13; **175.** 8; **179.** 9; **285.** 1, 12; **306.** 8, 16; **307.** 10; **308.** 9; **313.** 3, 4; **363.** 6; **370.** 6; **371.** 5, 8; **372.** 6, 11; **377.** 14; **384.** 3; **395.** 3; **398.** 4; **401.** 1, 12; **406.** 16; **407.** 2, 4, 6; **422.** 13; **438.** 14; **439.** 16; **441.** 12; **452.** 8; **466.** 12; **467.** 11; **476.** 1; **482.** 2; **482.** 7; **483.** 4, 5; **487.** 10; **488.** 9; **492.** 13; **493.** 4, 8; **494.** 9, 10; **495.** 4, 12; **496.** 10; **502.** 11, 15; **503.** 8, 12; **504.** 14; **506.** 1; **507.** 4, 9, 16; **510.** 1, 12, 16; **511.** 7; **512.** 6, 8, 9; **513.** 1, 4, 8, 12, 16; **514.** 4, 8, 16; **516.** 4, 13; **367.** 4; **517.** 3; **486.** 11; **161.** 4; **476.** 12; **483.** 4; **458.** 10; **467.** 1

**ānχi** living one **1.** 10; **51.** 3; **133.** 13; a name of Osiris **323.** 2

**ānχu**, **ānχiu** the living, either men and women, or the blessed dead **24.** 2, 9; **26.** 5; **93.** 6, 7; **100.** 3; **113.** 3; **118.** 12; **141.** 4; **145.** 11; **155.** 16; **224.** 16; **249.** 11; **260.** 9; **269.** 10; **295.** 12; **300.** 4, 12; **359.** 7; **428.** 1; **478.** 4; **490.** 6; **497.** 13

**ānχ** ever-living **360.** 10; **468.** 7; life springs out of death **400.** 12

**ānχ** *ānχ uta senb* "life, strength, health!" **3.** 3; **57.** 1; **64.** 2; **110.** 6; **209.** 7; **365.** 3; **460.** 8; **479.** 1; **512.** 14; *ānχ usr* "life, power!" **484.** 13

**ānχet** life 125. 12

**ānχet** victuals 466. 12

***Ānχti*** a name of Osiris 320. 9

***Ānχet-pu-ent-Sebek-neb Baχau*** a proper name 265. 2

***Ānχ-em-fentu*** "Liver on worms", the doorkeeper of the fifth Ārit 328. 9; 360. 12

**ānχui** the two ears 10. 5; 290. 6; 463. 6; 511. 1

**ānχámi** flowers 34. 3; 402. 12; 403. 8; 448. 2

**ānt** ring 96. 15

**ānt** to be covered with 337. 15

**ānt** claw, hook, nail of the hand 393. 1; plur. 448. 12; a proper name 396. 11; a proper name 393. 1

**ānti** a kind of unguent 109. 10; 142. 3; 209. 7; 211. 8; 213. 9; 268. 2; 340. 14; 349. 3; 375. 10; 414. 3; 495. 1; 417. 7; 248. 5

ānṭu ⟨hieroglyphs⟩ light 46. 8; 146. 10

ānṭ ⟨hieroglyphs⟩ evil 68. 16

ānṭu ⟨hieroglyphs⟩ darkness 283. 4

ānṭi ⟨hieroglyphs⟩ one of the forty-two assessors 255. 1

ār ⟨hieroglyphs⟩ an animal of the goat species 292. 12

ār ⟨hieroglyphs⟩ to bring, to come, to arrive 68. 16; 1
āri ⟨hieroglyphs⟩ 9; 124. 1; 214. 12; 244. 1; 279. 5; 3
8; 492. 12; 494. 3; 495. 2

ārā ⟨hieroglyphs⟩ to find 233. 13

ārār ⟨hieroglyphs⟩ jawbone 466. 14

ārārt ⟨hieroglyphs⟩ uraeus 101. 5; ⟨hieroglyphs⟩ ārāti 1
uraei 6. 9; ⟨hieroglyphs⟩ 118. 21; ⟨hieroglyphs⟩
⟨hieroglyphs⟩ two huge uraei 53. 15

ārit ⟨hieroglyphs⟩ a tool 392. 12; lintel of a door 264. 6

ārit ⟨hieroglyphs⟩ hall, chamber 273. 8; 358. 6; 425. 1
plur. ⟨hieroglyphs⟩ 329. 5; 330. 12; 475. 15

ārit ⟨hieroglyphs⟩ 358. 3; ⟨hieroglyphs⟩ 359. 2; ⟨hieroglyphs⟩ 359. 10; 1
360. 3; ⟨hieroglyphs⟩ 360. 12; ⟨hieroglyphs⟩ 361. 5; ⟨hieroglyphs⟩ 361. 14

ārert ⟨hieroglyphs⟩ hall, mansion 362. 8

ārfi ⟨hieroglyphs⟩ bundle, purse 25. 6

ārertu ⟨hieroglyphs⟩ halls, mansions 165. 14; 166. 9; 16
1, 8; 168. 15; 172. 7; 299. 6, 9; 329. 5, 6; 331. 9, 13

**ārerit** hall, mansion 309. 3; 327. 11; 327. 15; 328. 1; 328. 5; 328. 9; 328. 13; 329. 1; plur. 333. 6

**ārq** to bind, to tie 443. 8; girdle 176. 8; to be completed 296. 12; 296. 3, 8

**ārq** to swear 10. 4

**ārq** end 512. 6; end of the earth 389. 11

**ārqi** last day 252. 5

**ārt** jaw 31. 14

**ārti** jawbones 89. 12; 302. 6; 360. 16; 467. 5; 507. 7

**āḥ** the moon 502. 8

**āḥā** to stand up, to withstand 15. 10; 20. 16; 25. 3; 32. 10; 57. 3; 87. 2; 95. 2; 96. 2; 100. 12; 104. 11; 108. 5; 129. 3; 152. 8; 158. 2, 3; 170. 14; 180. 4; 202. 11, 12; 203. 10, 11; 219. 6, 7; 239. 13; 282. 16; 283. 9; 294. 3; 310. 3, 4; 348. 1; 370. 7; 376. 13; 380. 4; 383. 9, 10; 417. 9; 424. 16; 425. 9; 455. 16; 473. 16; 478. 12; 492. 1; 501. 6; 502. 13; 506. 10; 516. 4; 189. 9; 190. 3; 392. 2; 415. 10

**āḥā** as an auxiliary verb 56. 3; 60. 4; 60. 3; 452. 2; 69. 7; and see *passim*.

***Āḥā-àn-urṭ-nef*** a proper name **286.** 16

**āḥā** stability **96.** 7

**āḥā**
**āḥāu**
**āḥāṭ**
duration of life, life, a contemporary **13.** 8; **216.** 9; **357.** 7; **412.** 6, 8; **460.** 9; **459.** 4; **459.** 5

**āḥāu** condition, state **101.** 17

**āḥāu** stores, provisions **137.** 16

**āḥāu** supports **262.** 2; **483.** 3

**āḥāu** noon-day **333.** 16

**āḥait** boat **507.** 3

**āḥāt** tomb **278.** 2; **285.** 6; **326.** 14; **327.** 3; **345.** 11

**āχ** to stretch out or support heaven **49.** 3; **485.** 11

***Āχtuset*** a class of divine beings **244.** 13; the variants are , , , **244.** 13

**āχa** to fly, to soar **63.** 13

**āχa** to sleep **228.** 10

**āχanet** to close the eye **113.** 16

**āχu**
**āχ**
altars **63.** 11, 16; **381.** 5; **425.** 11; **428.** 7

**āχem** / **āχemu** — to quench, to extinguish 86. 4 ; 251. 11 ; 263. 16 ; 302. 11 ; 303. 13 ; 340. 8 ; 378. 8, 11 ; 343. 14 ; quenched 353. 4 ; those who extinguish 320. 8

***Āχemu*** — a class of divine beings 490. 3

**āχemet** — river banks 208. 3

***Āχen-maati-f*** — a proper name 135. 15

**āχeχa** — serpent-fiends 349. 1

***Āχeχu*** — a proper name 257. 10

**āś** — . . . . . . 248. 9

**āśt** / **āśau** — many, much, manifold, multitude, crowd 22. 2 ; 26. 2, 12 ; 158. 14, 15, 16 ; 159. 1 ; 302. 7 ; 314. 2 ; 332. 1 ; 361. 1 ; 398. 12 ; 400. 3 ; 401. 1 ; 408. 9 ; 409. 16 ; 443. 13 ; 502. 9

**āś** — with 301. 8 ; 276. 14 ; 37. 11 ; 257. 10, 14

**āś** — to call, to invoke 28. 13 ; 408. 13

**āś** — evil speech 515. 7

**āś** / **āś** — the cedar or acacia tree 246. 9 ; 310. 9 ; 335. 1

**āś** cedar gum (?) **346.** 12

**āśāśet** a part of the body **117.** 10

**āśāt** knife **391.** 6

**āśemu** the forms in which the gods appear upon earth **122.** 4; **123.** 1; **128.** 14

**āśemu**, **āśemiu** crocodiles **177.** 9; **319.** 2; **364.** 12; var.

**āśaśat** gullet **447.** 2

**Ākeś** name of a city **325.** 7

**āq** to go in, to enter **18.** 6; **19.** 16; **21.** 9; **23.** 7; **29.** 10; **33.** 13; **60.** 2; **61.** 5; **66.** 11; **90.** 4; **103.** 11; **111.** 4; **114.** 1; **135.** 8; **165.** 1; **179.** 14; **185.** 1, 10; **223.** 15; **238.** 8; **241.** 17; **242.** 8, 14; **246.** 5; **264.** 2, 3, 6; **269.** 15; **270.** 3, 6, 14; **302.** 12; **305.** 14; **306.** 1; **309.** 5, 7; **313.** 8; **337.** 10; **341.** 9; **348.** 4, 8; **349.** 4, 11; **351.** 14; **362.** 8; **374.** 15; **394.** 8; **407.** 13; **414.** 14; **428.** 5; **431.** 4, 5, 11; **432.** 11; **435.** 3, 8; **439.** 8; **451.** 15; **460.** 15; **467.** 10; **470.** 12; **472.** 8; **473.** 1; **474.** 12; **475.** 13; **477.** 15; **481.** 7; **489.** 3; **490.** 17; **491.** 10; **492.** 2; **494.** 2; **509.** 1, 4, 10; **513.** 9, 14

**āqiu** those who enter in **374.** 4; **376.** 2; things which enter **464.** 15

**āq pert** entrance and exit **14.** 11; **70.** 5; **194.** 9

**Āq-ḥer-àmi-unnut-f** a proper name **59.** 9

**āqu** cakes, loaves **449.** 11 ; **467.** 9

**āq** just **39.** 9

**āq** to keep the mean ; **114.** 5 ; to be in the middle **130.** 5 ; exactly over the heart **420.** 9

**āqi** part of a boat **87.** 12

**āqa** etc. etc. **207.** 7

**āqa** / **āqu** rope, cordage, tackle of a boat **190.** 7 ; **204.** 6, 13 ; **210.** 16 ; **436.** 10 ; **483.** 15

**āqa** . . . . . . **503.** 8

***Āqan*** a proper name **503.** 12 ; **504.** 2, 3, 13 ; **507.** 3. 15

***Āqennu*** name of a city **439.** 13

**āḳa** unguent **338.** 11

**āḳu** to be burned **133.** 5, 8 ; **134.** 3

**āṭ** / **āṭet** a pole of a net with forked ends **391.** 2 ; **392.** 12, 14 ; **393.** 3 ; **394.** 6, 13 ; **396.** 9

**āt** domain **224.** 11

**āt** hall, palace **125.** 13 ; **224.** 11 ; **272.** 13 ; **341.** 10 ; **437.** 14

***āt*** member, limb 113. 4; 262. 10; 508. 7; plur. 15. 13; 29. 11 *(ter)*; 51. 14; 91. 4, 7; 96. 5; 120. 6; 132. 13; 140. 7; 150. 16; 195. 15; 196. 3, 8; 289. 6; 316. 14; 340. 13; 361. 5; 367. 7; 385. 4; 406. 12; 411. 16; 414. 6; 426. 12; 439. 16; 440. 16; 468. 15; 478. 10; 479. 13; 482. 6

***Āti*** the ninth nome of Lower Egypt 255. 3, 14

***āteptu*** grain 333. 10

***āter*** provisions (?) 436. 8

***Āṭ*** a proper name 346. 14

***āṭ*** domain, region 105. 15

***āṭu*** soil 453. 10

***āṭ*** to divide, to split 128. 2

***Aaṭi*** one of the forty-two assessors 255. 1

***Āṭetet***, ***Āṭ***, ***āṭeṭet*** the morning boat of the Sun 2. 4; 3. 4; 4. 6; 6. 8; 7. 8; 35. 14; 40. 5; 103. 13; 125. 9; 164. 13; 214. 15; 284. 14; 319. 7; 382. 9; 386. 8; 387. 12; 489. 15

***āṭu*** name of a mythological fish 243. 2

***āṭurt*** (?) . . . . . . . (a mistake ?) 275. 6

***Āṭ-ur*** "Great Splitter", name of a god 111. 2

***āṭet*** fixed 304. 7, 9

# U.

*u* . . . . . . . . 432. 16

*u* they, them, their 411. 16; 416. 6, 7; 509. 11, 12; 512. 5

*Ua* a proper name 441. 7

*ua*
*uau* to depart, to go away 56. 2; 97. 4; 219. 16; 229. 7; 334. 13; 421. 14; 436. 8; 42. 3

*ua*
*uau* way, path, road 204. 16; 350. 3; plur. 135. 10; 10. 8; 296. 7

*uau* water-course, stream 297. 15; 378. 16

*uauau* radiance 138. 8

*uau* flame 344. 13

*uau* chains, fetters 452. 2

*uauu* to speak evil 512. 11

*uaui-uait* hair 356. 16

***uai*** to destroy, to vanquish, to be master of 131. 11; 350. 3

***Uaipu*** a cow-goddess 462. 5

***uab*** flower, blossom 167. 10; 505. 14

***Uamemti*** one of the forty-two assessors 255. 5

***uaret*** rope, cordage, tackle 393. 5

***Uart-neter-semsu*** a proper name 393. 6

***uaḥ*** to place, to set, to fix, permanent, enduring, abiding 5. 10; 95. 12; 139. 2; 144. 2; 165. 3; 365. 3; 392. 6; 438. 15; 439. 1; 460. 4; 501. 13; to add to 251. 2, 3; 180. 13

***uaḥit*** libation vessels 180. 3

***uaχ*** a pool in the Elysian Fields 228. 14, 16

***uas*** sceptre, staff of office or honour 158. 13; 201. 3; 263. 12; 277. 16; 438. 2

***uasm*** (or ***smu***), ***uasmu*** refined copper of the finest quality 37. 16; 96. 14; 447. 1, 4

***Uast*** Thebes in Egypt 45. 4; 248. 16; 443. 10

***uaś*** to worship, to be adored 271. 4; 298. 7; twice adored 169. 8

***Uaḳ*** name of a festival 440. 3; 497. 1

**uat** way, road, path 21. 4; 55. 3, 7; 103. 8; 104. 10; 134. 6; 196. 2; 233. 7; 239. 9; 283. 16; 332. 7; 370. 8; 382. 11; 468. 6; 491. 3; 493. 7; plur. 37. 5; 104. 10; 107. 9; 113. 12; 143. 14; 170. 16; 210. 11; 224. 6; 239. 3, 4; 311. 6; 320. 4; 369. 11; 105. 14; 106. 13; two ways 438. 12; 451. 7; 79. 2; each and every path 362. 6; fair ways 386. 16; 388. 1; 388. 4; 448. 10

**uat àbtet** eastern roads 319. 15

**uat àmentet** western roads 319. 16

**uaṭ meḥtet** northern roads 319. 15

**uat reset** southern roads 319. 14

**uaṭ** sceptre 502. 14

**uaṭ** tablet 263. 8, 14, 16; amulet 216. 15; 405. 9, 15; 406. 3, 4; amulet of green *faïence* 291. 2

**uaṭ** unguent 333. 12

**uaṭu** a green mineral substance, mother-of-emerald (?) 367. 3, 11; 369. 6, 15; 371. 2, 13; 372. 7; 373. 4; 375. 15; 377. 5; 378. 2

**uaṭ qemā**, **uaṭet qemā**, **uaṭ qemāt** mother-of-emerald of the south 164. 11; 353. 13; 414. 4

**uaṭet** a kind of linen 414. 5

**uaṭ** to make to flourish, to be green or vigorous; to blossom, to sow seed, vigour, new, fresh **13.** 14; **23.** 10; **64.** 16; **104.** 1; **128.** 13; **137.** 10; **143.** 9; **161.** 16; **173.** 2; **217.** 1 *(bis)*; **232.** 13; **243.** 11; **258.** 15; **268.** 7 *(bis)*; **310.** 7; **311.** 1, 7, 16; **349.** 2; **375.** 4; **379.** 8

**uaṭet** green **211.** 7

**uaṭet** green things, plants, herbs **124.** 9; **379.** 8, 10

**uaṭu** = *uṭu q. v.*

**Uaṭ-urȧ** "Great Green", the Mediterranean sea **54.** 13, 16; **55.** 1

**Uaṭ-maati** "Green Eyes", a proper name **99.** 14

**Uaṭ-nes**[**ert**] one of the forty-two assessors **254.** 1

**Uaṭit** a goddess **68.** 15; **69.** 8; **117.** 9; **148.** 10; **298.** 15; **303.** 3; **470.** 4; **508.** 10; , *Uaṭti* the two uraei goddesses, *i. e.*, Isis and Nephthys **8.** 7; **447.** 3

**uaṭṭet** herbs, plants **493.** 3

**uȧ** I, me **22.** 8, 15; **23.** 1; **122.** 2; **143.** 11; **153.** 11; **317.** 7 *(bis)*, 8; **375.** 14; **473.** 1, 13, 14

**uȧa** boat, boat of the Sun **4.** 9; **5.** 3; **6.** 9; **7.** 7; **12.** 15; **15.** 4; **25.** 1, 10; **40.** 14; **49.** 2; **66.** 5; **67.** 1; **111.** 2; **148.** 12; **149.** 7; **186.** 11; **190.** 4; **195.** 8; **203.** 10, 11; **210.** 7; **212.** 6, 8, 9; **214.** 5, 6, 7;

219. 8; 221. 9; 224. 10; 247. 10; 269. 5; 280. 16; 283. 3, 6; 284. 3, 6, 8; 289. 4; 291. 1, 5, 7, 8; 292. 10; 293. 6; 294. 4; 295. 16; 296. 5, 10, 13; 297. 10; 299. 1, 2, 16; 300. 2, 16; 301. 4, 12; 316. 4, 15; 318. 5; 330. 6, 7; 332. 6, 15; 349. 3; 368. 11; 395. 1, 12; 423. 10, 14; 424. 11; 425. 8; 441. 16; 479. 11

**aȧaiu** the Āṭet and Sektet boats, *i. e.*, the boats of the rising and setting sun 392. 10

***uȧa en Maāti*** the boat of Maāti 103. 12

***uȧa en ḥeḥ*** boat of millions of years 415. 6; 459. 14; 460. 2; 481. 12; 490. 12; boat of Rā 103. 7; 104. 11; boat of Kheperȧ 103. 5; 107. 8; boat of Tem 104. 10; boat of the divine father 415. 11

***uȧn*** to become worms 399. 10

***Uā*** One, the One 2. 1; 9. 9; 25. 16; 26. 1; 26. 10 *(bis)*; 97. 13; 167. 12, 15; 169. 1; 210. 14; 240. 7; 291. 13; 329. 15; 362. 3, 13; 377. 2; 497. 16; One God, *i. e.*, Osiris 452. 7; One (of a goddess) 415. 5; One of the gods 173. 8

***uā*** one, any one 5. 10; 62. 6; 167. 2, 14; 271. 10; 286. 8, 13; 317. 1; 364. 15; 440. 9; 462. 9; being one 10. 3; being alone 41. 16; one (fem.) 333. 7, 14

***uā*** .... one .... the other 62. 7; 97. 13; 54. 13, 15; 55. 1; 417. 3, 4, 5; 420. 5, 8; 452. 2; one to her fellow 449. 16; 485. 4; .... 407. 10, 11; 413. 4, 5, 15; 414. 1; 114. 7; 115. 9; 137. 4; 143. 4; = indefinite article a star **492.** 3; a follower **409.** 12; **405.** 3

**uā** to be one 51. 6; *uā neb* any one, each one, every one **222.** 4; **317.** 5; **368.** 4; **407.** 12; **408.** 2; **57.** 11; circling one **241.** 2

**uā uāu** one alone **363.** 14

**uāu** alone **392.** 6

**uāuti** solitude, alone **413.** 9; **461.** 15

**uāiu** alone **107.** 13

**uā** with 7. 6; and see *sub*; with **470.** 15

**uāt** a piece of cloth **420.** 8

**Uāau** the herald of the third Ārit **328.** 3

**uār** passage **203.** 4

**uār** to depart **219.** 10

**uārt** passage (of souls) **187.** 2; name of a place **284.** 7

**uārt**, **uārt** thigh **87.** 6; **162.** 11; **202.** 9; **207.** 9; **215.** 5, 7; **297.** 1, 15; **373.** 11; **375.** 1; **378.** 3; **376.** 13; **392.** 1; **392.** 2;

380. 5; 397. 5

**uārti** the two thighs **447.** 7

**uārt** stream **218.** 4

**uu** evil, evil one **414.** 12

**uu** district of a nome, of **324.** 15

**ui** sign of the dual two very mighty gods **272.** 15

**Ui** a proper name **207.** 12

**uben** to rise (of a luminary), to shine **1.** 3, 6; **3.** 13; **4.** 1, 2; **6.** 13; **8.** 14; **25.** 16; **52.** 1; **61.** 8; **85.** 14; **102.** 13; **114.** 1; **115.** 8; **137.** 8; **207.** 8; **235.** 8, 13; **238.** 4; **292.** 5; **296.** 11; **314.** 15, 16; **315.** 9; **408.** 9; **423.** 11, 15; **425.** 9; **456.** 9; **484.** 14; **486.** 15; **502.** 8; **513.** 3; rising and setting **411.** 12; **426.** 10; **39.** 6

**ubennu**, **ubentu** rays of light **120.** 18; **292.** 5; **446.** 2

**ubennu** to flow **392.** 15

**ubeχ**, **ubeχt** to shine, shining, blazing **301.** 2, 5; **307.** 8

**ubes** water-flood **279.** 11

**ubesu** fiery beings **283.** 9

***Ubes-ḥrȧ-per-em-χetχet*** a proper name **59.** 11

***ubeṭ*** to be scalded **133.** 16; to set fire to, to burn up **341.** 16; **344.** 5; **354.** 11

***ufa*** to be in restraint (?) **493.** 15

***umet*** a garment **448.** 15

***umetet*** middle (?) **135.** 5

***un*** , lightness **21.** 14; defect **273.** 11

***un*** to be, being, existence, what shall be, things which are, to become **2.** 8; **4.** 15; **24.** 8; **53.** 3, 5, 13; **57.** 2; **61.** 1, 13; **64.** 8; **80.** 14; **89.** 15; **94.** 3; **95.** 2; **120.** 13; **152.** 11; **164.** 3; **218.** 13; **232.** 6; **285.** 1, 14; **308.** 8; **309.** 4; **318.** 1; **347.** 11; **364.** 15; **366.** 11, 12; **374.** 11, 14; **377.** 14; **382.** 14; **401.** 5, 8; **406.** 15; **414.** 7, 8; **436.** 9; **425.** 11; **431.** 2; **433.** 5; **455.** 14; **459.** 1; **461.** 4; **462.** 2; **468.** 1; **481.** 3; **484.** 4; **487.** 12; **490.** 6; **493.** 15; **497.** 16; **501.** 5; **507.** 12; **517.** 3; as an auxiliary verb see *passim*

***unt, unenet*** , ***untet*** being, existence **10.** 13; **14.** 3; **51.** 10; **226.** 8; **471.** 1; **479.** 15; **482.** 12; **504.** 7, 8; **505.** 8; **75.** 15; being **450.** 3; rising (?) **96.** 11; those who are **159.** 14; **208.** 10; **249.** 10; **252.** 9; **270.** 3; **376.** 6; **389.** 3; **486.** 6; , , **36.** 14; **174.** 5; **295.** 7

***un***, ***unen*** with *maā*, in very truth **16.** 1; **95.** 4; **366.** 15

***un*** to open, opener, opening, opened 5. 11; 19. 12; 21. 6; 26. 3; 30. 4; 89. 10, 12; 103. 7; 105. 16; 110. 13; 119. 9; 131. 7; 143. 14; 148. 16; 149. 2, 11, 12, 14; 150. 6, 10; 170. 16; 194. 12; 241. 17; 244. 10; 264. 14, 16; 265. 3, 8; 272. 9; 373. 7; 275. 9; 278. 13, 14, 15, 16; 346. 3; 374. 7; 376. 16; 436. 2, 7; 438. 7; 470. 10; 474. 2; 493. 7; 502. 10; 514. 1, 6; 37. 6; 235. 2; 372. 2; 380. 8; 473. 16; to burst open 124. 13; opened 213. 4; 295. 1; 374. 15; 420. 4; 128. 8; 194. 15; 195. 1; 351. 14

***uniu***, ***uneniu*** openers, scatterers 21. 4; 320. 7

***un*** appearance 41. 16; 86. 7, 8, 12; 154. 11; *un ḥrà* to open the face (*i. e.*, to uncover?) 100. 5; 119. 13; 234. 5; 236. 12; 336. 6; 433. 9; 467. 2; 234. 8

***un*** shrine 323. 3

***un*** shaved 401. 16

***un***, ***unenu*** to pull out hair 469. 3; 471. 11

*un*, *uni*, *unt* — to rise up 32. 8; 51. 6; 62. 5; 120. 6, 18; 162. 8; 388. 10; those who rise up.

*unun*, *unenunen* — to lift up 120. 16, 18; 155. 7

*uni* — light, defective 288. 15

*Unen-em-ḥetep* — a division of the Elysian Fields 228. 3, 8; 229. 6

*unām* — unguent 311. 8

*unun* — to sow seed 227. 8

*unb* — flower, blossom 91. 16; 115. 12; plur. 157. 3

*Unpepet-ent-Ḥet-Ḥeru* — a proper name 266. 2

*unfu*, *unf* — to remove, to uncover, to unloose 115. 4; 125. 10

*unem*, *unemi*, *unemet* — the right side, opposite of left 34. 4; 43. 1; 56. 15; 111. 12; 152. 6, 7; 264. 6; 284. 14; 382. 8; 386. 7; 387. 11; 389. 13; 395. 13; 420. 8; 436. 1

*unnu* — . . . . . . 128. 15

***Unnu***
***Unenu*** Hermopolis 28. 5; 30. 4; 127. 10; 131. 1; 183. 1; 203. 14; 309. 14

***unnut***
***unnut*** (?) a brief space of time, moment, hour 10. 11; 59. 9; 85. 8; 136. 4; 137. 5; 143. 5; 262. 13; 302. 4; 315. 7; 333. 15; 380. 6; 437. 12; 467. 3; 508. 11 *(bis)*; plur. 42. 5; 97. 14; 99. 11; 137. 2; 228. 15; 315. 8; 468; 5; hours (?) 10. 11

***Unnut*** goddess of the hour 309. 14

***Un-nefer***
***Unen-nefer***
***Unen-neferu***
***Unen-nefer*** a title of Osiris 13. 7; 14. 4; 16. 14; 23. 2; 37. 10; 114. 6; 182. 5; 249. 13; 276. 10; 285. 8; 298. 3; 320. 8; 323. 1; 347. 4, 11; 366. 11; 452. 2; 471. 1; 476. 3; 479. 14; 481. 6, 10; 482. 12, 16; 484. 4, 6; 489. 2, 4; Un nefer-Rā 48. 6; 70. 2; 78. 9

***Un-ḥāt*** a proper name 359. 2

***unχ***
***unχu*** to dress, to put on a garment 180. 3; to array oneself 229. 3; arrayed, girded with 239. 5; 267. 14

***unχ*** to be loosed, to untie 294. 16; 295. 1; 359. 15

***unχ*** garment 339. 6

*Unes* the capital of the XIXth nome of Lower Egypt 256. 5

*uneśu* wolves 87. 7

*Unt* a city of the twelfth Aat 377. 7, 10, 14, 15; 381. 14

*Unti* name of a god 38. 5; 298. 4

*un tini* be ye 114. 14

*unṭu* kinsfolk, relatives 18. 13; 19. 2; 68. 10; 250. 2

*Unθ* name of a district or country 257. 7

*Ur* , a proper name 165. 10; 179. 12

*ur* to be great, great, mighty, supreme, powerful, might, mighty one 9. 12; 16. 2; 359. 1; 392. 10; 504. 6; 506. 10; fem. 27. 12; 194. 2; 281. 12; greatly, exceedingly 421. 13; *ur-ui* two great (plumes) 6. 2; 330. 9; *urtiu* might (?) 332. 10

*ur* , great man, chief, prince, nobleman 22. 16; 38. 16; 116. 18; 119. 1; 174. 3; 493. 12

*uru* , , , chiefs, nobles 25. 3; 31. 12; 103. 11; 236. 11; 260. 11; 275. 14; 398. 6; 478. 3; 509. 5; *urt* princess 295. 13; mighty ones or things 345. 11; 169. 7

*ur*, *uru*, *uru*, *uru* — divine being 38. 6; 98. 10; 119. 16; 133. 11; 136. 2; 139. 5; 144. 5; 172. 9; 201. 10; 214. 6; 217. 16; 229. 8; 240. 12; 286. 14; 358. 7; 367. 6; 372. 3; 377. 11; 392. 9; 403. 6; 418. 9; 468. 3; 476. 1; 478. 8; 496. 2; 512. 2; plur. 111. 12; 128. 5; 131. 12; 165. 2; 201. 7; 245. 3; 271. 6; 289. 5; 301. 10; 439. 7; 440. 1; 455. 8; 459. 16

*urt* — goddess, great lady 200. 7, 9; 210. 12; 286. 12, 15; 404. 10; 405. 11; 455. 12; 490. 14; 504. 5; 506. 7

*ur sep sen* — doubly great 419. 9; 483. 5; 513. 9

*ur* — oldest, greatest 487. 4

*ur* — ..... greater than 106. 9; 442. 9

*ur* — 86. 15; most mighty one 188. 13; 227. 2; 396. 4; 501. 13; most great 43. 14; 194. 1; 343. 5; 482. 10; 17. 1; 171. 14; 27. 4; 259. 2; 367. 13; 373. 7; 378. 9; 293. 3; 131. 15

***Ur-Ȧnnu*** prince of Heliopolis **406.** 8; **406.** 8

***Ur-urti*** the two great goddesses **136.** 7; **142.** 16

***ur χerp āb*** (or ***ḥem***) "the chief president of the worker[s]", a title of the high priest of Memphis **20.** 9

***ur . . . . . .*** chief of the . . . . . . ? **63.** 3

***ur*** large joint of meat, haunch **23.** 8; **130.** 8; **161.** 13; **242.** 6; **268.** 9; **434.** 14

***Ur-at*** a proper name **515.** 3

***Urit*** name of a city **256,** 1, 12

***urit*** hall **313.** 4; **506.** 7

***Ur-peḥui-f*** a proper name **332.** 10

***urma*** (?) ornaments (?), gear (?) **236.** 14; **237.** 13; **450.** 7

***Ur-maat*** a proper name **237.** 13

***Ur-maat-s*** a proper name **215.** 1

***Ur-mertu-s-ṭeśert-śeni*** name of a cow-goddess **318.** 12; **364.** 2

***Ur-ḥekau*** "mighty one of enchantments", a proper name **220.** 3; **376.** 7; **415.** 6; **439.** 3; **481.** 12

**urer** / **ureret** / **urertu** } name of a crown 13. 10; 38. 10; 65. 4, 5; 177. 4; 239. 5; 289. 14; 293. 10, 14; 361. 11; 367. 9; 408. 7; 469. 4; 471. 8; 477. 4; 482. 11; 476. 6 *(bis)*; 318. 7

**urḫ** / **urḫu** } anointed 268. 1; 294. 7; 308. 4; 335. 1, 11; 336. 7; 337. 2, 14; 338. 11; 339. 5; 340. 1, 14; 341. 10

**ur-ḥefati** two goddesses of Heliopolis 495. 9

**ures** pillow 420. 16

**urś** / **urśu** } to pass the time, to watch (?) 186. 8; 236. 10; 357. 7; 515. 1

**urt** hall 287. 9

**urt** funeral chest 2. 9

**urt** pylon, hall 506. 7 *(bis)*

**urt** funeral mountain 490. 19

**urt** flood 132. 10

**urt** = *ureret* crown 359. 16

**Urt-urt** a proper name 469. 7

**urṭ** to be motionless, to rest, inert, helpless 6. 5; 66. 12; 120. 6; 133. 12; 221. 9; 282. 16; 290. 4; 368. 11

***Urṭ-àb*** "Still-heart", a name of Osiris 19. 13; 139. 8; 144. 8; 334. 9; 335. 4, 15; 336. 11, 14; 337. 7; 338. 2, 8, 15; 339. 9; 340. 5; 341. 2, 14; 342. 5, 12; 343. 3, 7, 12; 344. 2, 10; 345. 1, 9, 16; 346. 7; 351. 6; 352. 7; 356. 6; 402. 8 *(bis)*; 435. 2; 480. 11; 481. 9, 10; 489. 4; see 99. 13

***uh*** to be troubled 149. 16

***uhau*** to supplicate 349. 5

***uhen*** decay, failure 482. 1

***uhen-tu*** overthrown 436. 14

***uḥeset*** to beat down, to slay 357. 4; 481. 14

***uḥet*** baked meats, stew 449. 9

***uχa*** to lay or set down, placed 152. 8; 214. 16; to seek 178. 7

***uχa*** darkness, night 183. 12

***uχa*** pillar 445. 1, 3

***uχeb*** to shine, bright 219. 4

***uχert*** a wooden implement 296. 13; 297. 9; plur. 296. 4

***uχeṭ*** to be angry or pained 458. 1, 14

***uχeṭet*** boat 89. 7, 8

***us*** to do away with 274. 10

***usfa*** snarers 395. 10

*us* power, strength 1. 10; 14. 2

*user* to be strong, mighty, strength, might, power, strong 6. 8; 32. 12; 38. 16; 47. 7; 100. 4; 103. 15; 122. 1; 174. 16; 182. 16; 196. 15; 198. 2; 225. 6; 228. 4; 240. 15; 269. 7; 286. 16; 298. 12, 13; 303. 1; 353. 12; 362. 5; 376. 9; 425. 12; 426. 13; 445. 7; 454. 13; 465. 14; 484. 13; 496. 15; 357. 8; 376. 11

*useru* powers, mighty ones (human or divine), strength 171. 13; 176. 16; 196. 15; 198. 2; 298. 14; 303. 2; 358. 10

*usert* strength 92. 10

*usert*, *user* a strong place, a part of the head or neck, brow 33. 4; 98. 15; 173. 3; 193. 6; 307. 14, 17; 325. 13; 119. 12; 191. 14, 16; 192. 3; 169. 7; 171. 3; 192. 16; 204. 11, 12; 332. 10; 345. 12; 191. 8

*User-ȧb* "Strong-heart", a proper name 299. 13; 475. 5

*User-ba* "Strong-soul" a proper name 146. 13

*useru* oars 130. 4; 206. 9; 242. 11

*useru* to steer a boat 488. 12

*Usert* "Strong-one", name of a goddess 230. 2; 339. 12

**useḥ** to advance 151. 12

**useχ** collar, neck ornament 404. 16; 405. 4

**useχ** breadth 218. 17

**useχ** to be in a wide space 124. 13

**useχ** breadth, broad, wide space 151. 12; 218. 15; 338. 5; 352. 5; 370. 4; 493. 7

**Useχ-nemtet** "Broad of Stride", a proper name 515. 2

**Useχ-nemtet** one of the forty-two assessors 252. 13

**Useχ-ḥrá** "Broad Face", a name of Rā 92. 6

**useχt** hall 14. 8; with 182. 17; 246. 5; 259. 9, 15, 17; 260. 7; 264. 2; 444. 16; 467. 8; 476. 9 *(bis)*

**useχti āat** the great double hall 509. 6

**useχti Maāti** the double hall of Maati (var. ) 249. 3, 10; 259. 15; 260. 7; 264. 2; 265. 13; 266. 5; 267. 13; 424. 8; 434. 3; 509. 1

**useχt Śuu** the hall of Shu 509. 8

**useχt Seb** the hall of Seb 425. 12; 509. 7

**useχu** plated 447. 11

***useśt*** urine 125. 1, 6; 238. 16; 465. 10

***useś*** to evacuate 414. 8

***usten***, ***ustennu*** to walk, to follow 424. 12; 431. 6; 432. 12; 433. 4

***Usṭ*** a proper name 359. 4

***uś*** to cry out 471. 15

***uśau*** night, darkness 136. 1; 472. 7

***uśā*** to eat, to gnaw, to crunch bones, to inhale the smell of food 100. 14; 209. 15; 446. 6; 449. 9

***uśeb*** to answer 197. 6; 198. 12

***uśeb sep*** to make an answer at the right time 443. 4

***uśeb*** to be begotten 227. 4

***uśen*** to net 453. 16; 480. 5

***uśennu*** feathered fowl 229. 2

***Uḳa*** a festival 278. 6; 513. 10

***uḳaiu*** wooden pegs or legs 206. 14

***ut*** the city of embalmment, the abode of Anubis 327. 5; 385. 15

*utu* embalmment **205.** 11

*Utu* the god of embalmment, *i. e.*, Anubis **208.** 6

*ut* coffin **407.** 9

*uta* to act the part of an embalmer **450.** 6

*Utet-meḥt* the northern Oasis, el-Baḥriyeh **324.** 12

*Utet-reset* the southern Oasis, el-Khargeh **324.** 11

*Utau* (?) a proper name **427.** 2; **431.** 13

*utu*, *utut* to set out on a journey **40.** 5; to command, to order, command, order, decree, to copy, behest **24.** 5; **27.** 7; **41.** 6; **52.** 11; **77.** 14; **78.** 1, 2; **89.** 15; **103.** 3; **110.** 4; **114.** 4; **161.** 15; **195.** 1; **199.** 15; **201.** 5; **215.** 8; **243.** 2; **250.** 10; **273.** 3; **283.** 11; **287.** 1 *(bis)*; **315.** 3; **331.** 4; **385.** 1, 2; **401.** 2, 4; **404.** 7; **421.** 3; **428.** 9; **431.** 15; **445.** 11; **448.** 3; **451.** 2; **455.** 15, 17; **459.** 3; **464.** 1, 2; **465.** 1; **471.** 3, 4; **472.** 3; **485.** 10; **488.** 2; **503.** 16, 17; **505.** 12; **514.** 16

*uṭeṭ* to order **24.** 7; **65.** 6; **91.** 9

*utut*, *uṭeṭet* commands, behests, things ordered or decreed **21.** 12; **105.** 6; **151.** 6; **152.** 4; **172.** 8; **220.** 10; **369.** 12; **371.** 1, 7; **461.** 16

***Utu-reχit*** one of the forty-two assessors **258.** 7

***uṭun*** (?) . . . . . . . . **52.** 10

***utu*** unguent (= [?]) **333.** 13

***utu*** flowers **449.** 9

***utuit*** oar-rest **205.** 12

***uteb*** mutable **173.** 9

***uteb*** to go or come round about **166.** 5; **201.** 12

***uteb***, ***utebu*** furrow **151.** 3; **152.** 2; **263.** 10, 11; **494.** 16; plur. , **29.** 1; **158.** 3; **177.** 7; **288.** 4; **384.** 9, 13; **453.** 8

***uteḥ*** altar **214.** 16; **439.** 13; plur. **154.** 13; **155.** 6

***Utent*** name of a country **144.** 16

***utet*** to beget **9.** 11; **13.** 9

***utet*** to beget **11.** 11; **442.** 8; begotten **442.** 13; *uta* begetter **321.** 15

***Utet*** Begetter, a name of Osiris **324.** 8

***Utet-ḥeḥ*** "Begetter of millions of years", a proper name **55.** 1

*uṭ*
*uṭet* — to shoot out, to cast out, to dart forth from 36. 12; 56. 11; 105. 12; 110. 3; 136. 7; 143. 1; 191. 15; 192. 14; 193. 10; 271. 10; 311. 13, 14; 383. 5, 6; to put forth the hand with hostility against anyone 453. 3; 497. 11

*uṭaiu* — strong 195. 4

*uṭit* — chamber 504. 5, 6

*uṭebtu* — burned 206. 7

*uṭen*
*uṭennu* — to drive back 86. 11; to make an offering 247. 8; 268. 2; 284. 15; 294. 7; 299. 14; 312. 6; 318. 3; 332. 16; 333. 6; 359. 8; 395. 14; 423. 12, 15; 424. 3, 6, 9, 12, 15; 425. 4, 7, 10, 13, 16; 426. 3, 5, 8, 11, 14; 427. 1, 4, 7, 9, 13, 16; 428. 3, 6, 9, 12; 429. 1, 4, 7, 10, 13; 430. 1, 4, 6, 10, 12, 15; 431. 3, 6, 8, 11, 14; 432. 1, 4, 7, 9, 12, 15; 433. 2, 5, 7, 10, 15; 434. 3, 6, 9, 12, 15; 435. 2, 5, 7; 440. 10; 450. 12; 486. 4; 422. 5, 7, 8, 10, 13, 15; 423. 3, 5; 423. 1

*uṭen*
*uṭennu*
*uṭent* — offerings, things offered 278. 15; 316. 12; 317. 2; 375. 11; 437. 15

*uṭeṭ* — to void (filth) 64. 6

*uθes* — to raise up, to lift up, to support, 43. 11; 134. 2; 220. 7; 286. 15; 370. 14; 456. 1; 472. 9; 503. 15

*ufa* — to go out, to set out, to escape from, to journey **2.** 11; **35.** 13; **55.** 9, 14 *(bis)*; **190.** 9; **205.** 4; **209.** 2; **212.** 9, 15; **213.** 3, 6; **267.** 8; **312.** 10; **414.** 15; **419.** 7; **450.** 8; **451.** 6; **465.** 10

*ufat* — journey **159.** 2

*ufa* — to be in a good state or condition, to preserve, sound, healthy, well **2.** 14; **7.** 13; **29.** 16; **57.** 6; **63.** 9; **77.** 3; **112.** 7, 8; **113.** 10; **116.** 6; **220.** 2; **290.** 2, 3; **305.** 10, 13; **370.** 10; **406.** 5, 6; **411.** 3; **421.** 15, 16; **425.** 5, 15; **429.** 12

*ufau* — strength **479.** 13

*ufau* — amulet **213.** 11; plur. **402.** 14

*ufau* — magical powers **403.** 5

*Ufa-re* — "Strong-mouth", a proper name **22.** 4; **347.** 1

*ufa sep* — strong with good fortune **289.** 16

*ufat* — the eye of the Sun **38.** 15; **56.** 7; **57.** 9; **113.** 15, 16; **114.** 2, 8; **139.** 14; **158.** 7; **211.** 3; **252.** 5; **267.** 10, 11; **314.** 13; **315.** 4, 9, 10, 11, 15; **316.** 10, 14; **317.** 3, 4; **386.** 4; **408.** 10; **421.** 10, 11, 12

*ufati* — the two eyes of the Sun **413.** 1, 3

*ufat* — the Utchat with legs and wings **413.** 4; **416.** 13

***ufā*** to weigh, be weighed, to estimate, to consider, to reckon up, to make a decision, to release **16.** 1, 16; **96.** 9; **101.** 17; **104.** 14; **177.** 1; **201.** 13; **235.** 9; **242.** 16; **296.** 4, 13; **297.** 8; **302.** 1; **314.** 4; **358.** 16; **360.** 9; **447.** 16; **493.** 3

***ufā-meṭet*** to consider or estimate words **18.** 12; **19.** 5; **79.** 9; **285.** 13; **309.** 8; **359.** 6; **471.** 9; **475.** 1

***ufā senemem*** to weigh hair (?) **79.** 9; who maketh the water to make to balance his throne **239.** 8; to estimate the fields **124.** 9

***ufāiu*** weighers, those who try something in a balance **1.** 13; **422.** 3

***ufāti*** judgment, decision **233.** 7

***Ufā-aābet*** a proper name **126.** 9

***ufefau*** to delay **189.** 7; **190.** 1

## 𓇋𓇋, 〃 I.

*i*

*iu*

to come, comer, coming, come 1. 5; 4. 13; 11. 8; 31. 1; 41. 1; 54. 2; 58. 1; 67. 14; 69. 12; 70. 2, 7; 85. 5; 86. 3, 9; 88. 14; 93. 5; 97. 7, 10; 98. 6, 9; 102. 14; 109. 8; 129. 4; 137. 6; 239. 5; 301. 5; 302. 5; 303. 14; 304. 1; 305. 10; 310. 2; 311. 12; 312. 14; 313. 1; 331. 7; 334. 13; 347. 4, 12; 348. 2; 349. 1; 350. 3; 358. 7; 359. 15; 361. 9; 362. 2; 363. 14; 370. 14; 372. 1; 374. 14; 375. 13; 379. 4, 6; 382. 12; 383. 16; 384. 16; 389. 5; 392. 11, 13; 394. 6, 8; 398. 5; 399. 1; 404. 4; 408. 12; 429. 8; 432. 10; 442. 15; 452. 8, 13, 14; 453. 1, 2, 10, 13, 15; 454. 1—16; 456. 6; 457. 1; 459. 7; 462. 5; 466. 10; 480. 11; 482. 4, 14; 483. 7, 10, 14; 484. 10; 487. 7; 488. 1; 490. 4; 491. 1; 494. 10; 495. 5; 503. 9, 10, 13; 504. 2, 14; 505. 2; 506. 2, 10, 16; 507. 4; 507. 5; 510. 4, 9; 511. 6; 512. 4; 516. 2; 𓂝 〃 𓅱 come, come! 261. 8

*i-tu*

*iu-tu*

coming, a coming 75. 4; 97. 12; 109. 8; 192. 4; 192. 10; 304. 5; 372. 5, 6; 379. 9, 14; 478. 17; advance 33. 7; 441. 10

*it*    𓇋𓇋 𓂝 a coming 112. 4; 468. 14; 469. 1, 6; 479. 13; 480. 1; 512. 2; 𓂝 356. 6; 𓇋𓇋 〃 1. 5; 48. 8, 9; 406. 7; 𓇋〃 𓂝 ▭ 8. 3

*iu* comers **193**. 5; **342**. 7; **355**. 3; **492**. 3; **46**. 3; *iu āq* going in and coming out **194**. 9

*iu* to end (of a book) **380**. 14

***Iupastu*** a class of divine beings **231**. 3

*i* / *it* hail, O, **107**. 10, 11; **108**. 2

*iu* O verily **409**. 8

*iumā* sea **412**. 3 *(bis)*

***Ireqai*** a name of Åmen-Rā **419**. 11

*iχ* to stretch out the heavens **412**. 3

*isu* abodes **436**. 7

# B.

*ba* soul 3. 5; 14. 10; 30. 14; 37. 3; 40. 4; 90. 3; 145. 8; 171. 5; 194. 4; 194. 12; 195. 1, 10, 12, 13; 285. 1, 11; 307. 9, 10; 315. 14; 325. 12; 347. 11; 363. 6; 399. 14; 409. 6, 9; 432. 5, 7; 438. 9; 459. 16; 460. 2; 461. 13; 462. 3; 471. 14; 472. 2; 480. 6; 491. 7, 10, 16; plur. 44. 2; 363. 9; , 62. 3; 74. 13; 166. 6; 190. 6; 194. 7; 195. 8, 14; 276. 12, 14; 277. 8; 381. 14; 454. 12; 490. 2; 430. 14

*ba* soul 21. 3; 51. 2; 65. 16; *ba* with and 194. 12; *ba* with 194. 12; *ba* with 189. 12; *ba* with 196. 3; *ba* with and 487. 15; a perfect soul 145. 4; 194. 5, 8; 433. 3; 491. 14; 147. 6; 183. 16; 268. 15; with 384. 1; 470. 13; 475. 16; 493. 8; soul of souls 48. 9; 185. 8; 38. 8; 412. 12; 308. 9; a soul made of gold 191. 1; 436. 4

**Ba** divine soul 20. 8; 28. 6; 60. 2, 8; 184. 2, 3, 7; 185. 1, 11; 194. 1; 271. 9; 272. 14; 273. 8; 296. 7; 509. 11, 12; 510. 1, 11; 512. 6; 516. 13, 14; plur. 20. 12; 21. 1, 5; 58. 15; 94. 10; 472. 1; 474. 4; 510. 7, 13; 511. 3, 13, 14; 512. 9; 513. 12, 16; 514. 4, 8, 15

**Ba** 60. 9; 94. 11; *Ba* 94. 9; *Ba* 60. 9; *Ba* 66. 4; (*i. e.*, Smam-ur); *Ba* 60. 10; *Ba-šeps*, holy soul, a name of Osiris 323. 8; *Ba-ṭeser*, a name of Osiris 471. 1; 475. 10; 481. 9; 420. 1; 429. 15; 413. 12; 397. 13; 65. 11; 430. 11

**baiu** souls souls in the gods 474. 11; of the East 12. 16; 221. 3; 222. 5; 369. 5; of the West 13. 1; 218. 11; 220. 13; of 7. 4; 86. 16; 181. 12; 201. 8; 215. 1; 236. 10, 14; 237. 14; 238. 12; 449. 11; 451. 6; of 7. 5; 230. 18; 232. 14; of 7. 5; 233. 3; 235. 1, 2; of 235. 7, 15; 236. 2, 6; 238. 3; living divine souls 416. 4; souls who have come forth by day 427. 14; souls of the damned 486. 8; souls of his father (Osiris) 324. 16

**Ba** divine soul with plumes 413. 16

**Ba** a proper name (?) 177. 14

**ba** to be strong 174. 16; 216. 10

**Bai** a proper name 272. 7; 275. 7

**Bati** the double soul 60. 10; 516. 16; 517. 2; the divine double soul in the Tchafi 59. 16; 60. 4, 8

**Bati-erpit** a name of Osiris 321. 2

**ba** to force a way through 31. 10; 33. 7

**Bau** a proper name 449. 14

**Bai** name of a god 38. 8

**baba** to work 137. 2

**babau** den 373. 2

**babau** caverns, caves, lairs, dens 104. 9

**Baba**, **Baba**, **Babai** the firstborn son of Osiris 64. 13; 133. 9; 260. 11; 504. 9, 11; 505. 9

**Ba-neb-Ṭeṭṭeṭ** a title of Osiris 112. 13; 117. 8; 247. 6; 340. 12

**Bareka θåfaua** a proper name 409. 10

**baḥ** see

**Baχau** the mountain of sunrise 218. 12, 15; 220. 14; 265. 2; 446. 7; 496. 7

**Bast** the city of Bubastis 254. 11; 295. 13

**Bast** the goddess of Bubastis 415. 3

**Basti** one of the forty-two assessors 256. 6; var.

**bak** to labour, to toil, to be strong 173. 6, 13; 199. 9; to work for 486. 1

**baku** works, labours 250. 4

**baḳ**, **baḳi** to be weak, feeble, helpless, wretched 177. 11; 376. 10

**baḳ**, **beḳa**, **baḳi** feeble one, helpless one (*i. e.*, the mummy [?]) 165. 16; 166. 13; 172. 11; 352. 14; 353. 14; 354. 14; 355. 5, 12; 356. 3, 8, 13; 357. 1, 5

**bat** boughs, branches, plants 213. 15; 466. 9

**Bati** name of a fiend 356. 3

**båaq** a kind of grain or fruit 317. 6

**bȧa** iron, a name of the sky, firmament, iron weapon or tool 8. 6; 44. 5; 135. 6; 138. 7; 185. 6; 279. 5; 280. 10; 281. 14; 286. 10; 309. 11; 332. 3; 367. 14; 376. 4; 392. 2; 485. 9; *bȧa en pet* meteoritic iron (?) 86. 14; 396. 15

**bȧt qemāu** iron of the south 97. 1; 140. 14; 141. 7

**bȧat**, **bȧau** wonderful things 37. 4; 141. 13

**Bȧbȧ** name of a god 198. 1

**bȧbȧ** a cry of joy 435. 16

**bȧn** evil 197. 2; 257. 12, 16; 260. 2; 365. 10; 416. 8, 15; 419. 7

**bȧk** hawk 5. 15; 33. 11; 63. 13; 134. 16; 156. 4, 8; 164. 7, 9, 10, 16; 165. 9; 168. 3; 170. 9, 10; 171. 7; 179. 10; 202. 14; 226. 1; 242. 8; 287. 4; 290. 14, 17; 294. 3; 375. 9; 376. 12; 386. 11; 397. 2; 414. 1, 3; 417. 10; 438. 6; 461. 12; plur. 113. 3

**Bȧkui** (?) the double divine hawk 142. 13; 323. 4

**Bȧket** name of a city 321. 7

***bābāt*** stream 44. 10

***bāḥ*** to flood, to overflow, to be flooded with, to be abundant, abundance, harvest 2. 11; 36. 13; 132. 5. 136. 1; 165. 4; 227. 13; 228. 13

***Bāḥ*** the god of the Inundation 128. 6; 145. 2; 146. 9; 201. 5; 298. 4; 315. 12

***bu*** not 105. 6; 233. 13; 412. 16; 413. 10

***bu*** place 124. 3, 13; 129. 9; 169. 11; 221. 6; 332. 5; 434. 5; 441. 3; 448. 4; 450. 16; 452. 10; 438. 12; 493. 8; 505. 6; a holy place 151. 10; a place 7. 6; this place 492. 14; place of law 264. 5; = 179. 3

***bu neb*** everywhere 3. 6; 23. 4; 87. 9; 150. 12; 189; 6, 8, 13; 211. 16; 276. 16; 277. 15; 294. 10; 312. 10; 362. 13; 366. 14; 491. 12; 492. 1

***bu nebu*** people, folk, all men 350. 10; 408. 2; 498. 3

***bu nefer*** prosperity, happiness 15. 13; 96. 6; 480. 1

***bu ṭu***

***bu ṭut*** evil thing, calamity 250. 3; 252. 7; 480. 15; 488. 12

***but*** evil things, evil 66. 14; 67. 3; 232. 3, 4; 309. 9; 480. 6

| | |
|---|---|
| ***buṭ*** | = *uṭeb* offering 3. 7 |
| ***bi*** | name of a fiend 429. 5 |
| ***biu*** | strength 314. 8 |
| ***bebait*** | the mantis 216. 2 |
| ***bebuu*** | strong 407. 4 |
| ***Bebi*** | name of a god 75. 14 |
| ***bebet*** | flowers 99. 9 |
| ***bebet*** | fountain head 300. 16 |
| ***bebet*** | hollow place, cavity 310. 8; 311. 2, 10; 312. 2 |
| ***bepi*** | . . . . . . . . 430. 8 |
| ***benānā*** | to bathe 293. 4 |
| ***benben*** | a kind of wood 335. 13 |
| ***benben*** | bier, funeral couch 448. 15 |
| ***benbenet*** | a hall, pylon chamber 314. 16; 325. 5, 15 |
| ***ben*** | to pass away, to dissolve, to go on 120. 8; 339. 13 |
| ***ben*** | union, to be united with 106. 10 |
| ***benen*** | to beget, to be begotten 68. 6 |
| ***benen*** | ring 34. 3, 4 |
| ***benen*** | a wood 340. 16 |

**bennu** a bird commonly identified with the phoenix 14. 11; 33. 12; 53. 2; 138. 1; 144. 4; 165. 1; 181. 3; 210. 9; 242. 9; 243. 9; 247. 7; 252. 2; 347. 12; 474. 12; *Bennu ba en Rā*, the *bennu* the soul of Rā 94. 9

**bennut**, **benentu** matter, pus 197. 8; 198. 13

**bennu** cakes (?) 494. 6

**Bener** name of a city 325. 1

**benerȧ** pleasure, sweetness 68. 11; 298. 5

**benerȧut** sweet-smelling thing 469. 14; *benera* (?) 504. 5

**benśu** bolts 264. 4

**bent**, **bentet** divine apes 67. 2; 302. 12

**beḥ** to cut, to split 106. 14

**beḥen** baleful one 114. 9

**beḥen** to cut, to pierce 2. 15; 68. 7; 80. 1, 3, 5; 225. 1; 294. 11

**beḥennu** murderous 298. 11

**beḥennu** an animal of the wolf or dog species 87. 8

**beḥes** }
**beḥeset** } calf 222. 6; 505. 10

**Beχennu** a proper name 418. 9

**beχeχu** fire 125. 3

**bes** form 308. 14; 353. 14

**bes** to pass, passage 28. 6; 45. 8; 110. 14; 163. 5; 235. 2, 10; 236. 14; 285. 5; 310. 2; 339. 4, 12; 497. 3

**bes** }
**besu** } flame, fire 263. 8, 13; 340. 7; 344. 6; 369. 9; 378. 7; 408. 5; 409. 4, 8; blazes 353. 4; 409. 16

**Besu-χas** a proper name 266. 1

**besesu** humours, excretions 493. 11

**besek** }
**besku** } internal organ of the body 95. 7; 163. 2; plur. 64. 16; 254. 7, 14; 260. 11

**beś** to vomit 219. 12

**beśu** (?) metal plates or scales 219. 4

**beka** to shine 126. 10

**beka** to-morrow 134. 11; 142. 9

**bekau** weakness 100. 4

**beq** olive tree, olives 59. 4; 263. 2, 4; 333. 12; the olive tree in Ȧnnu 463. 12

***Beq*** a proper name 336. 4; 347. 1

***beqsu*** eyeball, skin (?) 98. 1; 289. 2

***beqsu*** balance 367. 10

***beḳa*** defect, exhaustion 57. 1; 100. 4

***beḳa*** feeble one 339. 1; 342. 3, 10; 343. 1, 9, 16; 344. 7, 14; 345. 6, 13; 346. 4

***beḳa*** crime, evil, sin 66. 3; sinners 24. 13

***baḳai*** evil-doing one 43. 4

***beḳsu*** part of a boat 104. 11

***beḳasu*** guilty (?), wicked (?) 360. 9

***beḳset*** . . . . . . . 302. 1

***bet*** place 511. 1

***bet nebt*** everywhere 513. 3; 516. 14; 517. 3

***bet*** incense 436. 16; 444. 6

***beta*** to sin, to commit a fault, wrong, iniquity 16. 3, 9, 14

***betau*** sin 509. 3

***betu*** abominable thing 94. 4; 98. 14; 99. 3, 7, 11; 108. 12, 14; 109. 2; 410. 10; plur. 39. 4; 91. 17;

92. 10; 100. 13; 123. 6, 7, 13, 15; 125. 4; 151. 8; 179. 12 *(bis)*, 13; 184. 4, 10; 192. 9, 10; 214. 10, 11; 238. 15; 243. 13, 14; 250. 7; 269. 11; 279. 11; 283. 16; 330. 10; 397. 14; 406. 5; 460. 14, 16; 465. 9; 466. 3, 4; 467. 12; 488. 12; 492. 9, 10; 493. 9, 16; 494. 1, 2; 411. 3

**betau** to do harm 403. 6

**Betȧ** name of a city 110. 16

**bet**, **beti** barley 14. 14; 23. 10; 151. 9; 160. 16; 209. 6; 230. 8; 244. 3; 368. 2; 369. 2; 389. 11; 454. 10; 464. 4; 493. 4

**beti ḥeṭet** white barley 124. 10; 214. 14

**beti ṭeśert** red barley 454. 8

**betennu**, **betnu** swift 87. 10, 15; 88. 2

**beṭ** incense 216. 11; 508. 6

**beṭeś** to be disposed for evil but powerless to do it 372. 14

**beṭeś**, **beṭeśet** fiends 2. 8; 74. 13; 316. 8; 61. 3

**Beṭśu** name of a city 322. 6

**Beṭti** a proper name 97. 13

**beθet** (?) brought 462. 8

***Beq*** a proper name **336.** 4; **347.** 1

***beqsu*** eyeball, skin (?) **98.** 1; 28

***beqsu*** balance **367.** 10

***beka*** defect, exhaustion **57.** 1

***beka*** feeble one **339.** 1; **342.** 9, 16; **344.** 7, 14; **345.** 6, 13; **346.** 4

***beka*** crime, evil, sin **24.** 13

***bakai*** evil-doing one 4

***beksu*** part of a boat **104.** 11

***bekasu*** guilty (?), wicked (?) 36

***bekset*** . . . . . . . **302.** 1

***bet*** place **511.** 1

***bet nebt*** everywhere **513.** 3; **516.**

***bet*** incense **436.** 16; **444.** 6

***beta*** to sin, to commit a fa- quity **16.** 3, 9, 14

***betau*** sin **509.** 3

***betu*** abominable thing **94.** 3, 7, 11; **108.** 12, 14 10; plur.

ıkes, of-
452. 12;

:ff out of
the uni-
:. 14; 36.
5. 1

ngs 2. 1;

:ods 4. 4;
5; 15. 17;
. 9; 98. 9;
; 110. 15;
2. 12; 223.
4. 10; 250.
.. 10; 303.
.. 13; 342.
; 427. 12;
7; 432. 6;
7. 15; 477.
1; 496. 16;

.6. 3; 465. 7

of the gods

of the gods

# □ P.

*Pe* 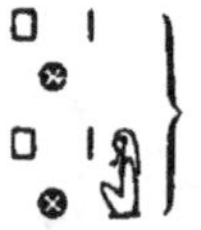 one half of the city of Buto (Per-Uat'it) 7. 5; 73. 1, 4; 79. 6; 81. 10; 83. 7; 109. 13; 160. 14; 163. 12; 209. 4; 230. 18; 231. 2, 4; 232. 14; 243. 11; 321. 6; 323. 12; 325. 7; 329. 11; 406. 8; 439. 7; 442. 5; 454. 7; 455. 16; 483. 10

*Pe* ....  .... 506. 15

*p* □ the 412. 7, 8; 413. 8, 10; 414. 5; 419. 14; 511. 4, 6;  all that is in his heart 411. 6

*pa*  the 11. 10; 58. 10; 236. 13; 249. 10; 263. 13, 14; 317. 2; 409. 4; 411. 7, 10, 11; 412. 3; 418. 9, 10; 420. 10; 468. 14; 506. 1; 507. 2; 507. 14;  413. 4;  the one who 399. 8; 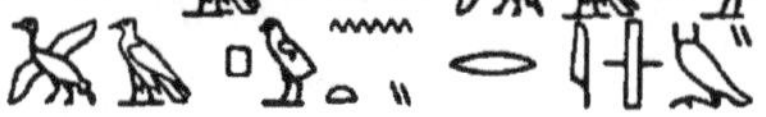  64. 9

*paif*  his 412. 4; 420. 10

*pa, pai*  to fly 138. 8; 140. 2; 148. 11; 164. 2, 10; 179. 9; 181. 4; 376. 11; 493. 12

*pai*  flight 390. 16

***paut*** nine 222. 4; 431. 16; 432. 3

***paut*** ninth 340. 5

***paut*** stuff, substance, matter, cakes, offerings 164. 14; 181. 5; 452. 12; 454. 6; 468. 7; 483. 11

***paut***, ***pauti*** primeval matter, the stuff out of which the gods and the universe were formed 12. 14; 36. 12; 49. 2; 66. 5; 185. 1

***paut*** company, aggregation of beings or things 2. 1; 318. 2

***paut neteru*** the company of the gods 4. 4; 6. 3, 16; 9. 13; 12. 5; 15. 17; 16. 6; 17. 1; 22. 6, 9; 98. 9; 107. 16; 108. 5, 13; 110. 15; 146. 7; 213. 5; 222. 12; 223. 3, 6; 224. 14; 244. 10; 250. 13; 277. 16; 285. 10; 303. 6; 315. 3, 9; 325. 13; 342. 14; 408. 11; 416. 9; 427. 12; 429. 6, 9; 431. 4, 7; 432. 6; 439. 11; 440. 8; 443. 2; 452. 10; 462. 11; 467. 15; 477. 4, 11; 478. 13; 485. 5; 486. 12; 490. 17; 491. 1; 496. 16; = of Nu 51. 13

***paut neteru*** = 455. 11; 456. 3; 465. 7

***paut neteru āat*** the great company of the gods 69. 16; 78. 3; 179. 4; 318. 6; 443. 11

***paut neteru nefeset*** the little company of the gods 318. 7; 443. 11

*pautti* the double company of the gods **174.** 7; **196.** 4; **107.** 14; **348.** 15; **87.** 2

*pait* bolt-hole **264.** 16

*Par* a proper name **408.** 6

*Pa-rehaqa-χeperu* a proper name **408.** 6; **415.** 8

*pas* ink-jar **199.** 6, 11

*Paśakasa* a proper name **415.** 7

*pat* (?) light **442.** 9

*pā* sparks, fire **340.** 9

*pāu* flames **353.** 4

*pāt* a class of human beings alive or dead **12.** 6; **113.** 8; **388.** 4; **417.** 11; **489.** 16

*pāit ḥrȧ-f* human-faced **417.** 4

*pu* O, a mark of emphasis = this **10.** 13, 14; **11.** 10; **38.** 8; **179.** 13; **197.** 4; **333.** 1; **132.** 4; **39.** 8

*pui* that **12.** 15; **14.** 1, 3; **18.** 12; **19.** 4, 15; **30.** 7; **39.** 16; **52.** 4, 15; **53.** 2; **54.** 11, 12; **56.** 8, 9; **58.** 5; **60.** 10, 11, 12, 14; **64.** 3, 14; **65.** 1; **71.** 7; **72.** 1. 13; **73.** 1, 10; **74.** 1, 9; **75.** 1, 11, 15; **76.** 4; **88.** 11; **97.** 12; **101.** 15; **110.** 16; **121.** 17; **128.** 2; **132.** 12; **133.** 7; **134.** 1; **158.** 7; **175.** 8, 9; **178.** 6; **184.** 3, 7, 8; **192.** 6, 8; **196.** 13; **197.** 17; **198.** 10; **201.** 11; **204.** 5, 10; **215.**

4; 216. 13, 14; 236. 5; 249. 13; 252. 2, 3, 4; 260. 11; 261. 9; 277. 11, 12, 13; 284. 6; 286. 13; 287. 8; 296. 8; 298. 1; 301. 14; 313. 13; 336. 3; 368. 14; 370. 2, 12; 372. 9; 373. 11; 374. 5, 10, 13; 376. 7; 378. 16; 379. 3, 6; 389. 5, 8; 391. 16; 397. 4; 398. 1; 400. 15; 406. 10; 409. 12; 456. 13; 460. 10; 484. 1, 2; 494. 16; 495. 6; 496. 7; 505. 9; 507. 8; 516. 16; that divine one 88. 12

***Punt*** the land about the most southern parts of the Red Sea and Somali land (?) 8. 5; 41. 15

***putrȧ*** to explain, to shew forth explain it then 51. 8, 13, 16; 52. 3, 10, 14; 53. 3, 9; 54. 3, 5, 8, 12; 55. 4; 56. 1, 9, 14; 57. 6, 13; 58. 6; 60. 1; 66. 3, 16; 69. 1.

***pef***, ***pefi***, ***pefi*** that thing, that one 3. 6, 9, 11, 14; 4. 9; 61. 4, 14; 62. 1; 65. 7, 10; 77. 11; 78. 12; 79. 1, 4, 12; 81. 6, 8, 11, 12, 14, 15; 83. 4—10; 84. 3—9; 98. 2; 108. 3; 122. 11; 131. 12, 14; 136. 3; 147. 12; 148. 3; 186. 12; 218. 12; 219. 1, 2; 231. 14; 232. 2; 298. 11; 365. 9; 441. 12; 461. 2; 467. 14; 469. 16; 503. 6; 507. 11

***pef*** that 503. 14

***pefa*** that 179. 11; 231. 10

***pefes*** a fiery dart 232. 2

***pefsit*** baked 449. 9

***pefses*** baked 449. 8

***Pen*** a proper name 203. 4 *(bis)*

**Pen-ḥeseb** (?) a proper name **494.** 9, 15; **495.** 3, 7, 12, 15

**pen** this **2.** 12; **15.** 17; **20.** 7; **24.** 7; **51.** 8; **67.** 14; **77.** 1; **80.** 10; **90.** 12; **91.** 1; **92.** 1; **93.** 16; **96.** 16; **97.** 1; **98.** 2; **99.** 11; **137.** 1; **141**; 15; **143.** 3; **145.** 16; **178.** 12 *(bis)*; **209.** 5; **248.** 9, 11; **260.** 2; **288.** 1; **294.** 6; **299.** 15, 16; **308.** 7, 8, 16; **310.** 7; **311.** 1, 8; **316.** 1, 15; **317.** 2; **322.** 14; **366.** 1, 2; **371.** 12; **380.** 2; **393.** 3; **399.** 2; **402.** 14; **403.** 9; **404.** 11, 12; **405.** 4, 16; **408.** 16; **436.** 16; **444.** 1; **447.** 3; **459.** 7; **461.** 4; **463.** 12; **465.** 8, 9; **474.** 3; **477.** 13; **482.** 8; **486.** 8; **488.** 10; **501.** 9; **502.** 11

**penā** to overturn, to capsize, to overthrow **105.** 10; **139.** 4; **143.** 3; **219.** 7; **346.** 10

**peni** land (?) **369.** 10

**pennu** rat **100.** 13

**penq** to wipe away **206.** 12

**penq** to beat to pieces (?) **494.** 5

**Penti** name of a god **123.** 2

**pert** a season of the Egyptian year **252.** 5; **314.** 13, 14; **315.** 8

**per** house, abode, temple, habitation **67.** 12; **107.** 1, 2; **137.** 16; **288.** 1; **314.** 3; **385.** 1; **450.** 5; **492.** 2; plur. **466.** 11; celestial mansions **160.** 16; **177.** 2; **217.** 16; **450.** 9; **478.** 6

**perui** double house **405.** 12

**perit** temples **43.** 10

**Per-Ȧusȧr** temple of Osiris **20.** 5, 13; **21.** 2, 6, 12; **63.** 7; **246.** 14; **247.** 16; **334.** 8; **349.** 2; **365.** 14; **426.** 2

***Per-Åuset*** temple of Isis **169.** 14

***Per-Åmsu*** the temple of Åmsu **255.** 7

***Per-Åsṭes*** temple of Åsṭes **348.** 8; **349.** 5

***per åbu*** place where hearts are judged **89.** 4

***Per-unnut*** temple of the goddess Unnut **309.** 14

***per-ur*** the "great house", a name of the tomb **88.** 10; **319.** 11

***Per-en-Ptaḥ*** the temple of Ptaḥ at Memphis **222.** 10; **223.** 12; **386.** 1; **445.** 3; **451.** 5; **461.** 9; **463.** 11, 14

***per menå*** the abode of the dead **134.** 16

***per-neḥeḥ*** house of eternity, *i. e.*, the tomb **442.** 4, 16

***per neser*** house of fire **88.** 10; **319.** 11

***per neter*** house of the god (*i. e.*, Osiris) **405.** 11

***per neter āa*** the house of the great god **125.** 9

***Per-rerti*** the temple of the double Lion-god **169.** 13

***per ḥāt*** the house of hearts, *i. e.*, the judgment hall **89.** 4

***Per-ḥapṭ-re*** a proper name **261.** 11

***Per-Ḥeru*** the temple of Horus **495.** 6

***Per-ḥet*** "White House", a proper name **357**. 9, 13

***Per-χenti-menȧtu-f*** a proper name **149**. 5

***Per-Sabut*** the temple of Sabut **509**. 13

***Per-Satet*** the temple of Satet **247**. 9

***Per-suten*** royal house **164**. 1

***Per-seḥāptet*** = Per-sektet (?) **216**. 2

***Per-kemkem*** the temple of Kemkem **163**. 6

***Per-keku*** temple or house of darkness **165**. 16; **439**. 1

***per qebḥ*** house of coolness **14**. 13

***Per ṭep-ṭu-f*** the temple of "him that is on his hill", *i. e.*, Anubis **247**. 14; **348**. 3

***Per Tem*** the temple of Tem **347**. 6

***Per Teḥuti*** the temple of Thoth **495**. 6

***per***, ***peru*** to come forth, to appear, appearance, proceeding from, exit, manifestation **3**. 5; **11**. 12; **19**. 16; **21**. 11; **36**. 16; **66**. 10; **77**. 4; **103**. 1; **104**. 1; **106**. 1; **107**. 2, 16; **108**. 3; **109**. 13; **113**. 10; **114**. 1; **115**. 12; **313**. 13; **315**. 6; **335**. 10; **343**. 6; **344**. 6; **347**. 12, 16; **356**. 4, 12; **359**. 16; **363**. 6; **374**. 15; **376**. 8; **378**. 14; **380**. 13; **382**. 13; **390**. 14, 15; **395**. 4; **397**. 12; **399**. 14; **404**. 6; **405**. 10; **410**. 15; **411**. 5, 16; **414**. 15; **416**. 9; **430**. 4; **432**. 5; **435**. 3; **436**. 9; **437**. 9; **439**. 8; **440**. 7; **443**. 3; **444**. 8; **449**. 7; **450**. 13; **451**. 6; **455**.

6; 456. 2; 462. 14; 465. 5; 469. 1, 2; 471. 6; 472. 6; 473. 12; 474. 13; 477. 15; 481. 6; 497. 13 *(bis)*; 505. 14; 506. 3

***per ā*** *per ā* to act with violence 257. 4; to come forth retreating 253. 10

***peri*** he who cometh forth 44. 5; 103. 11; 111. 4; 138. 4; 147. 12; manifestations 398. 4

***perer***
***pereru*** to come forth 208. 7; 221. 13; 309. 7; 368. 6, 15

***pert***
***perert*** exit, appearance, a coming forth, what comes forth 1. 10; 6. 16; 18. 5; 51. 2; 166. 5; 211. 12; 221. 10; 223. 10; 368. 13; 374. 4; 376. 2; 390. 3; 395. 9; 424. 6; 432. 8, 11, 13; 435. 8; 438. 1; 451. 15; 485. 12; 489. 2; *pert* exit 226. 9

***peru*** things which come forth, manifestations 53. 8, 11; 56. 2; 139. 16; 143. 8; 144. 15; 176. 3; 251. 13; 379. 9; 441. 4

***perti*** to come forth 292. 15

***per*** to come forth into the presence 70. 5

***pert em hru*** "coming forth by day" 18. 4; 25. 15; 26. 1; 30. 13; 77. 1; 80. 9; 82. 16; 300. 10; 320. 15; 322. 16; 410. 16; 469. 15; 470. 9; 491. 7; 502. 7; 511. 8; 515. 2, 4, 6, 8, 10, 12, 15

***per ḥer ta*** to be born into the world 487. 6

***peri*** strip of linen, bandage 414. 5; 417. 8

*perχeru* — offerings of oil, wine, beer, bread, cakes, oxen, feathered fowl, incense, etc., offered to the *ka* 182. 6; 223. 7; 268. 2; 277. 5; 300. 1; 318. 3; 387. 1; 430. 12; 486. 6; 510. 3; 514. 13; 516. 8

*pert-er-χeru* offerings 150. 16; 261. 4; 269. 9; 366. 7; 380. 1

*pertu-er-χeru*
*perθu-er-χeru* — offerings 217. 7; 267. 10

*persen* — cakes 80. 15; 130. 8; 209. 13; 223. 9; 242. 6; 333. 9; plur. 449. 8

*pert*
*perti*
*pert* — grain, corn 14. 14; 23. 9; 124. 11; 151. 9; 209. 6; 244. 4; 319. 13; 367. 15; 369. 1; 379. 15; 389. 10; 454. 10; 464. 4; 485. 12; 493. 5; 504. 11; 505. 4; red grain 215. 15; black grain 494. 11; white grain 494. 11

*peḥ*
*peḥu*
*peḥt* — to arrive at, to attain to, to reach forwards, attainment, end 2. 13, 4. 6; 12. 13; 22. 4; 36. 10; 41. 5; 67. 13; 163. 4; 171. 11; 185. 4; 280. 11; 282. 4; 284. 7; 286. 14; 288. 4; 299. 8; 331. 12; 449. 14; 451. 2; 488. 6

***peḥu***
***peḥui***
***peḥui***
***peḥtet*** — hinder parts, buttocks, thighs, the lower part of the back **153.** 8; **179.** 8; **262.** 9; **414.** 8; **436.** 16; **508.** 6

***peḥuit*** stern of a boat **3.** 4

***peḥu*** swamp **233.** 10, 13

***peḥuu*** marshes, swamps **411.** 10

***Peḥu*** name of a god **277.** 13

***peḥrer*** to run **36.** 14; **408.** 11; **475.** 2

***Peḥreri*** "Runner", a name of Rā **189.** 5

***peḥti***
***peḥtet*** — strength, strong one, might, power **68.** 2; **92.** 11; **126.** 10; **170.** 9; **173.** 2; **220.** 7; **233.** 15; **314.** 2; **325.** 11; **332.** 2; **370.** 12, 13, 14; **408.** 6; **478.** 8; **481.** 11; hinder parts **220.** 5, 6

***peχa*** to separate **249.** 4

***Peχat*** name of a goddess **417.** 4

***peχes*** to cover over, to fall on **68.** 5

***pes*** ink-jar **458.** 4

***pesaḳs*** to spit upon **57.** 4

***peseḥ***, ***pesḥet*** to eat, to bite, to devour 101. 3; 372. 13; 437. 5

***Pesχeti*** divine envoy 137. 16

***peseś*** to divide, to cleave, to spread over, to be allotted, reparation 86. 2; 101. 17; 225. 14; 261. 12; 289. 3; 451. 1; divisions 287. 11

***pesek*** to spit on 302. 8

***Pesek-re*** a proper name 321. 11

***pest*** to shine, to illumine, light, radiance 1. 6; 4. 2; 8.15; 26. 1; 26. 11; 36. 4; 61. 7; 101. 5; 115. 9; 149. 7; 150. 2; 286, 4; 292. 5; 305. 10; 363. 5; 420. 13; 502. 8; to shine 312. 15

***pest***, ***pestetu*** rays of light 49. 16; 292. 5

***Pestu*** the god of light 162. 11

***pest*** to spread out like light 69. 6

***pest*** back, backbone 36. 4; 112. 14; 118. 12; 164. 11; 372. 11; 402. 7; 447. 3

***pest***, ***pestu*** backbone, back 144. 4; 361. 1; 506. 5

***pest ȧmu Ȧnnu*** the back in Ȧnnu 302. 7

**pesṭ ṭep** (?) to move the head 68. 1; 69. 4

**peś** to spread out 467. 16

**peśen**, **peśeni** to divide, to cleave (?) 60. 11; 61. 2

**Peśennu** name of a city 102. 6

**pequ** food 372. 4

**peqet** . . . . . . 401. 14

**peqet** garments, apparel 451. 8

**peḳ** to explain 348. 2

**peḳ** byssus, very fine, semi-transparent linen 34. 5; 440. 4

**Peḳa** name of a city 439. 1

**peḳes**, **peḳas** to spit upon 215. 6; 361. 2

**Peḳas** name of a city and god 324. 4

**pet** the sky, heaven 1. 3; 2. 3; 3. 14; 52. 2; 58. 10; 61. 5, 6; 63. 8; 67. 9; 88. 13; 89. 11, 15; 97. 14; 107. 5; 115. 5; 127. 1; 131. 9; 147. 13; 201. 14; 224. 6; 278. 13; 281. 12; 291. 3; 292. 11; 296. 6, 14; 297. 12; 314. 16; 317. 14; 333. 16; 334. 2; 358. 11; 362. 3; 366. 14; 368. 7; 376. 11; 377. 2; 390. 13; 398. 5; 406. 15; 412. 8, 9; 422. 5; 438. 7; 439. 8; 440. 7; 443. 2, 15; 446. 6; 447. 16; 450. 14; 464. 6; 465. 11; 474. 15; 489.

16; 501. 13; 505. 8; 512. 9; 509. 16; 515. 12; 324. 6; the heaven of Rā 384. 2

*pet ȧbtet* eastern heaven 319. 3; 364. 12

*pet ȧmentet* western heaven 319. 2; 364. 11

*pet meḥtet* northern heaven 318. 16; 364. 10

*pet reset* southern heaven 319. 4; 365. 1

*pet* , heaven and earth 1. 13; 8. 4; 69. 13; heaven, earth, and hell 69. 13; 273. 5, 7; 482. 1

*petti* heavenly beings, denizens of the sky 114. 14

*Peti* a proper name 122. 4

*pet* to see 455. 14

*peti* to explain 60. 13; 61. 15; 62. 16; 63. 15; 64. 7; 65. 1, 4, 8, 13; 62. 15

*petpet* crusher 325. 11

*Petrȧ* name of a god 150. 8

*petrȧ* to see, to look at, to observe, to shew forth, to declare, to appear 6. 10; 127. 4; 262. 16; 263. 1, 4, 5, 7, 9, 11, 12; 413. 10; 266. 8, 15

*Petrȧ-sen* the name of a river 208. 2

*Ptaḥ* the great god of Memphis 27. 11; 32. 11;

86. 8; 135. 6; 179. 7; 180. 7; 218. 1; 222. 10; 223. 12; 321. 2; 336. 5; 385. 1; 386. 1; 396. 12; 421. 3; 442. 13; 445. 2, 10; 509. 10

***Ptaḥ*** Ptaḥ 113. 2; 118. 19; 323. 6

***Ptaḥ en per*** temple of Ptaḥ 28. 4; 224. 3

***Ptaḥ-ḥet*** temple of Ptaḥ 28. 11; 312. 13

***Ptaḥ-ḥet-ka*** "house of the *ka* of Ptaḥ", a name of Memphis 116. 6, 7; 254. 1; 325. 11; Memphis of the underworld 217. 6

***Ptaḥ-ȧneb-res-f*** "Ptaḥ of his southern wall", a name of Ptaḥ of Memphis 440. 10; 442. 11; 444. 14

***Ptaḥ-Seker***, ***Ptaḥ-Sekri*** "the coffined Ptaḥ" 386. 4, 14; 387. 9, 15; 441. 8

***Ptaḥ-Sekri-Tem*** name of a triad 37. 11

***Ptaḥ-tanen*** name of a great cosmic god 485. 10; 325. 14

***Ptaḥ-mes*** a proper name 274. 1, 15; 275. 9; 276. 4

***peṭ*** to open out, to extend, to stretch out 38. 7; 195. 2; 288. 2; 394. 10; 475. 2

***peṭ*** a kind of unguent 175. 1

***Peṭet*** name of a city 324. 1

***peṭsu*** opener, breaker 132. 12

***peṭ-śe*** name of a shrine 321. 10

# F.

*f* he, him, it, his, its **1. 3**; **3. 13**; **5. 4, 12**; and see *passim.*

*f* + *ui* *i. e.,* with the mark of the dual **61. 13**; **64. 4**; **89. 12**; **115. 16** *(bis)*; **116. 5**; **121. 17**; **134. 16**; **142. 14**; **164. 11**; **279. 14**; **355. 10**; **370. 12**; **437. 11**; **448. 3**; **451. 11**; **461. 12**; **479. 15**; **482. 12**; **484. 4**; **503. 6**

*fa*, *fa*, *fat* to bear, to carry, to be carried, to lift up **33. 6**; **171. 5**; **207. 13**; **217. 3**; **230. 9**; **264. 8**; **449. 12**

*faiu* bearers, carriers **244. 9**; **423. 10, 13**

*fa* to diminish through decay **401. 6**

[illegible] to raise the hand **28. 5**; **413. 15**; **414. 2**; **417. 10**

[illegible] the god of the lifted hand **420. 3. 9**

[illegible] a proper name **381. 5**

[illegible] "[illegible] of heaven", name of the god of the sev-

[illegible]

***Fa-Ḥeru*** a name of Osiris **324.** 14

***Fau-ḥrâu-sen*** those who lift up their faces **462.** 15

***Fat-Ḥeru*** name of a city **322.** 10

***fenχu*** offerings **250.** 13

***Fenχu*** the name of certain dwellers in Syria **263.** 7

***fent*** worm, serpent, reptile **167.** 15; plur. **24.** 10; **185.** 7; **360.** 13; **400.** 3; **401.** 6, 7, 10

***fenṭ*** nose **37.** 1; **446.** 5; **451.** 11; **467.** 11

***fenṭ*** nose **407.** 13; plur. **511.** 15

***fenṭ*** nose **8.** 6; **112.** 10; **207.** 14; **208.** 6, 15; **217.** 4; **252.** 3; **360.** 10; **483.** 3; **484.** 12; plur. **374.** 9; **50.** 6

***Fenṭi*** one of the forty-two assessors **253.** 1, 14; **515.** 5

***feχ*** to proceed from **333.** 8

***feχeχ*** to burst through **464.** 7

***feqat*** to feed **353.** 14

***feḳa*** to make water **398.** 9

**fetu**          worms  459. 10

**feṭ áb**          languor  411. 11

**fetetu**          fish  395. 9

**fṭu**          four 109. 3 ; 121. 15 ; 136. 10, 16 ; 143.
                  3 ; 155. 11 ; 164. 11 ; 201. 4 ; 222. 3 ;
**fṭut**          252. 1 ; 269. 5 ; 291. 1 ; 303. 10, 11 ;
                  306. 1, 2 ; 308. 3 ; 317. 4, 5 ; 320. 7 ;
**fṭu**          336. 11 ; 407. 9 ; 435. 14 ; 439. 12, 13 ;
                  462. 5 ; 464. 16 ; 494. 11, 13, 14 ; 495.
**fṭut**          6 ; IIII ☉ fourth 328. 1 ; 360. 3 ; 435. 14

**feṭqu**          destruction, damage  496. 5

# M.

**em** sign of the participle, see *passim*

**em** particle of negation, no, not 15. 10, 11; 95. 2; 95. 5; 96. 2, 3; 100. 12; 109. 7; 501. 6, 7; let not make to stink (my name) 96. 6

**em** , in, into, from, on, at, with, out from, among, of, upon, as, like, according to, in the manner 1. 3, 8, 13; 2. 4; 3. 2, 7, 17; 4. 3; 11. 13; 15. 11; 18. 10; 26. 1 *(bis)*; 26. 2; 27. 10; 32. 7; 87. 13; 120. 6, 7, 15; 122. 14; 124. 2, 3; 142. 13; 146. 11; 151. 10; 157, 8; 205. 3; 243. 12

**mā** } from, with 24. 1; 32. 6; 61. 12; 62. 12; 64. 3; 65. 16; 66. 6; 90. 8, 9; 91. 14; 92. 1; 93. 3, 13; 97. 9; 98. 7, 10, 12; 105. 4; 113. 15; 116. 17; 119. 3, 4; 121. 4; 128. 16; 129. 16; 130. 7; 132. 3; 135. 15; 136. 9; 139. 4; 153. 2; 160. 2; 166. 15, 16; 170. 6; 215. 4; 224. 9; 225. 14; 245. 3; 260. 11; 262. 4; 282. 3; 298. 10; 314. 8; 315. 4; 331. 5, 6; 340. 2; 335. 2, 12; 336. 9; 337. 4, 15; 338. 12; 339. 7; 340. 16; 341. 11; 359. 10; 365. 8, 9, 10; 366. 9; 370. 13; 392. 12, 13; 394. 6, 7; 408. 13; 411. 1; 417. 6; 424. 13; 426. 16; 427. 15; 457. 4; 468. 3; 469. 9; 470. 2; 473. 6; 495. 15; 496. 1; 501. 3; 503. 7; 507. 5, 12, 13; 513. 11; 517. 2; *māmā* 181. 9

**emmā** among 4. 16; 26. 5; 30. 10; 40. 5; 44. 6; 119. 11; 120. 17; 127. 7; 152. 11; 155. 13, 15; 195. 9; 200. 10; 203. 6; 236. 11 *(bis)*; 244. 13; 245. 2; 266. 13;

267. 5; 280. 3; 286. 8; 290. 13; 298. 10; 299. 14; 300. 4; 302. 9; 307. 13; 314. 7; 331. 1, 2, 3; 333, 2; 362. 10; 377. 2; 389. 5, 9; 433. 8; 452. 10; 466. 1; 490. 6; 491. 3; 492. 13; 497. 14; 509. 13; 516. 12 *(bis)*

**em āb** — opposite 292. 16; 309. 4; 461. 14; 464. 16; 474. 2; 501. 1; 466. 14

**em ābu**

**em baḥ** — before, in the presence of 3. 8, 9; 15. 12; 70. 5, 16; 71. 6; 78. 7, 9—16; 79. 2—14; 80. 15; 81. 4; 82. 6; 83. 4—10; 84. 3—9; 85. 16; 92. 4; 95. 3, 5; 96. 4, 10; 110. 15; 111. 10; 122. 4; 138. 6; 147. 11; 159. 8; 179. 4; 208. 13; 249. 13; 252. 6; 260. 4; 260. 10; 261. 7; 272. 1; 275. 3; 276. 5, 6; 290. 17; 300. 1; 316. 12.; 333. 1, 4; 366. 6; 378. 2; 386. 9; 386. 12; 388. 4; 417. 9; 427. 9; 437. 9; 439. 3; 440. 8; 443. 2; 451. 1; 465. 5; 468. 10; 477. 4, 10, 16; 501. 7; 505. 10; 511. 11; 516. 9

**em baḥ ā** — before, in the presence of 13. 15; 65. 7; 75. 6; 76. 14; 271. 3; 274. 4; 315. 9; 461. 2; 462. 11; 485. 5

**em nem**

**em nem-ā** — a second time 120. 2; 285. 2, 12

**em ruti** — outside 149. 2, 15; 497. 10

**em ḥāt** — before 6. 10; 40. 14; 148. 12; 269. 5; 304. 6, 8; 387. 15; 397. 11; 423. 10, 14

**em ḥāti ā** — before 195. 8

**em ḥer**  in front of, upon 219. 1

**em χennu** / **em χen** 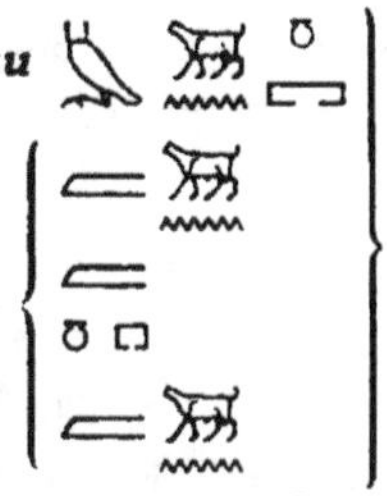 within 11. 6; 12. 4; 13. 2; 24. 8, 11; 25. 1; 44. 8; 46. 16; 66. 2; 107. 4; 109. 12; 112. 5, 7; 115. 14, 15; 119. 10; 133. 10; 142. 2; 156. 9; 192. 7; 195. 7; 195. 13; 219. 8; 227. 16; 243. 3; 245. 6, 7; 261. 13; 299. 10; 313. 4; 315. 1; 331. 14; 341. 6, 15; 342. 14; 343. 5, 13; 344. 12; 345. 2, 10; 348. 9; 349. 6; 354. 6, 11; 355. 2, 9, 15; 393. 16; 408. 11; 411. 12; 412. 1, 2; 428. 10; 429. 1; 441. 1; 468. 7; 479. 3; 488. 3; 490. 13; 497. 10; 502. 2;  455. 13

**em χert** 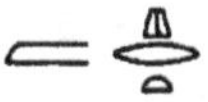 on behalf of 143. 3

**em χet**  behind, after 6. 16; 18. 7; 25. 9, 15; 49. 16; 51. 3; 56. 2, 5, 15; 58. 14; 68. 8; 77. 2; 82. 16; 88. 15; 103. 14, 15; 104. 16; 111. 6; 119. 2; 130. 11; 182. 3; 219. 6; 228. 4; 243. 3; 260. 3; 286. 16; 304. 3; 312. 3; 331. 16; 333. 14; 376. 10; 385. 12; 399. 11, 14, 15; 421. 5, 6, 12. 14; 431. 8; 461. 11; 466. 7; 474. 14; 479. 13; 481. 16; 487. 10

**em sa**  after, behind, at the back of 58. 9; 59. 6; 67. 5; 88. 14; 92. 3; 134. 6; 140. 6; 191. 13; 193. 5; 282. 11; 372. 5, 6; 495. 16; 506. 2

**em qeṭet** 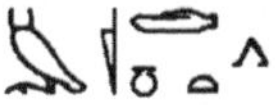 throughout 409. 16

**ma** / **maiu** / **mat**  new, to be new or renewed 41. 3; 165. 12; 188. 7; 291. 5; 294. 5; 298. 2; 389. 5, 9;  made new 91. 4;  289. 7, 9; 483. 4

**maa**, **maau** to see, to observe, sight 1. 11; 2. 10, 14; 5. 7; 7. 12; 12. 6, 7; 20. 6; 22. 9; 38. 1; 40. 6; 57. 4; 92. 2; 102. 14; 106. 12; 111. 4; 119. 16; 134. 14; 138. 9; 139. 15; 142. 12; 144. 13; 145. 15; 147. 3; 170. 1; 191. 9; 216. 3; 217. 6; 219. 15; 231. 8, 9; 241. 2; 246. 7; 247. 4, 11; 248. 1; 249. 5; 252. 6; 257. 15; 270. 15; 271. 6; 273. 9; 283. 2; 285. 8, 9; 287. 16; 289. 11; 290. 5; 291. 8, 13; 293. 10; 301. 7; 308. 14; 313. 12; 334. 1; 348. 3; 358. 12; 362. 3; 370. 8; 372. 1; 376. 3, 4; 378. 10; 380. 6; 386. 9; 387. 16; 388. 15; 389. 14; 403. 12, 14; 405. 2, 3; 423. 11, 15; 426. 10; 431. 1; 433. 10; 435. 4; 438. 15; 439. 1; 441. 2; 442. 16; 450. 13; 451. 5; 452. 1; 455. 8; 456. 15; 458. 1; 459. 3, 4; 462. 2; 464. 8; 467. 2; 468. 10; 473. 4, 11, 13; 476. 4; 487. 8; 491. 11; 492. 1; 497. 8, 9; 498. 2; 509. 8; 511. 1, 5, 10; 513. 9; seen 41. 14; 59. 15; 145. 5; to see 274. 7

**maat** to see, sight, visible 136. 8; 143. 1; 167. 1; 186. 10; 202. 10; 263. 4; 375. 5; 446. 7; sight 10. 15; 386. 4; 387. 9

**maat** eye 63. 7; 115. 1; 133. 10; 167. 10, 15; 212. 13; 231. 7, 13; 235. 9, 14; 283. 5; 382. 8; 386. 7; 387. 11; 401. 13; 406. 11; 455. 11 eye to eye 144. 14

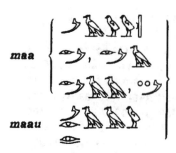

***maati***, ***maatiu*** the two eyes **35.** 12; **50.** 2; **53.** 16; **89.** 12; **101.** 16; **112.** 9; **117.** 3; **135.** 15; **159.** 3; **191.** 10; **219.** 7; **224.** 5, 6, 8; **230.** 2; **290.** 5; **370.** 11; **372.** 14; **375.** 5; **419.** 3; **436.** 2; **446.** 6; **447.** 8; **454.** 15; **462.** 6 *(bis)*; **463.** 6; **469.** 4; **511.** 1, 10; **514.** 1; **515.** 14

***maat*** eyes **237.** 13

***maat-nebt*** any body **410.** 10

***maat-neb*** every body **334.** 1; an eye **236.** 12

***maat Rā*** Eye of Rā **57.** 8; **63.** 16; **69.** 9; **56.** 15; **58.** 13

***maat Ḥeru*** Eye of Horus **30.** 5; **64.** 1; **67.** 11; **109.** 14; **113.** 1; **117.** 16; **119.** 11; **148.** 10; **170.** 13; **176.** 16; **189.** 9; **190.** 3; **192.** 7; **195.** 2, 10; **206.** 12; **232.** 3; **288.** 3; **304.** 10, 13; **305.** 3, 7, 10; **306.** 12; **307.** 6, 10; **330.** 3; **371.** 10; **376.** 9; **503.** 5, 6

***maat Śu*** Eye of Shu **401.** 4, 10

***maat Tem*** Eye of Tem **46.** 6; **192.** 7; **197.** 8; **198.** 14

***Maa-ȧntef*** name of a plank or peg **207.** 1

***Maa-ȧnuf*** one of the forty-two assessors **255.** 7

***Maa-átef-f-χeri-beq-f*** 
 a proper name **59. 4**

***Maati-f-em-χet***  one of the forty-two assessors **253. 15**

***Maati-f-em-ṭes***  one of the forty-two assessors **253. 8**

***Maa-em-ḳerḥ-án-nef-em-hru*** 
 a proper name **59. 11**

***Maa-ḥa-f***  a proper name **390. 4**

***Maa-ḥeḥ-en-renpit***  a proper name **113. 11**

***Maatuf-ḥer-ā***  a proper name **69. 2**

***Maaiu-su*** (?)  a proper name **261. 9**

***Maa-θet-f*** 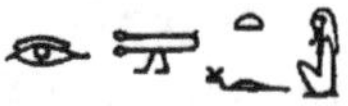 a proper name **374. 1; 382. 3**

***maár***  restraint, misery, affliction, wretched one, oppressor **170. 15; 269. 7; 408. 13; 488. 16**

***maā***  limb **404. 6**

***maā*** 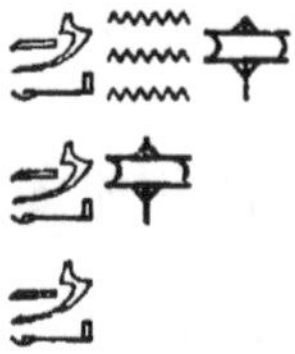 wind, breeze **4. 7; 12. 12; 108. 15; 489. 2**; plur. 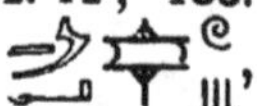,  **9. 8; 35. 14**; with  fair wind **36. 10**

***maāutu***  stalk **222. 1, 16; 368. 1, 3; 369. 2, 4**

***Maāt*** — the goddess of law, and right, and truth 1. 9; 2. 5; 3. 3; 4. 14; 9. 5; 39. 3; 260. 4, 15; 262. 7, 10; 315. 14; 318. 5; 326. 6; 415. 12

***Maāt*** — the goddess of law, and right, and truth 156. 15; 238. 5; 249. 16; 511. 10, 11

***Maāti*** — the two goddesses of right and truth 509. 2, 6

***Maāt*** — the region of Maāt 433. 14

***Maāti*** — the cities or place of the two Maāt goddesses 246. 5; 254. 9; 259. 15, 18; 322. 11; 324. 15

***maā***
***maāti***
***maāu*** — to be straight, right, justice, what is right, to pay what is legally due, law, truth 16. 8; 33. 6; 58. 6; 61. 3; 62. 7, 8; 70. 3; 119. 4; 147. 14, 16; 160. 3; 229. 13; 235. 8, 13; 272. 5; 289. 12; 290. 6; 361. 11; 427. 12; 440. 8; 446. 10, 11; 452. 8, 9; 465. 8, 9; 487. 11; 506. 5, 14; 511. 10; to be right 486. 11; doubly true 272. 14; *āp maāt* righteous judge 15. 16; the scales balance exactly 467. 8

**maā**, **maāt** real, genuine real lapis-lazuli 140. 15; 141. 7; 446. 8; a genuine friend 497. 8; real royal scribe 17. 9; 37. 6; very truth 16. 11; 161. 4; 294. 11; 356. 15; really true 413. 7; most truly a mystery 498. 2

**maāt** *maāt àb* right of heart 259. 14; 269. 11; *ses maā* uniformly and regularly 77. 5; 80. 16; 82. 18; 152. 13; 159. 8; 182. 8; 187. 14; 294. 12; 308. 10; 356. 15; 135. 7; 122. 3

**Maāti** (?) the Maāt gods 359. 7

**maā-χeru**, **maāt-χeru** to triumph over, triumph, victory, to be triumphed over 1. 10, 12; 9. 10; 13. 14; 137. 6; 143. 6; 178. 5; 189. 11; 414. 15; 476. 15, 16; 483. 5; 510. 4; , 93. 13; 94. 5; 269. 4; 363. 5; fem. 4. 13; 28. 13; 194. 14; 363. 4; 387. 8; 73. 9, 16; 91. 10; a crown of triumph 77. 9

**maā** to stretch out (?) 32. 7

**maā** to journey, to follow on 451. 9; 474. 4

**māài** to come 4. 9

**Mafțet** the lynx 101. 7; 105. 11; 373. 3

***mama*** palm tree 243. 12

***Manu*** the mountain of the sunset 1. 9; 2. 12; 36. 2; 46. 5; 47. 3; 49. 12; 434. 16; 50. 7

***maha*** a part of the head 503. 8, 11; 504. 1, 13; 505. 1; 507. 3, 9, 15

***mahu*** part of a boat 212. 7, 8

***mahu*** a crown, wreath 77. 9; 80. 10; 83. 1

***mast*** leg, thigh 195. 3; 283. 6; 391. 9; 507. 8

***masti*** the two legs 89. 14; 154. 10; 191. 11; 193. 3; 448. 7

***Masti*** a class of divine beings 280. 5; 319. 10; 281. 6

***maqet*** ladder 377. 2; plur. 395. 5

***maḳ*** a precious stone 316. 11

***matu*** incense (?) 445. 2

***Mafat*** name of a city 238. 4

***mȧ*** as, like, concerning, even as 3. 8; 4. 16; 10. 3; 27. 9; 38. 2; 42. 6; 58. 2; 63. 14; 70. 10; 83. 2; 84. 2; 104. 16; 107. 5; 113. 14; 128. 3; 138. 3; 156. 6, 11; 157. 5, 11; 218. 5; 231. 9; 270. 2, 9; 300. 10, 12; 305. 10; 306. 6; 308. 10; 312. 15; 313. 14; 317. 1; 329. 12; 331. 7; 362. 5; 364. 15; 365. 5; 378. 13; 379. 5; 385. 1, 2; 399. 7; 402. 15; 409. 11; 414. 8; 420. 13; 424. 2; 428. 2; 432. 12; 440. 9; 441. 5; 442. 14; 444. 16; 445.

1, 2; 446. 6; 459. 8; 465. 10; 471. 13; 476. 4; 481. 6; 485. 9; 488. 2; 497. 16; 506. 3; 510. 5; 511. 13; 513. 3; 168. 7

**mȧ** likeness, like 120. 8; 166. 1

**mȧ** like that same one 399. 12; inasmuch as, even as 10. 5; 272. 7; 409. 6; 275. 7; 275. 8; 409. 16; *mȧ qeṭet* in the manner of 314. 17; 33. 11; 242. 8; 313. 11, 14

**mȧti** what is like, copy, type 27. 3; 399. 3; divine counterparts 399. 5

**mȧtet** picture, likeness, similitude, like unto, copy of 42. 1; 130. 5; 187. 5; , likewise, even as 242. 3; 271. 6; 317. 2; 379. 9; 400. 9

**mȧn** daily 37. 5; 112. 3; 169. 13; 183. 11; 301. 6; 347. 5, 12; 361. 9; 389. 5, 9; 405. 11; 469. 1, 6; 483. 10, 14

**mȧn** daily 223. 1; daily 488. 2; 2. 5

**mȧu** to be like 60. 15

**mȧu** cat 60. 11, 14, 15, 16; 261. 10, 16; 100. 14

**mȧu** cat's skin (?) 340. 3

**mȧu** lion 417. 7; lions 134. 5

**em mȧu** kneaded, moulded 310. 16

***mā*** give, grant 57. 16; 174. 14; 195. 9; 301. 15; 302. 5; 303. 5; 360. 8

***māk*** behold, verily 17. 5; 22. 4; 29. 2; 30. 14; 33. 4, 6; 44. 1; 96. 10; 100. 12; 114. 5; 115. 11; 119. 14; 128. 5; 136. 5; 139. 10; 144. 9; 187. 9; 196. 5; 199. 8; 216. 9; 241. 3; 248. 6; 249. 15; 281. 13; 282. 1; 295. 4; 296. 2; 297. 6; 358. 13; 370. 13; 384. 10, 15; 394. 6, 16; 403. 14; 419. 1; 421. 6; 445. 4; 446. 16; 447. 9; 448. 13; 450. 16; 451. 9; 476. 4; 478. 14; 488. 13; 503. 9; 504. 14; 507. 10; 172. 2; 260. 12

***mā*** the bringer (?) 10. 3

***mā***, ***māȧ***, ***māȧi*** come! give! bring! 47. 4; 77. 15; 107. 15; 134. 5; 136. 4; 165. 10; 204. 6; 264. 1; 266. 9, 16; 270. 4; 302. 3, 10; 399. 4; 408. 14; 409. 7, 11; 419. 3; 508. 12; 512. 15; 514. 7, 11; 516. 9, 10, 13, 15; 288. 4; come ye! 107. 11; 121. 5, 6; 140. 6; 313. 11; 58. 5; 59. 5

***Māāat*** name of a place 54. 15; 263. 11

***Māāu-taui*** name of a god 266. 8, 9, 15, 16

***māb*** thirty 219. 3; 237. 5; 370. 4

***mābit*** name of a place or abode 237. 6; 254. 7

***māfket*** turquoise 11. 10; 44. 10; 107. 15; 177. 5; 182. 13; 221. 10; 230. 8; 368. 13; 512. 7, 12

***Mānāat*** a proper name 263. 10

***Mārqaθȧ*** a proper name 419. 12

***māhaiu*** generations (?) **43. 9**

***māhaṭeti*** fire **410. 3**

***māhui*** vessels **450. 11**

***māhenȧ*** vessel **242. 5**

***māḥā*** (?) standard **474. 7**

***Māḥu*** a proper name **148. 8**

***māχait*** sledge **20. 10**

***māχȧt***
***māχa*** scales, balance **1. 13; 15. 12; 16. 2, 15; 21. 15; 33. 5; 61. 13; 96. 4; 158. 6; 217. 3; 251. 5; 288. 15; 467. 8;** balance of the earth **218. 17**

***māχa*** to weigh **248. 7**

***māχatu*** intestines **67. 5**

***māχiu*** burning altars **320. 7**

***māχent*** a boat **87. 11; 130. 3; 202. 8; 204. 3, 4, 5, 12, 13; 218. 3; 241. 10; 261. 3; 483. 15; 503. 3, 4**

***māśā*** bowmen, soldiers **107. 6**

***māśeru*** evening, eventide **6. 4; 27. 8; 40. 3; 41. 11; 42. 16; 104. 14; 111. 3; 135. 16; 175. 14; 185. 15; 220. 9, 15; 302. 4; 345. 5; 357. 4; 370. 16; 509. 9**

***māku***, ***māket*** strength, strength which protects, to be protected against, protector 29. 13; 38. 11; 80. 16; 100. 6; 114. 1; 135. 15; 140. 12; 145. 11; 212. 6; 298. 15; 299. 2, 3; 303. 3, 4; 314. 7, 8; 330. 6, 7, 11; 359. 6; 366. 12; 410. 1; 420. 2; 447. 13; 463. 7; 476. 14; 479. 12; 480. 12; 481. 13; 482. 7; protector 114. 13

***mākefiti*** turquoise 14. 7

***mākḫa*** back of the head 386. 10; 387. 13

***māket*** station 473. 16

***māqet*** ladder 203. 1

***māta*** weapon, harpoon 190. 8; 219. 11

***mātennu*** ways, roads 21. 5, 7

***Māṭes*** a proper name 64. 12

***māṭet***, ***māṭetet*** the boat of the rising sun 244. 4; 279. 2; 335. 10; 395. 13

***māθennu*** ways, roads 135. 10

***māfa*** phallus 408. 7; 417. 6

***māfab*** fetter, chain 454. 3

***māfabet*** part of a ship 130. 4; 206. 11; 242. 3

***Māfeṭ*** a proper name 63. 6

***mu*** water, essence 3. 17; 5. 9; 70. 9; 127. 7; 137.

5; **147.** 15; **148.** 1; **151.** 1, 16; **173.** 12; **227.** 5; **233.** 6; **239.** 8; **251.** 10; **292.** 15; **334.** 15; **335.** 8; **336.** 5, 16; **337.** 12; **338.** 9; **339.** 3, 15; **340.** 12; **341.** 8; **347.** 14; **373.** 6; **378.** 3, 5; **378.** 7, 10; **379.** 5; **397.** 10; **402.** 9; **417.** 14; **420.** 12; **435.** 16; **436.** 6; **444.** 16; **447.** 6; **458.** 9, 12; **464.** 15; **466.** 2; **468.** 10; **485.** 11, 13; **486.** 7; pool, drink **516.** 6; the water-god **448.** 7; **219.** 10; head of the water **381.** 15; **422.** 11; **450.** 10; that which [liveth] in the water **36.** 15; **439.** 6; **414.** 4

***mu nu ānχām*** ānkhām (flower) water **402.** 12; **403.** 8

***mu nu ānti*** ānti (incense) water **211.** 8

***mu nu ḥesmen*** natron water **82.** 16

***mu nu qamāi*** incense water **420.** 5

***mu [nu] sefit*** incense water **506.** 4

***mu ṭu*** foetid liquid **400.** 2

***mut*** mother **1.** 6; **4.** 8; **6.** 6; **11.** 7; **12.** 8; **13.** 4; **25.** 7; **37.** 2; **43.** 7; **49.** 10; **59.** 1; **87.** 7; **94.** 4; **95.** 2; **96.** 1; **115.** 12; **135.** 14; **153.** 2, 15; **154.** 1; **163.** 7; **229.** 11; **233.** 5; **293.** 8; **313.** 16; **317.** 15; **404.** 9; **405.** 2; **415.** 7; **417.** 3; **436.** 4; **478.** 15; **479.** 10; **487.** 3; **489.** 3; **493.** 6; **501.** 5; **502.** 4; **503.** 10; **505.** 5; **506.** 16; **415.** 9

*mutet* parents 502. 13; 365. 6; 365. 13

*mut* weight in a scale 251. 3

*Mut-resθȧ* a proper name 28. 13; 194. 14; 222. 12; 223. 13; 386. 2; 387. 8; 444. 12

*Mut-ḥetep-θ* a proper name 46. 2; 48. 4; 383. 1, 7, 11, 14; 384. 1, 2, 4, 5, 11; 384. 16; 385. 10; 455. 7; 456. 15

*mit* water 378. 13

*met* or *mit*, *meti*, *metti* to die, death, dead, the damned 6. 6; 25. 15; 26. 8; 27. 8; 93. 12; 95. 12; 103. 15, 16; 104. 16; 115. 1; 119. 8; 120. 2; 145. 8; 285. 1, 12; 295. 9; 300. 6; 371. 11; 395. 16; 397. 12; 399. 14; 400. 10; 406. 16; 407. 2, 4, 6; 414. 13; 417. 14; 431. 14; 438. 4; 457. 9; 460. 13; 461. 5; 469. 5; 476. 15; 501. 14; 515. 10; plur. 74. 2, 8; 79. 2; 81. 15 *(bis)*; 196. 1; 213. 1; and see 84. 3, 4; 113. 8; 196. 4; 213. 1; 291. 14; 293. 12; 298. 13; 308. 15; 356. 11; 366. 1; 370. 7; 371. 15; 376. 5; 389. 14; 477. 6; 490. 2

*Mi-śeps* a proper name 456. 8

*men*, *ment* to be stablished, stable, firm, permanent, abiding, firm, fixed 13. 12; 14. 13; 16. 11; 52. 7; 70. 16; 112. 4, 6; 136. 14; 139. 11; 166. 10; 205. 1; 275. 6; 385. 1; 386. 11; 427. 9; 441. 12; 446. 7, 15; 447. 13; 459. 15; 460. 9;

482. 9; 483. 1, 2; 505. 11; 509. 14; 512. 4; 25. 4; 38. 11; 6. 7; 8. 5; 40. 12; 173. 4, 5; 293. 11, 14; 402. 2. 436. 8; 483. 1; 485. 8; stablishing daily 448. 9

*mennu* . . . . 47. 9

*mennu* chamber 390. 8

*mennu* bases, pedestals 448. 11

*men*
*mennu* } possessions, things which abide 442. 1; 459. 16

*Ment* name of a god 75. 16

*men*
*menti*
*mentiu* } the two legs, thighs 113. 1; 118. 18; 122. 11; 397. 10; 456. 3; 502. 15

*men*
*ment* } pain, sickness, disease, affliction 53. 14; 154. 8; 215. 4; 280. 13; 358. 16; 360. 2

*ment*
*mennut* } disease, sickness, sick one 239. 7; 250. 11; 420. 16

*Menk* a proper name 324. 16

*menk* to arrive at a place, to come into port, ... 51. 4; 77. 2; 418. 7; 40. 5

post at which to anchor 205. 6; 230. 10, 11

**menȧt** ending **205**. 10; happy ending or death **63**. 10

**menȧ** death **182**. 4; **184**. 10; bier **135**. 2; **139**. 8; **144**. 8

**menȧ**, **menȧtu** the dead **134**. 16; **149**. 4

**menȧt** death **82**. 16; with *ȧn* deathless **202**. 10, 12

**menȧu** stakes of death **473**. 7, 8

**meni** slaying in honour of some one **155**. 5

**menāt** breast **25**. 8

**mennu** ministrants **389**. 2

**menmen** to go about **141**. 10

**menmen** cattle, farm-beasts **9**. 4; **251**. 13

**menḥ** wax **29**. 7

**menḥu** to offer up **155**. 1

**Menḥu** name of a god **69**. 2

**menχ**, **menχet** clothed, clothes, garments **223**. 7; **307**. 13; **335**. 2; **372**. 7; **373**. 4

**menχu**, **menχ** wrought, perfected, founded, perfect, beneficent, gracious, well done, wrought in, set in **20**. 12; **21**. 1, 5; **39**. 8; **272**. 6, 14; **275**. 14; **300**. 6;

307. 9; 362. 10; 402. 11; 442. 9; 482. 16; 485. 8; 486. 8; 489. 14; 496. 8; 402. 11

**Menχ** a proper name (?) 201. 9

**Menqet** a proper name 213. 16

**Ment** a proper name 326. 8

**ment** swallow 186. 3, 4; 187. 14

**mențet** apple of the eye 446. 8

**menț**, **mențti**, **menθ** the breasts 121. 17; 420. 10; 446. 14; 447. 11

**Menθ**, **Menθu** the god Mentu 315. 12; 443. 10

**Mențat** name of a city 235. 9, 14

**mer** overseer, superintendent *Mer per* major-domo 10. 12; 26. 9; 145. 13; 484. 9; and see *passim*; officer of soldiers 11. 3; *mer šenti* overseer of the granaries 37. 6

**mer** to moisten (?) 310. 9; water-course 132. 13

**mer** a pool 3. 2; 264. 1; plur. cisterns 453. 10

**Mer-țesțes** (?) name of a mythological pool 9. 6; 12. 10; 36. 7; 440. 6

**mer** sickness, pain, grief, deadly, disease 57. 2; 154. 8; 215. 4; 280. 13; 365. 9; 462. 7; 106. 9

***mer*** the dead 272. 4

***meru*** pain, sickness, cruel 62. 14; 169. 13

***meràu*** disease, diminution, decay 515. 1

***Mer*** a proper name 147. 7

***merāḥāt*** tomb, sepulchre (with ) 442. 5

***mer*** to love, to be loved, to desire, to wish for, to please, wish, will 10. 10; 161. 11; 235. 16; 273. 10; 279. 7; 357. 3; 385. 6; 429. 14; 433. 7; 450. 16; 460. 2; 467. 10; 482. 11; 511. 4; *meri* loving, lover 17. 9; 31. 1; 37. 6; 51. 1; 68. 15; 77. 12; and see 124. 14; 129. 9; 150. 12; 180. 5; 209. 9; 210. 3; 211. 16; 291. 6; 377. 15; 399. 10; 493. 8; loved one 21. 11; lover 57. 12; loving 441. 11; loved 7. 2

***mert***, ***merit***, ***mertu***, ***mert***, ***mertu***, ***merutu*** love, desire, wish, beloved, willingly 11. 14; 26. 5; 156. 8, 13; 157. 7; 158. 1, 4; 184. 12; 214. 1; 290. 13; 316. 15; 339. 1; 345. 2; 352. 14; 362. 4; 373. 10, 16; 374. 9, 11; 378. 7, 12; 411. 5; 448. 3; 452. 3; 480. 13; beloved lady 415. 10; friends 459. 15; 460. 6

***merer***, ***merer***, ***mereru*** to love 3. 6; 17. 8; 86. 3; 94. 12; 153. 12; 163. 15; 185. 4; 226. 3; 270. 9; 292. 6; 434. 6; 441. 3; 442. 6; 443. 13; *mereriu* those who love 235. 15

*merert* wish, will, love **26.** 14; **90.** 2; **225.** 7; **261.** 1; **489.** 11; **503.** 10; **479.** 8, 12; **94.** 11

*Mer* a proper name **7.** 1

*Mert* a proper name **117.** 10

*Merti* a name of two goddesses **102.** 10, 12; **129.** 16; **249.** 14

*meru* bound, tied **150.** 9

*meru* swathing **72.** 7

*Mer-ur* the Mnevis bull **206.** 7

*meruḥ* oar, paddle **133.** 7, 17; **339.** 7

*meriut* a kind of tree **439.** 2

*Meri-s*
*Mer-s* a proper name (?) **156.** 16; **245.** 12

*merḥ*
*merḥet* wax **161.** 3; **341.** 10

*Mert* name of a part of a boat **207.** 5

*Mert* name of a city **224.** 8

*Mert* a proper name **315.** 13

*meḥ* , cubit **143.** 4; **164.** 11; **212.** 13, 14; **218.** 16; **221.** 15; **222.** 1, 2, 3, 4; **226.** 1; **291.** 1; **339.** 13; **368.** 1; **369.** 2; **368.** 2; **368.** 3; **369.** 2; **367.** 15; **369.** 4; **219.** 9; **368.** 2; **369.** 3; **371.** 4;

***meḥti*** northern beings, gods, etc., **36.** 11; **99.** 10, 13; **106.** 4; **114.** 15; **319.** 8, 15; **443.** 14; **508.** 9; lords of the north (?) **226.** 15

***meḥit*** north wind **37.** 1; **87.** 12; **129.** 4; **155.** 9; **207.** 14; **289.** 2; **382.** 13; **389.** 10; **407.** 10; **481.** 5; **484.** 13; **489.** 2

***Meḥt-χebit* (?)*-sāḥ-neter*** name of a cow-goddess **318.** 11; **364.** 2

***Meḥt-ti*** name of a double district **443.** 12

***meḥṭet*** to bathe **201.** 13

***em-χent-maati*** = (?) **426.** 16

***meχsef*** name of a wooden instrument **391.** 3; **394.** 7, 12; **396.** 7

***mes*** to bring **200.** 1; **299.** 11; bearer of **102.** 6; brought **462.** 7; bringing **427.** 7

***mesu*** anointed **142.** 3; **502.** 3

***mes***
***mesu***
***mes*** to give birth to, to bring forth, to be born, produced **6.** 5; **11.** 11; **57.** 5; **123.** 1; **139.** 3; **140.** 3; **153.** 12; **188.** 5, 6; **230.** 3; **293.** 8; **296.** 3, 12; **297.** 8; **346.** 13; **352.** 7; **398.** 7; **455.** 10; **481.** 6, 13; **487.** 3; genetrix **449.**

15; 487. 3; birth 53. 11;  born of 28. 13; 77. 10; 80. 12; 386. 2; 387. 7; 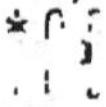 508. 4, 8, 12; 509. 4, 14; 510. 15; 511. 15; 512. 3, 10, 15; 513. 12; 514. 2, 6, 15; 515. 2, 4, 6, 9, 11, 13, 15; 516. 1; 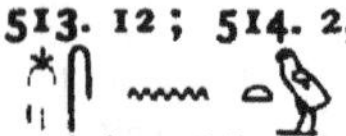 441. 6;  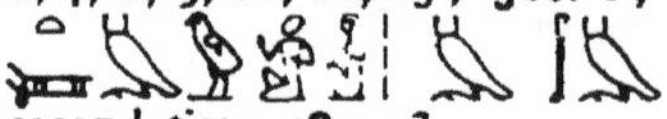 giving birth to mortals a second time 482. 13

***mesi***  one who is born 19. 7; 27. 9, 10; 240. 4; 329. 10; 466. 7

***mesu-tu*** / ***mestu***  birth 42. 12; 43. 6; 54. 9; 57. 8; plur.  11. 14; 114. 11; 115. 6; 170. 1; 478. 16; 513. 8;  455. 13;  497. 2

***mest***  birth 2. 13; 55. 9; 122. 3; 134. 11; 142. 10; what is produced 246. 9

***mes***  birth 409. 10

***mest*** 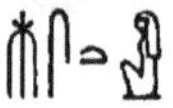 genetrix 456. 4; 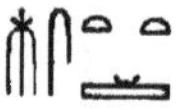 353. 12

***mestet*** 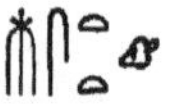 (sic) 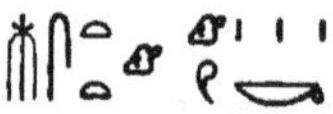 511. 15

***mes-ui***  . . . . . 274. 14

***mes***  child 147. 4

***mesu***  children 18. 14; 268. 7; 292. 8; 468. 4

***mesu***  producers (or children)   388. 11; 390. 7; 393. 15; 396. 2;  children of Nut 457. 11; 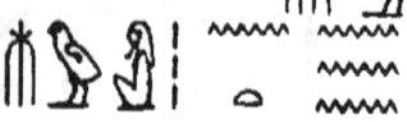 children of the water god, *i. e.*, plants **448.** 7; children of Horus **306.** 3; **462.** 4

***mesu beṭeś*** malicious but impotent fiends **2.** 8; **61.** 3; **74.** 13; **316.** 8

***mesu nebu*** all who are born, *i. e.*, the human race **450.** 3

***mes*** *hru mestu* birthday **278.** 11; **284.** 16

***mesi*** cakes **66.** 15; **67.** 6, 8, 10

***mesbeb*** (?) banded (?) **96.** 14

***Mes-peḥ*** a proper name **350.** 10

***Mes-Ptaḥ*** a proper name **335.** 7

***Mes-em-neter*** a proper name **34.** 11; **105.** 4

***mesmes*** to count (?) **42.** 5

***emseḥ*** , crocodile **97.** 7; **98.** 2, 8, 13, 15; **146.** 16; plur. **284.** 1; the eight crocodiles **98.** 11

***emseḥu*** crocodile of the East **99.** 1, 4; of the West **98.** 13, 15; of the North **99.** 10, 13; of the South **99.** 6, 8

***emseḥu*** to slay **345.** 4

*mesχen* — birth-place, birth-chamber 79. 11; 83. 8; 105. 7; 154. 7, 9; 226. 4, 6, 11; 348. 16; plur. 326. 7

*mesχent*

*Mesχen-āat* — a proper name 326. 7

*Mesχen-ment* — a proper name 326. 8

*Mesχen-nefert* — a proper name 326. 9

*Mesχen-seqebet* — a proper name 326. 8

*Mes-ṣepeχ* — a proper name 346. 16

*meska* — skin 206. 7

*Mesqen* — name of a place (?) 130. 1

*mesqet* — a place 66. 15; 67. 4; 160. 11; 209. 3; 461. 1

*mesqet* — weapons 107. 9

*mesṭemet* — eye-paint, stibium, *kohl* 268. 1; 333. 13; 446. 9

*mesṭeṭ* — leg 263. 5

*mesṭeṭ*
*mesṭeṭet* — what is hateful or abominable 106. 12; 399. 8

*mesθȧ* — palette 199. 6, 12; 458. 4

*Mesthȧ* — one of the four children of Horus

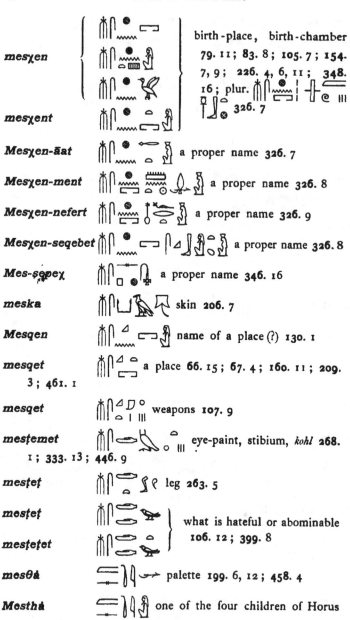

57. 13; 58. 8; 59. 2; 73. 5, 14; 384. 15; 206. 3, 15; 232. 8, 15; 306. 3; 319. 4

***mesṭemu*** painted with eye-paint **268.** 1

***mesṭer*** ear **34.** 4; **117.** 4; **217.** 6; **401.** 14

***mesṭer-ui*** the two ears **112.** 9; **135.** 13

***mesṭeṭ*** to hate **455.** 16

***met*** ∩ ten **76.** 13; **375.** 1; ∩ I eleven **354.** 9; **375.** 15; ∩ II **137.** 3; **143.** 4; **355.** 16; **377.** 4; ∩ III **355.** 7; **378.** 2; ∩ IIII **355.** 13; **379.** 11; ∩ IIIII **356.** 3; **333.** 9; **356.** 8; **357.** 14; **357.** 2; **333.** 9; **345.** 8; **358.** 6; tenth **341.** 2; **341.** 14; **342.** 5; **342.** 12; **343.** 3; **343.** 11; **344.** 2; **344.** 10; **344.** 16

***metu*** emission, venom **99.** 12

***met***, ***meti*** right, rightly, fittingly, exactly **16.** 8; **202.** 1; **371.** 9; to try the right **481.** 2

***metmetu*** sinews and muscles **29.** 10; **228.** 8; **372.** 15

***meter***, ***meteru*** to bear witness, to give testimony, evidence **15.** 10; **16.** 2; **95.** 3; **96.** 2; **261.** 11; **301.** 15; **302.** 3, 13; **360.** 8; **501.** 6; to give evidence against someone **260.** 4

***meṭu***, ***meṭ***, ***meṭet*** to speak, to say, to talk **21.** 13; **32.** 13; **85.** 7; **89.** 9; **98.** 9; **114.** 5; **115.** 8; **160.** 4; **166.** 3; **239.** 14; **377.** 2; **386.**

12; 438. 10; 456. 2, 7; 511. 2; 237. 2; 357. 15

***meṭ***, ***meṭu*** word, speech 27. 5; 34. 13; 115. 8; *meṭu ṭeref* word of wisdom 481. 1; 488. 14

***meṭu***, ***meṭeṭu*** words, speech 27. 7; 57. 12; 96. 9; 103. 3; 104. 13; 111. 3, 5; 165. 1; 168. 8; 195. 14; 243. 5; 261. 9; 281. 2, 10; 299. 11; 391. 15; 471. 4; 481. 1; 503. 16

***meṭet*** speech, decree, verdict, words, sayings 15. 17; 23. 14; 51. 5; 87. 1; 227. 2; 261. 15; 347. 12; 418. 9; 434. 7; 445. 11; 461. 13; 462. 10; 481. 2; 256. 4, 13; 245. 11; 426. 9; 427. 11; 91. 1

***Meṭu-ta-f*** a proper name 493. 6

***Meṭes-ḥrà-àri-śe*** the herald of the sixth Ārit 328. 15

***Meṭes-sen*** doorkeeper of the seventh Ārit 329. 1

***m θ u*** . . . . . . . . 471. 15

***meṯ*** to be deep 458. 9; doubly deep 339. 13

***meṯut*** abysses 136. 15; 143. 2

***meṯabu*** to fetter 454. 3

***meṯet*** oil 455. 1

# N.

*n* in, to, for, because 1. 4, 11; 2. 6; 9. 13; 12. 6; 16. 7; 49. 15; 137. 9; 145. 16; 413. 15; 417. 5; 420. 3; and see *passim.* 154. 3; 162. 1; 310. 7; 190. 7; 4. 13

*n* of see *passim.*

*n* = *ȧn* 63. 3, 4; 104. 13; 137. 15; 149. 6; 421. 5, 6; 449. 10; 463. 2; = 33. 10, 11; 62. 14; 91. 1; 132. 16; 135. 14; 139. 6; 144. 6; 225. 6, 11; 383. 4, 5; 406. 6; 447. 5; 451. 13; 462. 1; 467. 7; invisible 64. 7; = 255. 4; 259. 2

*n* we, us 16. 9; 52. 7; 96. 6; 107. 15, 16; 233. 10; 247. 1 *(bis)*; 264. 3, 5; 265. 6; 266. 3; 301. 9, 10; 486. 3; 233. 8

*na* the, these 178. 14; 248. 6; 259. 17; 410. 7; 511. 4, 6; 516. 7, 8; 58. 9; *na* . . . 142. 9

*Naȧrik* a proper name 418. 13

*Naȧrer-f*, *Naȧreṭ-f* see *Ȧn-ruṭ-f* 39. 1; 47. 12; 55. 5; 72. 13; 75. 11, 13; 59. 13

**Náarer**  see *Án-ruṭ-f* **82.** 1

**naik** 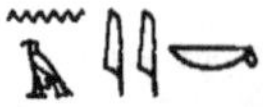 those of thine **262.** 4

**nar**  . . . . . . **306.** 10; **307.** 3

**Nasaqbubu**  a proper name **419.** 13

**Nak** (?)  name of a god **201.** 1

**NaΘkerΘi** 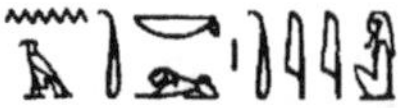 a proper name **418.** 11

**n-á** ,  I, me, my **2.** 14, 16; **3.** 2, 8; **4.** 15; **14.** 12; **16.** 14; **22.** 6; **69.** 13; **115.** 11; **120.** 8; **360.** 16; **361.** 1; **363.** 14; **375.** 14; **452.** 9; **505.** 3; **506.** 3

**ná**  . . . . . **507.** 6

**náh** 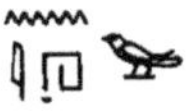 injury **353.** 6

**nás** 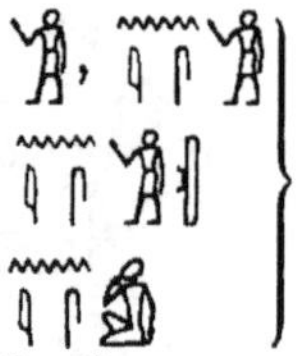 to invoke, to be invoked, to call, to cry out **22.** 10; **109.** 9; **128.** 13; **136.** 3; **271.** 7; **286.** 12; **302.** 4; **383.** 2; **388.** 13; **432.** 5, 6; **451.** 3; **486.** 4; 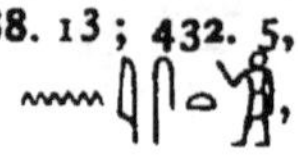,  invoked **3.** 6; **5.** 1; **44.** 7; **270.** 10; **355.** 2; **487.** 13

**Nák**  name of a fiend **6.** 7; **13.** 2

**nákiu** 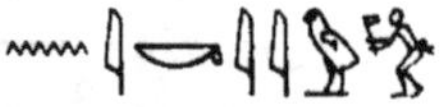 fiends who slaughter **473.** 9

**nā** 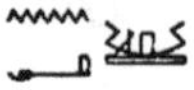 to sail in a boat **48.** 11; **289.** 4

**Nāáu**  name of a god or devil **98.** 16; **99.** 4; **315.** 12

**Nāu** name of a fiend 375. 12; 505. 11

**nāā** a decree 314. 4

**nāā** (?) (?) to advance 5. 3

**nār** a reed for writing with, pen 480. 6; 488. 13

**Nārt** a proper name 38. 13

**nāś** mighty one 408. 11, 12

**nāk̦** to break open 136. 14

**nāt** to journey 294. 9

**nu** of 1. 12; 18. 4; 19. 1; 20. 3; 52. 5; 58. 15; 60. 13; 125. 3; 158. 16; 173. 12; 270. 1; 271. 5; 307. 12; 336. 14; 446. 12; 70. 13; 173. 12; 223. 14; 441. 9; 449. 6; 512. 4

**Nu** name of a scribe 26. 9, and see *passim.*

**nu** the watery abyss of the sky 6. 15; 9. 2; 169. 9; 425. 3; 459. 8

**Nu** the god Nu 4. 8; 7. 11; 8. 1; 11. 13; 13. 4; 29. 13; 42. 1; 43. 3; 49. 7; 51. 6; 87. 7; 103. 1; 105. 5; 112. 8; 117. 1; 128. 18; 148. 12; 149. 1, 13; 156. 5; 167. 12; 176. 9; 183. 3; 184. 15; 185. 12; 258. 5; 290. 8, 12; 318. 5; 325. 7; 397. 13; 398. 1; 422. 12; 443. 12; 457. 6; 464. 8; 504. 6

**n-uȧ** I am 18. 12; 19. 2; 33. 14; 153. 11; 458. 5; and see *passim.*

**nuit** weapon 86. 13

*nub* gold **43.** 6; **116.** 5; **142.** 2; **164.** 8, 9, 16; **191.** 1; **289.** 8; **290.** 17; **316.** 11; **402.** 6, 10, 11; **404.** 3, 11, 16; **405.** 4; **440.** 3; **444.** 11; **446.** 3; **447.** 1, 4, 11; **448.** 8, 11; **502.** 2, 14; fine gold **409.** 14; golden light (?) **61.** 8

*Nub-ḥeḥ* a name of Osiris **321.** 1

*nub* to mould, to shape, moulder **36.** 15; **42.** 11; **115.** 1; **399.** 5; fashioned, inlaid **135.** 6; **449.** 6

*nubȧu* to mould **509.** 10

*nubḥeḥ* blossom **157.** 4

*Nubti* name of a god **505.** 15

*nun* to pay homage **170.** 11, 12; a proper name (?) **469.** 3

*nuk* I **7.** 12; **18.** 9, 10; **20.** 4; **27.** 16; **41.** 4; **51.** 5, 7, 11, 15; **52.** 2; **53.** 2 *(bis)*; **66.** 14; **86.** 15, 16; **87.** 6; **88.** 12; **91.** 8; **92.** 8; **93.** 14, 15; **94.** 9; **98.** 12, 15; **101.** 5; **102.** 5, 13; **107.** 3; **109.** 3, 9; **110.** 4, 5; **113.** 14; **114.** 12; **115.** 8; **116.** 18; **119.** 16; **120.** 8; **125.** 6; **226.** 5, 17; **133.** 1, 17; **134.** 10; **142.** 9; **148.** 10; **152.** 15; **153.** 5, 14; **167.** 2, 14; **170.** 5; **178.** 5, 13; **188.** 4, 5, 12, 14; **215.** 12; **224.** 10; **229.** 9; **239.** 9; **243.** 4; **252.** 3, 6; **261.** 7, 13; **273.** 7; **277.** 4; **288.** 3; **302.** 9; **310.** 3, 4; **313.** 12; **358.** 13; **361.** 10; **370.** 10; **375.** 9; **384.** 16; **397.** 13; **406.** 3; **411.** 7; **443.** 1; **452.** 13, 16; **456.** 8; **460.** 7, 16; **469.** 2, 3; **472.** 2; **474.** 5—13; **480.** 14; **488.** 11; **493.** 11; **503.** 10, 11, 13; **507.** 5; **132.** 4; **167.** 8; **169.** 9

*Nut* the goddess Nut, wife of Seb **15.** 6; **94.** 4;

107. 11; 130. 16; 294. 4; 443. 2, 9; 444. 14; 449. 14, 15; 474. 13

***Nut*** — the goddess Nut 1. 7; 4. 8; 7. 10; 11. 15; 12. 8; 13. 4; 38. 9; 49. 11; 78. 9; 108. 2, 5; 113. 2; 118. 18; 119. 16; 122. 2; 153. 11; 154. 1; 170. 12; 176. 4; 217. 9; 220. 3; 276. 10, 11; 288. 12; 296. 15; 297. 13; 298. 2; 315. 13; 318. 8; 326. 4; 375. 12; 418. 13; 420. 1; 457. 11; 461. 10; 461. 15; 467. 16; 478. 15; 479. 10; 481. 10; 483. 1; 484. 10; 486. 10; 487. 3; 489. 5; name of a sail of a boat 206. 5

***Nut*** — the night sky 36. 5; 37. 13; 43. 1; 165. 3; 174. 14; 176. 4; 190. 6; 289. 4; 474. 14

***nut*** — city 54. 3; 67. 16; 176. 14; 258. 11; 262. 12; 375. 2; 376. 1; 404. 5; 486. 3; plur. 43. 10; 183. 1; 224. 13; 225. 5; 226. 4; 227. 5, 14; 480. 1; 507. 12

***nut ent neter*** — city of the god 487. 14

***Nut-urt*** — name of a Pool in the Elysian Fields 228. 12

***nuti*** — citizens 437. 8

***nut*** — cords 393. 2, 7

***ni*** — . . . . . 495. 16

***nimā*** — who 129. 13, 15

***nini*** — to adore 1. 8; 4. 4; 9. 5; 11. 16; 36. 5

**Nin-åreref** see *Ån-rut-f* 64. 10

**neb** each, every, all, any 2. 6; 7. 6; 12. 1; 26. 14; 58. 2, 15; 64. 11; 65. 3; 76. 14, 15; 107. 2; 113. 8, 9; 138. 10; 153. 3; 194. 9; 271. 16; 294. 1, 2; 309. 3; 320. 15, 16; 333. 5, 6; 371. 10; 384. 7, 12; 407. 8; 437. 12; 444. 15; 509. 2, 3; 516. 3, 5; 517. 1; plur. , , 1. 4; 8. 8; 14. 12; 29. 13; 304. 12; 305. 8; 306. 14; 307. 7; 326. 4; 327. 1; 347. 5; 366. 13; 443. 13; 486. 14; every kind of green plant 454. 6; every kind of evil thing 197. 2; 198. 8

**neb** with *bu*, everywhere 3. 6; 23. 4

**neb** , lord, master 2. 2; 4. 13; 7. 9; 10. 13; 14. 5; 22. 4; 36. 2; 57. 12; 58. 4; 58. 7; 121. 5, 6; 137. 14; 170. 10; 249. 7; 445. 14; 512. 8; 514. 12

**nebt** lord 276. 11; 510. 9; 276. 14

**nebt** lady 15. 6; 309. 14; 343. 13

**nebu** , lords 14. 5; 21. 4; 70. 11; 137. 14; 159. 13

**neb** lord of, possessor of, owner of 426. 6; 428. 11

**neb åbu** "lord of hearts", a name of Åḥi 367. 8

**neb Åbtet** "lord of the East", a title of Rā 221. 12; 368. 15, 398. 3

***neb åmaχ*** "lord of veneration" 28. 11; 61. 12; 103. 1, 16; 134. 10; 139. 12; 194. 13; 199. 3; 217. 15; 222. 10; 223. 5, 13; 347. 6; 386. 1; 386. 7, 14; 387. 6, 16

***neb Åmentet*** a name of Osiris 434. 8; 179. 1

***nebt Åmentet*** a name of Hathor 490. 10

***nebu Ånnu*** lords of Heliopolis 439. 15

***neb āāui*** lord of two hands 427. 5; 185. 8

***neb ābui*** lord of the two horns, *i. e.*, Åmen 418. 12

***Neb ābui*** one of the forty-two assessors 257. 9

***neb ānχ*** a title of Osiris 34. 2; 48. 5; 110. 5; 137. 8; 166. 11; 242. 11; 320. 9; 321. 2; 323. 2; 325. 8; , lord of life 139. 10; 385. 16

***nebt ānχ*** a title of Isis 4. 10; 44. 15

***neb ānχ taui*** lord of the life of the two lands 468. 7

***neb uā*** the lord One 202. 2

***Nebt unnut*** a proper name 40. 12

***neb urert*** lord of the *urert* crown 32. 7

***neb useru*** lord of might 298. 13; 303. 1

***neb baiu*** lord of souls 276. 12

***neb pāt*** lord of mankind 388. 4

***nebt per*** owner of a house, *i. e.*, a married woman (?) 28. 13; 194. 13; 222. 11; 223. 13; 384. 5; 386. 2; 387. 8; 444. 12; 456. 15; 489. 8

***neb maau*** lord of eyes 387. 9

***neb maāt*** possessor of right and truth 57. 14; 58. 6; 298. 14; 363. 14; 481. 2; 70. 5, 15; 433. 9; 487. 14, 15; 34. 14; 254. 9; 303. 2

***Neb Maāti*** lord of the double city of right and truth 249. 7, 14

***meḥt en nebu*** lords of the north 226. 15

***neb nifu*** lord of air, a name of Osiris 252. 4; 262. 4; 399. 4

***neb nemtet*** the possessor of the power of walking 426. 5; 425. 16

***neb neru*** lord of victory, name of the heart of Osiris 64. 15

***neb neter meṭet*** lord of divine speech 228. 16

***neb renput*** possessor of years 185. 2

***neb Re-stau*** a title of Osiris 69. 16

**neb hennu** he to whom praises are sung 35. 16

**Neb-ḥrȧu** one of the forty-two assessors 257. 5

**neb ḥeḥ** lord of eternity 119. 5; 179. 2; 363. 14

**neb ḥeḥ** lord of millions of years 190. 4; a name of Osiris 323. 6; 324. 9; 90. 11; 174. 8

**neb χāu** lord of risings, a title of Rā 125. 2

**neb χut** a title of Rā 467. 3

**neb χeperu** lord of transformations 408. 9

**neb χet** lord of the universe 201. 4; 461. 2; 95. 3; 174. 9; 208. 10; 226. 16; 307. 13; 373. 14; 467. 13

**nebu χaut** those who possess altars 347. 9

**nebu χer-āba** lords of Kher-āba 112. 15; 118. 13

**nebt Sau** lady of Saïs, *i. e.*, Neith 112. 13; 117. 11

**neb satut** lord of light, *i. e.*, Rā 40. 1

**neb senṭ** he who inspires fear 46. 15

**neb seχti** possessor of the field 228. 15

**nebu kau** lords of food (or *kas*) 222. 14

**neb qerest** lord of the bier, *i. e.*, Osiris 399. 6

**neb kesu** he to whom homage is paid 188. 14

***nebt taui*** lord of the two lands **439. 14**; title of a king **484. 9**; **487. 6**; name of Osiris **325. 1**; **486. 14**; a pool in the Elysian Fields **228. 4**

***nebt taui em karȧ*** name of the anchoring post **205. 7**

***neb ta ānχtet*** lord of the land of life, *i. e.*, Osiris **323. 10**

***neb ta ṭesert*** lord of the holy land, *i. e.*, Osiris **482. 4**; **490. 10**

***neb tau*** lord of food **125. 7**

***neb tit*** (?) ...... **180. 15**

***neb temu*** lord of mankind **176. 2**

***nebu ṭuat*** lords of the underworld **432. 12**

***neb ṭeśert*** lord of the red land (or redness) **64. 15**

***neb ṭa*** possessor of a phallus **427. 13**; **428. 8**

***neb ṭefau*** lord of divine food **217. 15**; **487. 16**

***neb ṭetta*** lord of everlastingness, *i. e.*, Osiris **37. 10**; **70. 11**; **322. 1**; **324. 9**; **326. 6**; **489. 10**; plur. **428. 1**

***Neb-peḥtet-petpet-sebȧ*** a proper name **325. 11**

***Neb-peḥti-θes-menment*** a proper name **248. 14**

***Neb-maāt-ḥeri-reṭui-f*** a proper name 248. 13

***Neb-er-ṭer*** lord of wholeness, *i. e.*, Osiris 13. 15; 24. 5; 52. 5; 60. 13; 62. 11; 63. 12; 65. 7; 66. 7; 71. 9; 76. 14; 107. 13; 166. 8, 16; 187. 1; 260. 4; 269. 6; 282. 13; 320. 10; 323. 2; 461. 1; 480. 6; 486. 10; 488. 13; , 173. 15; 337. 9

***Nebt-ḥet*** Nephthys 12. 15; 15. 6; 53. 15; 67. 2; 68. 6; 72. 4; 276. 16; 293. 9; 294. 5; 315. 13; 318. 9; 339. 4; 375. 11; 382. 15; 407. 12; 443. 9; 447. 5; 478. 17

***Neb-s*** a proper name (?) 4. 11; 44. 16; 299. 13; 339. 12; 342. 8; 353. 12; 355. 4; 479. 16

***Nebseni*** a famous scribe 28. 4, 11; 61. 12; 62. 12; 71. 4; 81. 4; 82. 5; 103. 1; 132. 10; 134. 10; 138. 4; 139. 11; 156. 4; 159. 13; 194. 13; 215. 17; 222. 10; 223. 4, 12; 235. 7; 312. 14; 386. 1; 387. 6; 406. 3; 421. 1, 10; 444. 11, 13; 445. 3, 8; 461. 11; 462. 3; 463. 8; 464. 5; 465. 1, 15; 466. 1, 14, 16; 467. 12, 16; 468. 5; 466. 2

***Neb-qeṭ*** name of a scribe 239. 11

***neba*** a weapon 494. 5

***Nebȧ*** one of the forty-two assessors 353. 10

***nebȧu***, ***nebȧt*** flame, fire 101. 5; 346. 10; 357. 16

*nebeḥ* a kind of bird 127. 2

*nebt* hair, name of a cloud 47. 16; 85. 9; 284. 6; 286. 13; 299. 8; 314. 2; 331. 12; 388. 13; 445. 14

*nepu* a part of the body 391. 7

*neper* grain 323. 4

*Neperȧ* god of grain 165. 5; 380. 10

*nepert* irrigated land 36. 16; 450. 13

*Nepert* name of a city 322. 8

*nef* he, him 2. 12; 51. 8; 53. 11; 66. 2; 67. 14; 68. 6; 80. 14; 86. 12; 92. 2; 111. 5; 152. 12; 308. 8; 368. 11; 374. 11; 379. 6; 404. 7, 8; 438. 13; 448. 1; 464. 2, 4; 466. 4; 478. 5; 485. 2, 11; 487. 1; 488. 4; 489. 15; 492. 1; 495. 2; 497. 6; 503. 16 *(bis)*; 504. 3; 506. 1; 507. 13; 514. 6; 516. 5

*nef* air, wind, breath 24. 6; 37. 1; 38. 1; 61. 10; 70. 9; 102. 17; 104. 5; 109. 15; 111. 1; 126. 4; 127. 7; 139. 16; 144. 14; 151. 1; 155. 12; 159. 2; 169. 9; 207. 13; 221. 7; 223. 16; 224. 7; 225. 8; 228. 8, 9; 262. 4; 263. 12; 289. 1; 368. 9; 374. 7; 399. 4, 5; 425. 2; 436. 6; 438. 16; 446. 6; 458. 9, 12; 481. 5; 484. 12; 488. 1; 489. 1; 505. 8; 509. 10; 511. 6; winds, N. S. E. W., 407. 10, 11, 12; breath of life 429. 6

*nefu* sailor 207. 12

***Nef-ur*** name of a city 22. 14; 276. 11, 13; 287. 9; 324. 2; 512. 9

***nefai*** this, that 189. 9; 190. 3; plur. 405. 14, 15

***nefer*** to be good or happy 282. 12; 464. 8, 9; 11. 6; 386. 13; 36. 2; 406. 16; twice good, very good 15. 15; 40. 9; 112. 2; 139. 7; 144. 7; 290. 5; 442. 4; 444. 12; 459. 11; 514. 14

***nefer*** fair, beautiful, pretty, happy, good, well, 4. 2; 4. 7; 7. 2; 9. 8; 36. 4, 10; 63. 10; 77. 12; 78. 13; 96. 8; 108. 16; 139. 8; 139. 13; 224. 16, 280. 16; 295. 2; 318. 15, 16; 319. 1, 3, 4; 340. 15; 364. 9, 11, 12; 365. 1; 382. 11; 386. 3; 386. 9; 387. 9; 387. 16; 409. 14; 424. 1, 10; 479. 4; 489. 2; 505. 4; fine gold 409. 14; a gracious or comfortable word 501. 11; happiness 15. 13; 96. 6

***nefert*** fair, beautiful 50. 20; 91. 10; 100. 3; 130. 11; 137. 9; 138. 13; 159. 6; 284. 15; 289. 7; 295. 13; 362. 6; 382. 4; 473. 2; 488. 6; 493. 13; with 33. 13

***neferu*** beauties, splendours, fair things 2. 14; 7. 12; 12. 7; 35. 12; 41. 3; 95. 9; 176. 3; 195. 2; 208. 9; 229. 10; 246. 7; 249. 8; 283. 2; 301. 11; 308. 6; 439. 11; 442. 15; 444. 6, 15; 445. 1; 448. 3; 476. 5, 8; 479. 7; 486. 15, 16; 487. 2; 143. 14; 173. 1; 174. 4; 199. 15; 332. 7; 386. 16; 384. 2

***nefer ḥrȧ*** "fair face", a name of Rā 6. 1; 14. 8; 490. 11

***Nefer*** (?) the Lake of Nefer (?) 258. 9

***neferu*** to be glad (?) 44. 16

***Nefert*** a proper name 326. 9

***nefert*** name of a tree 495. 10

***Nefer-uben-f*** a proper name 128. 15; 149. 12; 407. 2, 3, 5; 435. 13; 437. 6, 11; 440. 11, 12; 441. 6, 8, 9, 14; 442. 1, 3, 11, 13; 503. 4, 13

***Nefer-sent*** name of a city 393. 16

***Nefer-Tem***, ***Nefer-Temu*** name of a god 62. 10; 178. 13; 257. 11; 456. 14; 468. 9

***nem*** (or ***uḥem***), ***nem***, ***nemm***, ***nemu*** to repeat, to report, to narrate 78. 2; 79. 15; 80. 1, 4; 168. 10; 180. 10; 195. 14; 235. 12; 238. 8; 245. 10; 290. 9; 298. 2; 302. 15; 341. 16; 414. 3; 439. 9; 446. 10; to converse 439. 8; voice 377. 4; to repeat 354. 11; 104. 13; 104. 16; 510. 16; × 510. 12; 478. 16

***nem*** with a second time, again 71. 14; 115. 2; 119. 8; 285. 2, 12; 295. 9; 300. 7; 395. 16; 431. 14; 457. 9; 460. 13; 461. 5; 482. 14; *nem ā* 120. 2

***Nem-ḥrȧ*** a proper name **243**. 5

***nem*** . . . . . . **417**. 7; girded, encircled **447**. 1, 4

***nem*** to defraud **250**. 16

***nem***, ***nemȧ***, ***nemȧ*** } to walk, to stride **9**. 6; **12**. 9; **35**. 15; **36**. 7; **42**. 16; **49**. 7; **431**. 11

***nemnem*** to march **289**. 5

***nemā*** who? **138**. 15; **143**. 15; **266**. 7, 14; **267**. 5; who then? **503**. 9; who then art thou? **241**. 18

***nemmȧ*** pigmy, dwarf **417**. 8

***Nem*** a proper name **6**. 5

***Nemu*** name of a god **62**. 4; **391**. 4; **394**. 12, 15; **396**. 10; **441**. 13

***nemeḥ*** to defraud **250**. 6; to falsify the reading of the tongue of the balance **251**. 4; a humble man **250**. 7

to grow young **443**. 3

***nemmes*** } name of a crown **168**. 5, 8, 12; **169**. 2, 5; **272**. 12; **275**. 12; **473**. 3, 10

***nemt*** block of slaughter **5.** 5; **24.** 13; **62.** 3; **69.** 4; **112.** 3; **121.** 14; **122.** 8; **254.** 5; **280.** 4; **373.** 15; **64.** 16

***nemt*** step, stride **22.** 7; **38.** 7; **49.** 9; **140.** 3; **408.** 12; **432.** 16; **487.** 1; plur. **2.** 8; **31.** 11; **45.** 13; **149.** 1, 13; **181.** 13; **182.** 17; **185.** 8; **187.** 7; **211.** 1; **252.** 13; **310.** 2; **320.** 15; **383.** 8; **470.** 12; **475.** 3; **497.** 6; **195.** 3

***nemtet*** slaughtering place **371.** 12

***n*** see *àn.*

***enen*** this, these **16.** 7; **24.** 1; **30.** 6; **31.** 15; **45.** 14; **51.** 14; **56.** 12; **101.** 15; **127.** 3; **147.** 7; **209.** 16; **231.** 8; **232.** 3; **270.** 2, 9; **301.** 2; **312.** 4, 6; **315.** 16; **316.** 16; **333.** 5, 6; **366.** 4; **448.** 13; **488.** 6; **505.** 16; this is he who **137.** 6; **143.** 6; **136.** 13

***enen*** unguent **337.** 3

***enen*** a stuff **340.** 2

***enen*** a weak or helpless being **28.** 5

***enen*** to be weak or helpless **162.** 12, 13

***eneni***
***eneniu***
***enentu***
***enenui***
weak and helpless beings, fiends, etc., **29.** 8, 9; **121.** 16; **122.** 11; **144.** 15; **196.** 14; **198.** 1; **371.** 5; **390.** 11; **394.** 3

***Enenaȧrerf*** see *Ȧn-rut-f* 157. 4

***ennu*** . . . . . . 25. 12

***eneniu*** . . . . . . 422. 7; 424. 7

***ennu*** this, these 28. 16; 41. 4; 57. 7, 11; 58. 2; 62. 12; 63. 15; 99. 16; 111. 11; 137. 7; 159. 3; 167. 2, 14; 203. 2; 215. 4; 218. 4; 231. 7; 235. 5; 244. 8; 263. 6; 286. 8; 306. 7, 15; 320. 4; 337. 4; 398. 7; 399. 7; 456. 8; 460. 8, 15; 503. 5; 506. 4; 66. 6; 67. 1, 3; 52. 12; 18. 11; 86. 3

***ennu*** season, period, time 140. 5; 280. 8

***ennu*** to watch, to observe, to see 189. 13, 14; 191. 14

***ennu*** to go away or about 196. 13; 197. 17; 226. 9; 283. 8

***ennu*** to be strong, to strengthen 226. 1; 373. 12

***ennu*** (?) adorations 313. 2

***Ennutu-ḥru*** a proper name 393. 7

***ennui*** canal, stream, watercourse 57. 7; 151. 2; 152. 1; 181. 12; 221. 6; 267. 8; 368. 8; 373. 6; 378. 15; 379. 5; 380. 5, 8, 10; 390. 9; 418. 8; 432. 15; 444. 15

***Enen-unser*** name of a cow-goddess 462. 4

***ennur*** a kind of bird 373. 10

***ennuḥ*** to masturbate 256. 9

***ennuḥ*** to bind, to tie, to fetter, to drag on 33. 14; 92. 9; 473. 7, 8

***ennuḥ*** cords, cordage, fetters 48. 1; 106. 3; 279. 10; 289. 11; rigging, tackle 295. 7; 391. 10; 396. 5

***ennuḥti*** horns 197. 1, 7; 198. 6, 9

***ennuχ*** to be burnt 133. 9

***ennuṭ*** to bear, to carry, to journey, 136. 12; 166. 9; 296. 4

***ennuṭiu*** a class of divine beings 166. 10

***Enenṭā*** a proper name 107. 7; … 107. 11

***Ner*** a proper name (?) 439. 4

***Nerȧu*** a proper name 334. 14

***neru***, ***neru***, ***nerȧu*** terror, strength, might, victory, strong one 108. 5; 200. 6; 286. 16; 315. 5; 341. 6; 417. 5; … victory 344. 4; … victorious one 354. 5; … 477. 11; …, … 43. 12; 64. 15; 68. 7; 157. 9; 171. 14; 188. 12; 194. 2; 245. 6; 373. 13; 454. 15; 477. 8; 487. 9; … 356. 10

***Neri*** a proper name 350. 4.

**Neràu-ta** a proper name 335. 7

**neràut** vulture 404. 3, 11

**neh** to conquer 109. 15; to be joined to 144. 12

**nehet** sycamore tree 124. 7; 130. 15; 139. 12; 144. 11, 12; 201. 14; 402. 12; 403. 9; 493. 1, 13; the two sycamores 221. 10; 368. 12

**neha** to alight 101. 13

**neha** to advance 227. 16

**nehaàs** to awake 511. 5

**Nehatu** name of a city 255. 9

**nehep** to copulate 224. 2; 227. 9; 229. 11

**nehep** to have power over 180. 12

**nehepu** strength 345. 11

**nehepu** light, fire, to shine 183. 8; 280. 7; 342. 8; 345. 11; 355. 3; 357. 7; 466. 7

**nehem** to rejoice, rejoicing 226. 8, 13; 315. 1

**nehemu** rejoicings 2. 9

**nehemnehem** to be destroyed (?) 105. 6

**neheh** flame, fire 283. 14

**nehehu** needy one 408. 13

***nehes*** to wake up, to rouse up, to lift up **341. 4; 354. 4; 404. 6; 465. 4**

***nehesu*** a class of divine beings **183. 2; 332. 13**

***Nehes-ui*** a proper name **242. 1**

***Neḥ*** name of a god **397. 12; 398. 1**

***Neḥa-ḥrȧ*** one of the forty-two assessors **253. 15; 515. 10**

***Neḥa-ḥāu*** a proper name **253. 4**

***neḥait*** flowers **263. 2**

***neḥeb*** to assert **173. 3**; **128. 18**

***Neḥeb-nefert*** one of the forty-two assessors **258. 9**

***Neḥeb-ka*** name of a deity **6. 8; 63. 14; 258. 11; 501. 12**; **95. 10; 367. 9; 375. 12; 469. 4**

***neḥebet*** neck **80. 7; 117. 9; 136. 6; 142. 15; 401. 15; 446. 16**; plur. **158. 8; 438. 3**

***neḥem*** to carry away, to deliver, deliverer **2. 7; 24. 1; 32. 6; 49. 9; 61. 11; 62. 12; 64. 2; 65. 13; 66. 6; 92. 10; 98. 10; 103. 16; 107. 15; 111. 6; 133. 12; 135. 14; 160. 2; 173. 11; 215. 3; 224. 8; 250. 13; 251. 5; 254. 1, 13; 256. 15; 260. 10; 262. 4; 282. 3; 298. 10; 334. 13; 365. 7; 366. 9; 369. 14; 375. 13; 411. 1, 14; 412. 10; 418. 3; 463. 15; 468. 2; 473. 6**; **261. 5;**

deliverer 350. 3; carried off, delivered 25. 6; 93. 3; 94. 1; 119. 2, 3; 132. 3; 383. 3; 421. 5, 6; 469. 8; 470. 1

***neḥeḥ*** eternity, for ever 53. 6, 7; 147. 2; 152. 12; 155. 16; 159. 14; 169. 12; 184. 2; 185. 1, 2, 9; 208. 10; 213. 15; 225. 16; 232. 12; 268. 16; 278. 12; 285. 1, 12; 308. 8, 9; 309. 5; 364. 15; 383. 3; 399. 7; 421. 7; 432. 1; 442. 16; 444. 1; 471. 2; 479. 15; 482. 12; 484. 4; 489. 8, 14; 498. 3; 504. 1

***neḥeḥ*** invoked 397. 15

***neḥes*** negro 416. 2

***neḥtet*** jaw-teeth 97. 16; 112. 17 jaws (?); 117. 7

***neχ*** to cry out 235. 1

***neχa*** sharp knife 448. 12

***neχaχat*** offerings (?) 201. 1 (var. )

***Neχebet*** the goddess of the city of Nekheb 508. 11

***neχebet*** plants 504. 7, 8

***neχen*** babe, child 126. 13; 232. 6; 502. 15; one of the forty-two assessors 256. 3

***neχennu*** children 251. 6; 265. 8

***Neχen*** a city of Upper Egypt 39. 6; 157. 14; 232. 11; 233. 3; 234. 7, 9, 13; 235. 4; 7. 5

***Neχen neter*** the god of Nekhen **234.** 13

***neχeχ*** whip **13.** 11; **408.** 7; **482.** 10; **487.** 5

***neχeχ*** to become old **33.** 7; **126.** 8

***neχt*** strong (in a bad sense) **100.** 7

***neχt*** to be strong, strength, mighty, power **32.** 11; **153.** 8; **182.** 16; **279.** 13; **313.** 15; **314.** 6; **338.** 6; **416.** 3; mighty deeds **180.** 11

***Neχt*** a proper name **11.** 3; **141.** 11; **315.** 13

***Neχtu-Ȧmen*** a proper name **23.** 16; **24.** 4

***nes*** she, her, it **12.** 12; **36.** 10; **57.** 4; **106.** 9, 10; **153.** 11; **192.** 8; **242.** 4; **304.** 5; **341.** 6; **343.** 14; **346.** 3; **374.** 3; **377.** 8; **389.** 1; **404.** 5; **461.** 10; **483.** 2; **487.** 4; **488.** 1; and see *passim.*

***nes*** to belong to **218.** 4; **219.** 2; belonging to the chancery **26.** 9; and see *passim.*

***nes*** tongue **5.** 13; **36.** 15; **180.** 7; **204.** 16; **401.** 16; **446.** 13; **511.** 11; **512.** 13; plur. **10.** 2; **152.** 8

***nes*** to devour, to consume **138.** 16; **143.** 15

***nes*** to arrange **449.** 3

***nesu*** said, spoken **135.** 1; **142.** 15; **370.** 4, 5; **372.** 11

***nes*** flame, fire **63.** 8; **186.** 6; **284.** 6; **369.** 9; **382.** 2

***nesu*** . . . . . . **466.** 7

***nesau*** tongue **465.** 8

***nes*** grain (?) **437.** 7; cakes (?) **437.** 8

***nesut*** weapons **107.** 10

***nesb*** to swallow **289.** 1

***nesbit*** devourer **350.** 9

***nesbti*** to devour **371.** 11

***nesbu*** eater **65.** 16

***nespu*** slaughterings, gashes, wounds, knives **106.** 1; **143.** 9; **204.** 11; **302.** 8; **361.** 2

***nesert*** to burn up, flame **58.** 14; **62.** 2; **99.** 1, 5; **119.** 1 *(bis)*; **156.** 15; **421.** 4

***Nesert*** the fire city **86.** 4; **87.** 13

***nest*** throne **13.** 12; **24.** 15; **77.** 16; **107.** 8; **114.** 3, 4; **116.** 2; **121.** 3; **149.** 5, 16; **194.** 2; **239.** 8; **284.** 3; **348.** 15; **458.** 15; **459.** 2; **460.** 5; **476.** 10 *(bis)*; **485.** 7; **512.** 14; plur. **165.** 12

**Nest** Throne 324. 6

**nesti** a class of divine beings 319. 14

**neś** to walk upon (?) 5. 12

**neśt** moisture 224. 7

**neśau** plates or strips of metal 448. 11

**neśu** a weapon 494. 5

**neśi** — making the hair to bristle 130. 3; 242. 1

**neśem** a precious stone (mother-of-emerald [?]) 405. 9, 16; 406. 3, 4; 406. 10

**neśmet** name of a boat of the sun 22. 12; 108. 15; 247. 11; 326. 5; 336. 3; 347. 14; 490. 13; 509. 12

**neśni** to make a storm, to stir up tempest 56. 14, 15; 109. 10; 128. 4; 200. 6, 11; 421. 13; 483. 7; 485. 2; 156. 15; 421. 13

**neśen**, **neśennu**, **neśni** storms, whirlwind 131. 12; 231. 12; 279. 11; 281. 15; 332. 3; 334. 13; 350. 2

**nek** thee, thou, thy 1. 7; 2. 5; 6. 3; 33. 4; 50. 2; 69. 6; 77. 11, 14; 98. 16; 99. 5; 100. 13; 115. 11; 304. 12; 305. 6; 312. 6; 361. 1; 379. 6; 393. 12; 402. 7, 8; 436. 2; 437. 4; 439. 2; 440. 1; 441. 4; 446. 10; 452. 7; 455. 1; 458. 1; 467. 15; 471. 13; 476. 4; 479. 2; 480. 3;

485. 1; 491. 9; 494. 10; 495. 8; 496. 1; 504. 15; 506. 2; 509. 3; 510. 10; 511. 6; 512. 4; 513. 16; 514. 1; 515. 1

***nek*** to copulate 180. 15; 225. 11; 250. 14; 255. 6, 14, 16; he had union with himself 53. 1

***nekek*** a sodomite 255. 15; 256. 9; to commit sodomy 256. 9

***nekau*** actions (?) 16. 5

***nekai*** injury 231. 12

***nekai*** harmful fiends 414. 9

***Nekȧ***, ***Nekȧu*** a fiend 9. 7; 418. 1

***neken*** to do harm or injury, injury, evil 34. 15; 105. 13; 165. 15; 166. 12; 202. 4; 228. 6; 402. 1; 406. 5, 6; 453. 3; 365. 9; 225. 3; 192. 8; 228. 7

***neqăut*** shackles 460. 7

***neqăiut*** those who steal away 90. 10

***Neḳa*** to chew 31. 13

***Neḳau*** a proper name 351. 8

***neḳeḳ*** to cackle 63. 14; 179. 10; 202. 13; 376. 12; 438. 6; 493. 12

***Neḳeḳ-ur*** the Great Cackler 131. 2

**net** thou **415**. 12; **416**. 3, 4

**net** the crown of the North **97**. 2; **415**. 4; **417**. 5; **495**. 16; King of the North **147**. 1

**Neti** a proper name **110**. 16

**net** the chancery, superintendent (or tongue) of the chancery **26**. 9; and see *passim*.

**ent** of **1**. 3; **3**. 14; **20**. 3; **28**. 5; **33**. 5; **52**. 2; **59**. 6; **67**. 6; **80**. 6; **87**. 11; **103**. 2; **124**. 11; **130**. 8; **149**. 13; **181**. 11; **197**. 3; **210**. 6; **223**. 11; **242**. 7; **262**. 7; **271**. 16; **281**. 7; **294**. 1; **297**. 1, 15; **304**. 5; **308**. 4; **315**. 7; **334**. 2; **343**. 11; **347**. 3; **360**. 8; **366**. 11; **375**. 3; **380**. 6; **389**. 4; **403**. 7; **420**. 12; **437**. 2; **445**. 2; **449**. 9; **464**. 16; **485**. 9; **493**. 2; **504**. 16

**net** waters **9**. 2

**Net** Neith **112**. 13; **148**. 9; **158**. 3; **235**. 8, 14; **238**. 4, 11; **326**. 6; **339**. 2; **348**. 10; **413**. 12; **414**. 2

**entā** statute, ordinance **42**. 6; plur. **274**. 14; **486**. 9

**netu** fastenings **86**. 8, 10

**entuten** ye **206**. 6

**entu** = not **462**. 1 *(bis)*

**neti** . . . . . . **109**. 11

**neti** to vanquish **236**. 15

***enti*** = *ȧnti* = *ȧti* a negative particle, not, without **81.** 16; **406.** 4; **66.** 10; **61.** 9

***Enti-śe-f*** a proper name **136.** 3

***enti*** who, which, that which **13.** 12; **15.** 17; **23.** 15; **24.** 7; **52.** 15; **53.** 5; **55.** 2; **64.** 3; **72.** 12; **129.** 15; **140.** 12; **162.** 2; **211.** 6; **218.** 12; **227.** 6; **260.** 2; **332.** 14; **336.** 2; **341.** 6; **343.** 5, 13; **358.** 16; **368.** 7; **390.** 13; **393.** 3; **406.** 4; **407.** 3; **441.** 6; **482.** 2; **488.** 3; **491.** 12; **492.** 1; **507.** 12; **508.** 9; **53.** 5

***enti***, ***ent***, ***entiu***, ***entet*** those who, the persons or things which are **24.** 16; **47.** 9; **99.** 14; **140.** 12; **166.** 2; **174.** 5; **213.** 1; **392.** 8; **440.** 6; **443.** 14, 15; **475.** 1; **478.** 4

***Enti-ḥrȧ-f-emmā mast-f*** a proper name **281.** 6

***entef*** he **25.** 7; **38.** 7, 9; **64.** 13; **65.** 3; **67.** 16; **68.** 4; **87.** 9, 10; **91.** 6, 7; **135.** 5; **271.** 9; **295.** 4, 5; **373.** 9; **379.** 1; **409.** 8, 12; **411.** 8; **412.** 12; **413.** 11

***netnet*** that which flows **175.** 1; **216.** 12

***neter*** god **2.** 12; **3.** 9; **121.** 14; and see *passim.*

***neteru*** gods **1.** 7; **4.** 3, 4, 14, 16; **6.** 3, 16; **7.** 9; **8.** 8, 16; **9.** 11; **11.** 14, 15; **12.** 3; **13.** 1; **21.** 3; **51.** 15, 16; **52.** 9, 11; **55.** 10; **64.** 2; **65.** 7, 8; **66.** 14; **67.** 3; **79.** 11; **318.** 1; **319.** 9, 13; **336.** 2; **365.** 6, 12, 13, 14; **367.** 10; **372.** 1; **374.** 3; **379.** 2; **382.** 4; **387.** 11; **462.** 10, 11,

12; **466.** 2; **487.** 3, 7; **514.** 2, 4; **515.** 16; **516.** 5, 7, 11 (see also *paut*); the company of the gods **162.** 2; gods **45.** 1; all the gods **54.** 7; **69.** 14; **74.** 7; **76.** 12; **459.** 11; **460.** 1; **511.** 13; the father-gods **365.** 6; the mother-gods **365.** 6, 13; the four gods **295.** 5; forty-two gods **249.** 10; gods celestial and gods terrestrial **485.** 14; gods of heaven and gods of earth **496.** 2; gods of the Ṭuat **424.** 13; **429.** 13; **434.** 2; gods of the **326.** 11; gods of Meḥen **434.** 5; **435.** 4; **326.** 10; **438.** 8, 13; **319.** 9; **455.** 12; **319.** 9; **455.** 12; **319.** 9; **443.** 14; **319.** 8; **443.** 14; gods following Osiris **422.** 14; **514.** 5; **515.** 16; gods of the shrine **422.** 10, 12; **87.** 2

***netert*** goddess **16.** 16; **78.** 6; **81.** 5; **82.** 6; **89.** 15; **112.** 12; **166.** 12; **169.** 14; **244.** 13; **246.** 1; **271.** 16; **275.** 2; **276.** 16; **294.** 2; **326.** 4; **399.** 12; **400.** 5; **410.** 6; **416.** 16; **444.** 15; **445.** 12; plur. **422.** 14; **480.** 6; **175.** 11; **111.** 9; **443.** 11

***neter*** great god, *i. e.*, Osiris **164.** 4; **208.** 13; **510.** 14; **512.** 8; self-created, great god **51.** 11; god One **9.** 1; god great **170.** 1; god of the city **24.** 4; **86.** 9;

226. 4, 5, 6, 11; 227. 5; 259. 12; 436. 15; 251. 1; god with a dog's face 64. 3

***neter-ui*** the two gods Horus and Set 475. 4; 449. 16

***neter***
***neteri***
***netert***
to make or become like a god, divine 8. 2; 9. 11; 37. 2; 43. 4; 67. 14; 80. 11; 154. 6; 165. 9; 168. 3; 170. 9, 10; 171. 7; 174. 15; 201. 14; 254. 6; 287. 4; 375. 9; 409. 5; 417. 12; 419. 6; 509. 12; 510. 13; 511. 3, 12; 516. 12; 416. 13; 47. 2; strengthener (?) 416. 7; divine one 491. 14; 49. 1

***neter ȧtef-ui*** the two divine fathers 449. 8

***neter meṭu*** sacred words or writings 151. 13; 228. 15; 441. 10

***neter nemmat*** divine block 24. 13; 91. 17; 122. 8

***neter ḥāu*** divine body 290. 12; 340. 14; 460. 3

***neter ḥet*** god's house, temple 219. 1; 242. 6; 326. 10; 347. 12; 441. 9; 464. 6; 472. 3; 489. 12

***neter ḥetepu*** holy offerings 1. 4; 58. 16; 261. 4; 269. 9; 380. 1; 453. 6

**Neter χert** the underworld, a region in the "beautiful Åmenṭet" **14.** 9; **18.** 5; **31.** 10; **43.** 16; **70.** 1, 5, 15; **90.** 9; **91.** 9, 15; **92.** 15; **93.** 13; **95.** 1; **97.** 9; **98.** 7; **116.** 18; **119.** 8; **120.** 2; **130.** 11; **162.** 10; **178.** 15; **179.** 1; **196.** 12; **197.** 16; **246.** 2; **285.** 5, 13; **295.** 9, 10; **310.** 2; **317.** 1; **334.** 3; **363.** 3; **365.** 7, 14; **370.** 7; **384.** 7, 13; **422.** 14; **424.** 15; **425.** 15; **426.** 7; **429.** 11; **435.** 3; **470.** 13; **480.** 13; **497.** 3; **501.** 4; **514.** 7, 9

**neter χet** property of the god **251.** 13; **253.** 11, 15; **337.** 14

**neter sentrå**
**neter senθer**
or **sentrå**
incense offered to the gods **80.** 11; **161.** 3; **175.** 1; **216.** 11; **223.** 7; **247.** 8; **268.** 2; **291.** 4; **294.** 8; **303.** 12; **310.** 16; **312.** 6; **317.** 7; **318.** 3; **382.** 16; **333.** 13; **366.** 7; **375.** 10; **437.** 1; **444.** 7; **300.** 1

**neter seḥt** divine hall **323.** 9; **348.** 4; **513.** 9

**neter śes** follower of the god **223.** 10

**neter ṭuai** divine morning star **222.** 7; **242.** 9

**neter ṭuau** to make like the divine morning star **277.** 12; **307.** 14; **300.** 11

**neter ṭept** the divine boat **218.** 5; **368.** 10

**neter ṭeṭ** sacred speech **135.** 13

**Neter** name of a pool **506.** 15

**Neteru**
**Neter** } name of a city **321**. 6; **323**. 12

**Neter ufat** name of a place **201**. 14; **491**. 10

**entek** thou **8**. 16; **10**. 5; **15**. 12; **38**. 3; **41**. 6; **96**. 4; **129**. 14; **241**. 18; **408**. 7, 12; **409**. 12; **421**. 4; **435**. 13 *(ter)*, 14; **440**. 9; **441**. 1; **442**. 13; **505**. 6

**Neteqa-ḥrȧ-χesef-aṭu** the herald of the fourth Ārit **328**. 7

**netet** cattle for sacrifice **182**. 12

**entet** which **67**. 5; **111**. 4; **141**. 13; **156**. 9; **157**. 8; **170**. 2; **190**. 15; **354**. 6; **355**. 2, 9, 15; **375**. 1; **376**. 3; **378**. 8; **394**. 9, 14, 15; **412**. 1

**neṭ** to bandage **414**. 5

**Neṭit** a proper name **324**. 3

**Neṭbit** name of a city **322**. 5

**Neṭet** name of a city **455**. 16

**neḟ**
**neḟet** ,
**neḟ** } to avenge, to protect **19**. 15; **46**. 14; **137**. 14; **153**. 1; **154**. 6; **195**. 4; **277**. 3, 4, 7; **306**. 12; **307**. 1, 3, 6; **346**. 11; **347**. 3; **361**. 4, 11; **385**. 7; **369**. 5; **478**. 13; **483**. 12; avenger **478**. 9; **482**. 15; to advocate **341**. 9

**neḟ ḥrȧ** to avenge **313**. 16; **452**. 9; **488**. 15; to pay homage to **442**. 5

***nefnef*** to gainsay **340**. 9; **353**. 5

***nef meṭu*** to exchange words **166**. 15

***neftu re*** to converse **140**. 8; addresses **451**. 14

***Nefeb-áb-f*** a proper name **107**. 5

***Nefefet*** a proper name **321**. 5

***nefem***, ***nefemu***, ***nefemet*** to be glad, to rejoice, happy, sweet **4**. 11; **6**. 9; **35**. 14; **76**. 8; **82**. 3; **126**. 5, 11; **127**. 9; **135**. 7; **173**. 3; **186**. 6; **298**. 2; **436**. 6; **437**. 6; **467**. 15; **481**. 5; **484**. 12; **485**. 16; **513**. 10; very pleasant, pleasant things **225**. 14

***Nefem*** name of a god **108**. 2

***nefemmit*** the pleasures of love **458**. 11, 13

***nefer*** to grasp, to hold fast, strong **149**. 4; **155**. 10; **196**. 4; **197**. 8; **282**. 5; **296**. 4, 12; **297**. 8; **395**. 6; to be restrained or held fast **309**. 8; **330**. 12; **467**. 6

***neferi*** clinchers **392**. 16; **429**. 3

***neferá*** to carve, to fashion **75**. 6

***nefeḥet*** to strengthen **225**. 12

**Nefeḥnefeḥ**  a proper name 59. 8

**nefes** 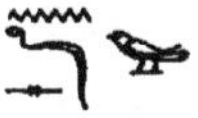

**nefeset**  weak, little 443. 11; 457. 15; 504. 7; 506. 7;  lesser gods 318. 7

**Nefesti** 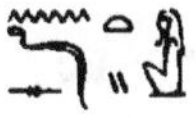 a name of Osiris 321. 14

**Nefses** 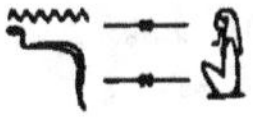 name of a god 339. 14

**Nefet**  name of a city 323. 11

---

## R or L.

**er** at, to, with, into, among, against, from, according to, near, by, towards, upon, concerning **1.** 9; **2.** 13; **3.** 5; **4.** 4; **10.** 5, 7; **15.** 10, 12; **34.** 11, 13; **43.** 13; **63.** 12; **64.** 10; **95.** 3; **96.** 2; **124.** 3; **126.** 13; **130.** 1; **136.** 3; **140.** 2; **147.** 13; **151.** 5, 6, 7; **210.** 9; **483.** 2; **501.** 6, 8; and see *passim.*

**er** more . . . . than more glorious than the gods **38.** 5; **48.** 10; **43.** 4; **87.** 10, 15; **88.** 3; **87.** 15; **88.** 4; **106.** 8; **277.** 2; **298.** 7; **330.** 9; **416.** 3; **442.** 9; **445.** 15; **446.** 13; see also **196.** 15, 16; **198.** 2, 3

**er-àmi** among **126.** 12; and see *passim.*

**er-àmi-tu** / **er-àmi-θu** among, between **64.** 9; **165.** 2; **215.** 16, 17

**er-åsu** in return for, as recompense for **231**. 6

**er-pu** or **23**. 6; **161**. 10; **316**. 11; **317**. 12, 16; **407**. 16

**er-mā** with, near **234**. 2; **266**. 10; **267**. 1; **509**. 9; **510**. 15

**er-men** as far as **31**. 15

**er-entet** because **244**. 3; **308**. 13; **396**. 2, 5, 7, 9, 10, 12, 14, 16; **397**. 2, 4, 6

**er-ruti**
**er-rut** } outside **26**. 2; **502**. 9

**er-ḥāt** before **505**. 5

**er-ḥenā** with **22**. 10

**er-ḥer** — remote from sight **372**. 9

**er-ḥeru** above **436**. 13

**er-χeft** in the face of **22**. 3

**er-χer** under **436**. 5, 13

**er-χerθ** on behalf of **136**. 16

**er-sa** by the side of **241**. 17

**er-ḳes** by the footprint of, near **15**. 15; **22**. 16; **60**. 12; **61**. 2; **70**. 15; **96**. 10; **154**. 12; **179**. 1; **215**. 11;

222. 5; 279. 12; 286. 3; 295. 10; 302. 13; 368. 4, 5; 425. 8; 427. 3; 430. 7; 433. 6; 436. 10; 487. 13

***er*** cake 466. 15

***re*** goose 451. 11; plur. 154. 15; 221. 6; 229. 1; 368. 8; 440. 10

***re*** worms (?) 418. 4

***re*** door, opening, mouth 8. 1; 11. 5; 61. 11; 63. 8; 107. 3; 108. 6; 150. 15; 151. 15; 191. 5, 8; 192. 1; 225. 6; 251. 6; 281. 8; 315. 6; 316. 15; 339. 5; 346. 15; 369. 14; 371. 12; 372. 13; 379. 15; 389. 11; 405. 12; 408. 15; 411. 16; 419. 2; 444. 8; 450. 3; 465. 7, 8; 467. 6; 479. 5; 510. 6; 511. 2; strong of mouth 22. 4; appearance 41. 16; plur. 22. 2; 115. 7; 269. 8; 374. 8; 510. 9; 444. 5

***re ȧpt*** (?) brow 68. 5; 69. 6

***Re-āa-urt*** name of a city 144. 10

***re uat*** entrance to the ways 37. 15

***re mu*** mouth of a stream 439. 6

***re Ḥāp*** mouth of the Nile 380. 3

***re χemennu*** the entrance to the city of Khemennu 92. 7

***re Seχait*** the mouth of the goddess Sekhait 326. 5

**Re-stau** 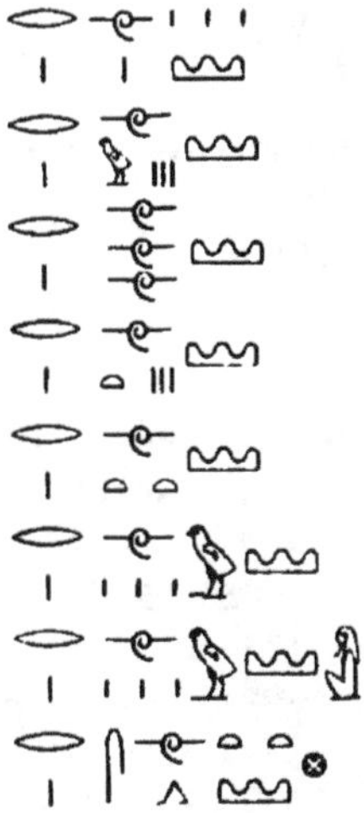 the entrance to the passages of the tomb, the underworld **19.** 14; **20.** 6; **23.** 2; **24.** 2; **27.** 15; **47.** 10; **55.** 5; **69.** 16; **70.** 11; **76.** 4, 7; **79.** 14; **82.** 1; **86.** 2; **138.** 16; **143.** 16; **223.** 11; **239.** 3, 4; **240.** 3, 4, 11; **248.** 1; **253.** 4; **261.** 13; **269.** 15; **270.** 3, 7; **302.** 6; **321.** 13; **322.** 2; **324.** 2; **329.** 10, 13; **348.** 4, 10; **358.** 9, 10, 15; **360.** 1, 16; **377.** 7; **426.** 1; **452.** 5; **477.** 9; **512.** 7; **515.** 10

**re** 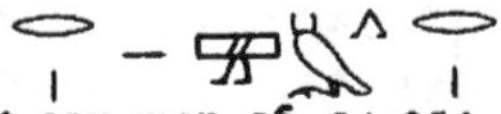 to set the mouth in motion against any man **16.** 5; **254.** 15; **255.** 1

**re**  chapter of a book **77.** 1; **80.** 10; **267.** 14; **316.** 15; **317.** 2; plur.  **18.** 4; **142.** 7; **223.** 14; **349.** 11; and see *passim.* 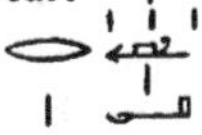 a single chapter **142.** 7; 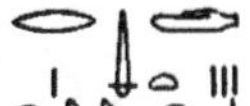 a chapter of words **23.** 14; **25.** 8; 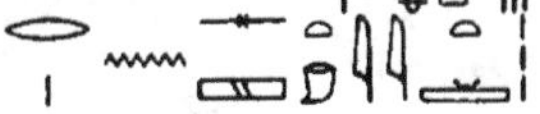 a chapter of mysteries **19.** 14

**ri** 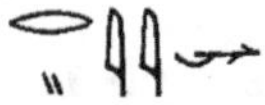 door **55.** 13

**erper** 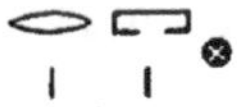 temple and the ground on which it stands **237.** 11; **472.** 2

**erperu** 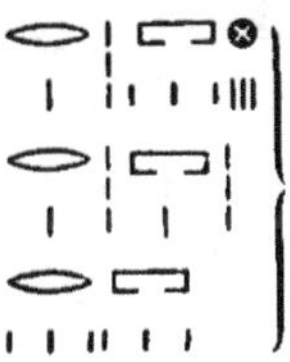 temples **16.** 4; **28.** 10; **97**; 4; **110.** 10; **138.** 4; **141.** 10; **250.** 12; **309.** 15; **486.** 2; 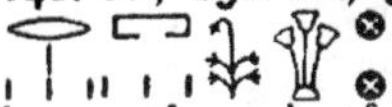 the temples of the south and of the north **223.** 4; **387.** 6

**Re** (?)  the Lion-god Rā **91.** 16; **139.** 6; **144.** 6, 16; **288.** 2; **435.** 13

**Re-iukasa** name of a god **418.** 10

**Re-Rā** the Lion-god Rā **132.** 13

**rā** storehouse **449.** 9

**rā** work **42.** 7

**Rā** the Sun-god **1.** 3; **2.** 7, 10; **3.** 13; **4.** 1, 7, 12; **5.** 4; **6.** 13; **11.** 3; **12.** 12; **20.** 5; **23.** 8; **27.** 9; **48.** 17; **52.** 4, 9; **75.** 14; **108.** 11; **117.** 2; **131.** 10; **295.** 4; **315.** 10; **359.** 10; **366.** 4, 8; **383.** 2; **409.** 5; **421.** 12; **426.** 10; **456.** 6; **457.** 1, 3; **470.** 9; **476.** 4; **486.** 12; **487.** 9; **490.** 11; **491.** 1; **496.** 13; **509.** 8, 11, 16; **510.** 13; **511.** 6, 13; **514.** 3, 16; **515.** 1

**Rā-Àusàr** Rā-Osiris **281.** 4

**Rā-Ḥeru-χuti** Rā - Harmachis **48.** 16; **318.** 4; **367.** 11; **381.** 3

**Rā-Tem** Rā-Tem, *i. e.*, the day sun and the night sun **46.** 3; **47.** 4; **64.** 1; **104.** 7; **317.** 4

**Rā-Maāt-men** the prenomen of Seti I. **10.** 16

**Rā-men-kau** the Mycerinus of the Greeks **97.** 2; **141.** 8

**Rā-meses-meri Àmen-meri-Maāti** the prenomen of Rameses IV. **271.** 8, 15; **272.** 8, 16; **273.** 2, 6

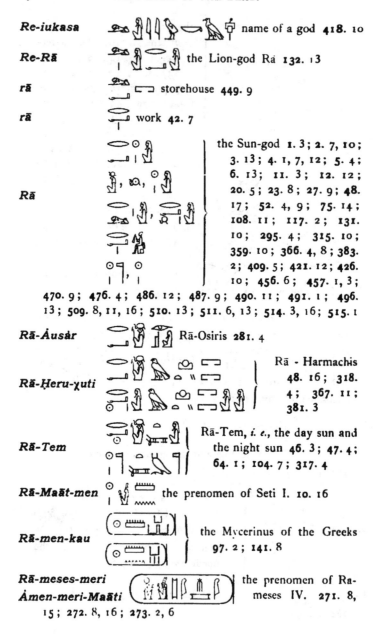

**Rā-er-neḥeḥ** a proper name **315**. 12

***rā*** day **2**. 6; **11**. 10; **28**. 2, 4; **138**. 10; **184**. 9; **289**. 7, 10; and see *passim* *rā mā* like the sun, daily **454**. 7; , *rā neb* daily **2**. 6, 13; **3**. 5; **33**. 6; **100**. 6; **104**. 17; **113**. 6; **199**. 15; **200**. 2, 11; **299**. 4; **329**. 7; **353**. 15; **397**. 15; **446**. 8; **456**. 15; **479**. 9; **480**. 14; **483**. 4; **494**. 13; **495**. 13

***ru*** . . . . . . . **463**. 9

***ru*** . . . . . . **468**. 10

***ruȧ*** to carry away, to separate from **105**. 15; **129**. 16; **160**. 10; **494**. 7

***rui*** journey **209**. 2 *(bis)*

***ruti***, ***ruti*** door (?) *er ruti* outside **25**. 4; **26**. 2; **134**. 11; **149**. 2, 15; **497**. 10

***rut***, ***rut̄***, ***rut̄***, ***rut̄*** to grow, to make to grow, to spring up **9**. 16; **127**. 11, 12; **133**. 12; **181**. 5; **379**. 7; **401**. 11; **408**. 8; **425**. 15; **460**. 5; **461**. 11; **509**. 15; **513**. 8; **514**. 16; things which grow **379**. 8; to be taut (of ropes and sails) **87**. 11; **235**. 16; **236**. 1; **447**. 7

***rut̄i*** strong, vigorous **41**. 12

***rut̄*** plants, things which grow **140**. 7; **181**. 6; **504**. 16; **505**. 5

***Ruṭ-en-Ȧuset*** a proper name **396.** 6

***Ruṭu-nu-Tem*** a proper name **391.** 11

***Ruṭu-neb-reχit*** a proper name **393.** 3

***ruṭ*** superintendent, overseer **392.** 3, 4

***ruṭ*** staircase **297.** 2

***ri*** bandage, strip of linen **414.** 5

***riu*** emanations **138.** 15

***eref*** then, therefore, an intensive particle **51.** 8, 13, 16; **52.** 3, 10, 15; **53.** 3, 9, 16; **54.** 5, 8, 12; **55.** 4; **56.** 1, 9, 14; **57.** 6, 13; **58.** 6; **60.** 13; **61.** 15; **62.** 16; **63.** 15; **64.** 7; **65.** 1, 4, 8, 13; **66.** 3; **69.** 1; **147.** 15; **148.** 1, 2; **183.** 8; **260.** 14; **444.** 1; **494.** 10; **495.** 5

***erpā***, ***erpāt*** hereditary tribal chief **13.** 9; **154.** 16; **325.** 16

***erpit*** Isis and Nephthys **323.** 6

***erpit*** image **409.** 13

***remu*** fish **147.** 15; **148.** 2; **198.** 6; **234.** 1, 3; **251.** 9; **292.** 12; **381.** 9; **392.** 4; **400.** 6, 11; **444.** 9

***remu*** the city of Fish **234.** 4, 7

***Remi*** the fish-god **188.** 13

***rem*** to weep **92.** 4

***remu*** to weep 467. 14;
*remt* lamented 445. 5

***remtu*** weeping, tears, 137. 15; 143. 13

***rem-θȧ*** studded 447. 4

***ermen*** , arm, shoulder 136. 4; 235. 8, 13; 450. 1 *(bis)*; 462. 8

***ermen-ui*** the two arms, shoulders 61. 13; 68. 11; 447. 13

***ermennu***, ***erment*** arms, shoulders 68. 9; 137. 3; 244. 10; 450. 14, 15; 495. 10; supporters 158. 6; the arms of a tree 244. 6

***ermennu-ui*** the two sides of a ladder 202. 16

***ermen*** to fall away from 217. 5

***ermenu*** to carry away 336. 6

***Remrem*** name of a god 163. 4

***ren*** , name 3. 6; 5. 1; 13. 16; 14. 1; 15. 14; 52. 16; 54. 13, 15, 16; 55. 1, 2; 60. 16; 63. 5; 64. 8, 12, 13; 69. 2, 3; 96. 6; 97. 11, 13; 98. 11; 132. 10; 133. 12; 136. 2, 16; 143. 2; 155. 16; 184. 7; 205. 6; 248. 8, 12; 262. 3; 263. 1; 264. 5, 7, 13, 15; 265. 7; 298. 2; 326. 4; 327. 1, 11, 17; 328. 3, 8, 12, 16; 329. 4; 334. 10; 335. 7; 336. 4; 337. 10; 345.

2; **346**. 15, 16; **347**. 1; **353**. 15; **355**. 4, 11; **356**. 2; **357**. 11; **358**. 3, 9; **359**. 2, 3; **360**. 12, 13; **361**. 14, 15; **370**. 5; **374**. 4; **391**. 10, 14; **406**. 10; **418**. 13, 14, 15, 16; **419**. 2, 8, 11, 12, 13, 14, 15; **438**. 9; **443**. 13; **462**. 10; **468**. 1, 3; **484**. 1, 2; **486**. 3; **509**. 3; **512**. 1, 14; **513**. 11; **513**. 8; plur. **24**. 5; **51**. 12; **317**. 13; **91**. 3; **158**. 10, 11; **160**. 6; **175**. 6; **206**. 10; **207**. 2; **260**. 1; **264**. 5, 8; **329**. 9; **377**. 10; **320**. 16

***ren*** to nurse **11**. 13

***renp***
***renpȧ***
***renpu***
***renpi***
to grow young, to renew youth **119**. 5; **154**. 10; **188**. 7; **294**. 15; **298**. 3; **482**. 14; **510**. 1; , , **8**. 2; **224**. 12; **467**. 2; **483**. 4; **486**. 11; **486**. 11; **11**. 6

***renpit*** year **158**. 14; **244**. 15; **366**. 2; **464**. 3; **505**. 15; **506**. 2; plur. **88**. 11; **92**. 10; **111**. 11; **113**. 12; **125**. 3; **158**. 14, 15; **168**. 11; **185**. 2; **188**. 4; **225**. 14; **359**. 8; **458**. 2; **195**. 9

***renpit*** herbs, plants **101**. 7; **454**. 5

***Renen*** name of a god **323**. 15

***renen*** to nurse, to suckle **7**. 1; **119**. 11; **293**. 8

***Renenet*** "nurse", a proper name **405**. 13

***Rennutet*** name of a goddess **443**. 1

***rer*** pig **231**. 10

***rer*** (?) territory **184**. 14

***rer***, ***reru*** to revolve, to go round about **26**. 9; **68**. 9; **77**. 5; **107**. 14; **114**. 7; **155**. 11; **165**. 11; **191**. 11; **282**. 7, 11; **283**. 3, 8, 11; **287**. 13, 16; **303**. 5; **315**. 2; **333**. 15; **358**. 11; **362**. 2; **382**. 15; **388**. 11; **389**. 12; **392**. 13; **405**. 11; **470**. 6; **497**. 15; encircled **448**. 7; those who revolve **390**. 8; journeyings **103**. 4; **104**. 10; go ye round **121**. 5

***rer χet*** to retreat revolving **487**. 8

***rert*** circle **468**. 7

***θes rer*** again, repetition **182**. 16; **211**. 3; **238**. 8; **373**. 3

***rert*** drugs, spices **67**. 13

***reru*** (?) . . . . . . . **154**. 4

***reru*** . . . . . . . **445**. 2

***rert*** men **420**. 6

***Rertu-nifu*** a proper name **324**. 9

***Rerek*** name of a serpent-fiend **100**. 12; **105**. 3; a serpent in the city of Åses **372**. 7, 10, 13

***Rerti*** the double Lion-god **27**. 5; **47**. 10; **103**. 4, 15; **104**. 7; **110**. 12; **125**. 4; **136**. 13; **161**. 6; **168**. 5, 12; **169**. 3, 5, 14; **281**. 16; **330**. 15; **391**. 9; **419**. 12; **435**. 13; **438**. 12; **515**. 12; one of the forty-two assessors **253**. 6

**Rereθå**
**Rereθi** } the double Lion-god 67. 13; 418. 16

**rehebu** flame 412. 4, 5

**rehen** } to rest upon, to sit on *or* in 258. 3, 13; 218. 13

**reḥ** to enter 103. 13

**Reḥu** name of a god 68. 1

**Reḥui** the name of a city 465. 10

**Reḥui** the two "combatant gods", *i. e.*, Horus and Set 27. 17; 56. 9; 242. 16; 359. 14; 439. 9; 483. 6

**Reḥti** } the two "combatant goddesses" 102. 12; 176. 11; the two sister combatants 485. 3

**Re-ḥent** a proper name 150. 10, 11 *(bis)*

**Re-ḥenenet** a proper name 321. 8

**reχ** to know, knowledge 4. 15; 52. 2; 55. 3; 63. 5, 6; 98. 11; 109. 3; 115. 15; 119. 14; 138. 1; 152. 10; 247. 1; 284. 8; 317. 13; 320. 16; 329. 8, 9; 334. 10; 335. 5; 338. 15; 339. 10; 342. 13; 343. 12; 344. 3; 345. 1; 346. 7; 349. 15; 350. 6; 351. 3; 363. 7; 365; 5; 368. 12; 374. 4; 391. 2—9; 392. 1—16; 393. 2, 4, 7, 9; 394. 4; 419. 1; 420. 11; 425. 14; 438. 9; 459. 10; 472. 11; 477. 13; 488. 9; 497. 5; 498. 1; 507. 12; knowing, known 10. 2; 24. 5; 248. 8, 12; 266. 3;

ye know 394. 9; 396. 2, 5, 8, 10, 12, 14, 16; 397. 2, 4, 6; to understand 89. 16; unknown 115. 3; 352. 4; knowingly 17. 6; 39. 10; 70. 4; 112. 3; 115. 15, 16

***reχu χet*** "knowers of things" 331. 1

***reχit*** beings who know, men and women, mankind 7. 3; 9. 2; 54. 11; 68. 9; 104. 12; 113. 9; 138. 10; 147. 7; 153. 9; 241. 2; 248. 6; 252. 4; 349. 4; 358. 12; 362. 3; 393. 3; 490. 1

***reχti*** to work for 101. 16

***Reχti*** name of two goddesses 249. 14

***Reχti-merti-neb-Maāti*** a proper name 249. 14

***res***, ***resu*** to watch, to be awake 6. 2, 5; 47. 2; 73. 11; 228. 10; 230. 5; 310. 11, 12; 401. 12; 465. 3; 505. 1; 79. 13; wake up! 431. 16

***resit*** the nine watchers 431. 16

***restu*** night-watchers 146. 15, 16

***Res-àb*** the warder of the fourth Ārit 328. 6

***Res-ḥrà*** the warder of the third Ārit 328. 2

***res*** south, southern 2. 1; 55. 5; 129. 4; 156. 14; 221. 5; 312. 3; 323. 11; 347. 7; 368. 7

***reset*** south **262.** 11; **311.** 4, 10; **317.** 14; **319.** 4; **365.** 1

***resu*** southern, those in the south **36.** 11; **99.** 6, 9; **106.** 4; **114.** 14; **319.** 8; **443.** 14

***Resu*** a proper name **321.** 5; **319.** 14

***resu*** south wind **129.** 5; **155.** 12; **389.** 10; **407.** 10

***Res-Meḥt*** South and North, *i. e.*, all Egypt **28.** 10; **110.** 10; **138.** 4

***Resenet*** a proper name **320.** 12; **323.** 5

***reś***
***reśi*** to breathe with joy **4.** 7; to rejoice **6.** 9; **236.** 1; **238.** 11; **12.** 6

***reśt*** to snuff, to inhale **351.** 13

***reśui*** the nostrils **488.** 4

then, an emphatic particle **7.** 7; **179.** 16; (bis)

fire, flame **340.** 7; **353.** 3; **412.** 2; plur. **351.** 13; **320.** 6

Seker (?) **106.** 6

***req***, ***req***, ***reqa*** to incline away from 15. 11; to fall away 91. 8; 501. 8; 96. 3

***Reqi*** fiend 6. 7

***reqau*** fiends 337. 11

***ret*** = to go about 313. 2 *(bis)*

***ret*** men and women, people, mankind, 235. 11; 463. 2; everybody 407. 16

***Retasaśaka*** a name of Åmen 419. 10

***reti*** doors 136. 10

***reṭ*** foot 162. 8, 10; 266. 2, 3

***reṭui*** the two feet 32. 8; 67. 15; 89. 9, 13; 90. 2; 96. 16; 113. 2; 118. 19; 136. 12; 140. 15; 141. 8; 150. 14; 153. 4; 157. 8, 9; 166. 7; 185. 5; 194. 15; 195. 6; 196. 7; 213. 2; 247. 14; 265. 15; 305. 13; 348. 3; 376. 8; 385. 8; 413. 13, 14; 420. 4; 436. 3, 12; 437. 10, 11; 439. 16; 449. 5; 491. 16; 502. 13; 511. 2; legs of an ape 116. 5

***reṭ*** men and women 64. 4; 250. 1

***reṭ***, ***reṭu*** staircase, steps 278. 1; 296. 7; 298. 1

***erṭā***, ***erṭāt*** to give, to set, to place, to put, the act of giving or placing, causing 20. 9; 223. 3; 333. 1; 334. 1; 370. 11; 406. 3; 447. 8; 470. 10; 492. 16; 497. 7, 9; 506. 16; 291. 5; 403. 9; *erṭāu* given 2. 6; 139. 5; 485. 6; given 386. 5; placed 34. 3; 65. 3, 5; 119. 1; 130. 7; 242. 7; 477. 4, 7, 10, 11; 490. 3; 494. 6; 133. 1; 25. 9; 67. 9; 231. 4; 293. 2; 75. 7; 337. 2; as an auxiliary verb 28. 9; 492. 7; 404. 12; 138. 1; 23. 13; 408. 5; 309. 2; 308. 6

***Erṭā-nifu*** a proper name 263. 12

***Erṭā-ḥen-er-reqau*** a proper name 337. 11

***Erṭā-sebanqa*** a proper name 350. 16

***erṭut*** places, abodes 214. 8

***erṭu*** (?) . . . . . . . 25. 4

***erṭu*** emanations 134. 3; 240. 13; 358. 8; 362. 2; 378. 14; 380. 13

***reθ*** men and women, mankind 9. 4; 13. 10; 24. 2; 96. 7; 113. 7, 8; 114. 12, 13; 145. 5; 175. 8; 237. 5; 238. 7; 245. 10; 253. 5; 260. 16; 285. 11; 291. 14; 293. 12; 356. 11; 365. 11; 388. 11; 389. 2, 13; 403. 14; 438. 12; 459. 10; 477. 6; 490. 2; 491. 8; everybody 366. 10; 497. 8

##  H.

*ha*  to go in, to enter, to embark, to advance, 22. 14; 24. 10; 89. 7; 106. 7; 147. 14; 149. 5; 178. 7; 203. 12; 210. 6; 248. 3; 273. 15; 282; 2; 284. 2; 287. 3; 295. 7; 335. 10; 346. 10; 348. 11; 411. 5; 491. 7

*hai*, *hait*  to enter, entrance, incomer or oncomer 18. 5; 23. 13; 25. 10; 50. 19; 52. 13; 59. 1; 62. 15; 63. 4; 75. 7; 103. 12; 149. 15; 357. 15;  106. 2

*ha*  =  O 441. 14; 442. 2, 11, 12

*ha*  to be strong 298. 6;  strength 131. 10

*ha*  time, period, reign 97. 2; 131. 9

*ha* ,  cry, shout, O 46. 13; 423. 5; 441. 6, 16; 442. 3; 452. 13, 16; 466. 16; 467. 7; 481. 9

*Hai*  a proper name 108. 11

*hai*  to shout 6. 3; 277. 3, 14; 289. 10; 290. 11; 316. 2, 4, 7; 508. 3; 509. 4; 510. 14; 511. 15; 513. 12

*hai*  rejoicing 49. 6

*haȧker* 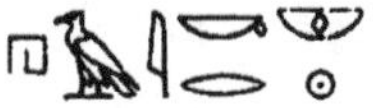 name of a festival 356. 1

***hau*** reign, time **141.** 8; **145.** 14

***hait*** heaven **267.** 6

***hab***
***habi*** to send **34.** 12; **56.** 16; **66.** 10; **111.** 12; **401.** 14; **421.** 12; **458.** 15; **459.** 1, 6; to advance **372.** 15

***Hab-em-atu*** a proper name **34.** 12

***habeq*** to fail **56.** 8

***hamu*** blemish, defect, sin **50.** 5

***Ha-ḥetep*** a proper name **373.** 5

***Ha-χeru*** a proper name **358.** 5

***Ha-sert*** a city of the seventh Åat **381.** 11

***Haker*** name of a god **74.** 2

***haker*** name of a festival **497.** 2; plur. **347.** 8

***Haqa-haḳa-ua-ḥrȧ*** a proper name **408.** 16

***hat*** cry, to shout **471.** 13

***hat*** to go in, entrance, to embark **211.** 12; **214.** 5; **243.** 16

***ha-ti*** to descend **292.** 14

***hatu*** brow (?) **413.** 6

***Hu-nefer*** name of a scribe 8. 13; 10. 16; 484. 9

***Hu-χeru*** the herald of the first Åat 329. 13

***hi*** acclamation 435. 15; 441. 4

***heb*** ibis 185. 16

***heb, hebt*** , to journey 91. 4; 348. 5

***hepu*** laws 481. 1, 12; 488. 13

***hem*** fire 219. 6

***hememet*** or ***hamemet*** name of a class of people on earth, and of beings in heaven with human forms 7. 3; 26. 3; 38. 4; 113. 9; 120. 16; 244. 11; 245. 5; 281. 11; 282. 15; 292. 6; 296. 2; 297. 7; 478. 6; 482. 2

***hemhem*** to roar, to cry out 338. 4; 340. 10

***hemhemet*** outcries, roarings 298. 6; 352. 4; 373. 8

***Hemti*** "Runner" 138. 12

***hen*** funeral chest, coffin 22. 11; 309. 13

***henå*** name of a city 322. 12

***hennu*** to sing songs of joy, to praise 103. 5; 315. 1; 342. 1

***hennu*** praises, shouts of joy 6. 4; 7. 4; 9. 13; 12. 5; 13. 1; 35. 16; 49. 2; 290. 11; 395. 3 *(bis)*; 416. 4; 429. 4; 435. 15; 441. 4; 481. 10; 489. 16

***henhennu***, ***henhenit*** the watery abyss of heaven 27. 4; 103. 2; 104. 10

***her***, ***hert*** to be pleased, to rest, content, gracious 332. 11; 339. 12; 353. 12; 415. 9; 438. 11; 516. 5

***herá*** a vessel 130. 7

***hru*** day 3. 9; 18. 4; 19. 4, 12; 20. 9; 23. 14; 52. 4; 53. 7; 56. 8; 58. 5; 148. 8; 262. 14, 15; 309. 2; 333. 15; 342. 1; 354. 13; 366. 1; 371. 12; 409. 4; 429. 5; 468. 15; 491. 7; 508. 11; plur. 158. 16; and see *passim*; to-day 112. 8; 114. 11, 12; 464. 13; judgment day 309. 8; birthday 278. 11; 284. 16; birthday of Osiris 395. 15; 497. 1; funeral day 402. 13; 403. 10; new-year's day 402. 15; daily 6. 6; 40. 1; 429. 3; 467. 2; 506. 2; 511. 5, 8, 10; 512. 9; 513. 8; a happy day 10. 8

***herlu*** . . . . . . 422. 16

***herert*** things which please 260. 16

***heh*** flame, fire 59. 9; 61. 10; 116. 1; 269. 8; 305. 12; 369. 14; 372. 9; 377. 7; 378. 6; 411. 6; 412. 2

***heker*** name of a festival 78. 16

***hekeru*** name of festivals 343. 14

***hetu*** to be addressed 397. 16

***hethet*** to go round about 453. 10

---

# H̱.

. . . . with . . . . . . 425. 1

ḥa head and neck 122. 9, 12, 16

ḥa behind 12. 16; 46. 5; 47. 2; 55. 10; 57. 14; 58. 8; 72. 6; 76. 5; 82. 7; 85. 6; 106. 12; 108. 11, 14; 109. 10; 121. 15, 18; 122. 2; 126. 9; 191. 12; 193. 4; 280. 4; 287. 13; 301. 3, 4; 302. 14; 310. 4 *(bis)*; 329. 14; 375. 11; 382. 15; 383. 2, 9, 10; 417. 9; 435. 1; 463. 1; 478. 15; 482. 8; to get back, back thou!, to put behind 44. 1; 68. 1; 93. 4; 97. 10; 98. 13, 15; 99. 1, 4, 6, 8, 10, 12; 105. 4, 7; 372. 12

ḥa, ḥat to invoke 445. 5, 13; 446. 16; 447. 9; 448. 4, 13; 450. 5, 16; 451. 9

Ḥaȧs a proper name 109. 2, 10; 463. 15

ḥaāu, ḥau, ḥeā dwellers in the marshes of the Delta 407. 15; 498. 3; 503. 7

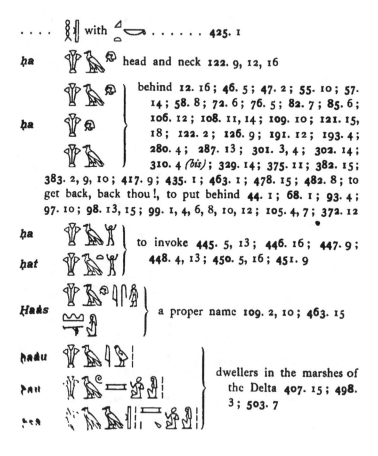

**ḥau** to dress, to be clothed, to cover over **202.** 4; **248.** 4

**ḥauu** naked, the naked, naked man **261.** 3; **348.** 12; **516.** 7

**ḥaiu**

**ḥau** things in addition **410.** 15

**ḥauatu** filth, dung **359.** 11

**ḥai** to shine **408.** 8

**Ḥai** a proper name **349.** 3

**ḥait** to grasp **160.** 14

**ḥan re** to have a care for **488.** 4

**Ḥa-ḥrȧ** a proper name **346.** 9

**ḥapu** to enshroud, to hide, to cover over **339.** 2; **376.** 1; **408.** 10; **410.** 11; **431.** 1; **512.** 7; with **416.** 10; covered over **174.** 8

**Ḥapṭ-re** a proper name **261.** 11; (var. and )

**ḥam**, **ḥamt** to snare **229.** 9, 12; **233.** 11; **251.** 8; **390.** 8, 9, 10; **391.** 10, 12; **393.** 8, 16; **394.** 2; **395.** 9; **397.** 7

**ḥamiu** snarers, fowlers **390.** 7; **393.** 15

**Ḥarpuḳakaśareśabaiu** a proper name **416.** 1

**Ḥareθi** a proper name **411.** 9

**ḥaqeṭ** to lead captive, to make a prisoner of someone **108.** 4; **280.** 3; captives **146.** 11

**ḥaqet** fetters **331.** 6

**Ḥaqu** name of a plank or peg **206.** 16

**ḥat** a place in the underworld **148.** 15

**ḥati** mourners, those who weep **19.** 8

**ḥaṭ** tomb **69.** 2

**ḥaṭ** net **233.** 14, 15 *(bis)*; **234.** 5

**ḥaθȧ**, **ḥaθȧtu**, **ḥaθetiu** storm, whirlwind **280.** 11; **283.** 2; **295.** 1, 3

**Ḥȧst** , name of a goddess **228.** 10; **229.** 15

**ḥā**, **ḥāā** to rejoice, joy **7.** 3, 7; **12.** 1; **27.** 10, 11; **39.** 15; **190.** 8; **272.** 16; **275.** 15; **289.** 10; **292.** 6; **299.** 6; **301.** 10; **314.** 17; **316.** 1, 6; **331.** 9; **388.** 9; **390.** 14; **438.** 6; **463.** 9; **484.** 11; **505.** 9; **208.** 8; **402.** 10; **471.** 14; **301.** 10; **50.** 3; **476.** 4; **479.** 6; **478.** 5

**ḥāā**, **ḥāāiu**, **ḥāātu** rejoicings, those who rejoice 2. 10; 4. 12; 12. 7; 40. 11; 44. 14; 46. 10; 49. 13; 175. 10, 15; 176. 2; 282. 11; 283. 10; 313. 11; 403. 11; 439. 10; 473. 14; 472. 12

**ḥāu**, **ḥāt** limbs, members 14. 6; 24. 2; 39. 4; 41. 3; 42. 12; 47. 2; 209. 16; 211. 9; 213. 7; 253. 4; 285. 9; 315. 5; 349. 1; 400. 1, 16; 401. 5, 8; 403. 11; 426. 12; 439. 4; 447. 11; 484. 16; 486. 12; 487. 3, 8; 502. 15; 505. 2; 509. 7, 10; 510. 4, 14 *(bis)*; 473. 12; 290. 12; 362. 13; thyself 291. 10; thine own self 308. 12; 366. 10

**ḥā** the front or beginning of anything 18. 4; 223. 14; 349. 11; 451. 2; of a book 50. 19; 334. 7; 444. 5; 508. 1

**ḥāt** breast, prow or bows of a boat, the fore part of anything 40. 14; 50. 7; 77. 12; 219. 3; 242. 2; 262. 8; 415. 11, 12; 436. 15; 456. 5; 490. 11

**ḥāp** to advance, to tarry 183. 11; 290. 3; 491. 16

**Ḥāp** Nile 342. 15

**Ḥāpi**, **Ḥāp** Nile 9. 3; 39. 5; 63. 9; 132. 11; 147. 13; 148. 1; 151. 10; 210. 10; 355. 10; 379. 7, 9, 14 *(bis)*; 380. 3; 440. 4; 447. 5; 465. 5

**Ḥāp-ur** Ḥāpi Great One 128. 1

*Ḥāpi*, *Ḥāp* — one of the four children of Horus 57. 13; 58. 8; 59. 3; 73. 5; 131. 9; 206. 15; 232. 8, 15; 306. 3; 319. 5; 326. 9; 385. 2; 505. 4

*Ḥāp* — name of a cow-goddess 437. 1

*Ḥāpiu* — Apis (?) 205. 8; 496. 2

*ḥāpu* — rudder 5. 3

*ḥāptu* — paddles, oars 281. 12; 283. 3; 290. 7; 298. 7

*ḥāti* — heart, breast, place of the heart, pericardium (?) 15. 9; 65. 2; 89. 4; 90. 1, 8, 13; 91. 14, 17; 92. 8, 12, 14. 93. 6, 7, 14; 94. 1; 95. 2, 7; 96. 1; 105. 11; 119. 13; 150. 13; 151. 14; 153. 8; 333. 9; 420. 9; 436. 4; 439. 10; 447. 14; 448. 1; 481. 8; 483. 3; 488. 8; 490. 5; 501. 3, 5; 502. 4; 505. 8; plur. 64. 6; 66. 1; 90. 17; 92. 9; 158. 8; 346. 3; 357. 12; 411. 15; 244. 12

*ḥātet* — rope of the bows of a boat 205. 10; 283. 10

*ḥāti*, *ḥātet* — unguent 308. 4; 333. 13; 335. 1; 336. 7

*ḥu* — for (?) 7. 4

*ḥu* — hair 343. 5

*Ḥu* — name of a god 15. 7; 56. 4; 176. 14; 348. 13; 439. 15

**ḥu** divine food 128. 19; 166. 16; 171. 16; 173. 9; 183. 10; 184. 4, 6; 228. 4; 286. 12; 397. 14; and see 43. 11; 161. 2; 230. 4

**Ḥui** a proper name 348. 8

**ḥu** to smite, to strike 2. 15; 28. 15; 92. 3; 200. 7; 271. 11; 274. 11; 281. 2; 287. 4; 303. 12; 306. 8, 16; 314. 1; 337. 16; 382. 11; 385. 4; 394. 8, 11; 440. 4; 453. 15; 475. 6; 480. 2; 496. 2; to slaughter 453. 15; to clap the hands 471. 2; 114. 11; 277. 6

**ḥuit Rā** smiters of Rā 422. 6; 424. 2

**Ḥu-tepa** a proper name 336. 15

**ḥua** to suffer corruption, to decay, to rot 120. 5, 7, 9; 399. 12, 16; 400. 2; 401. 5, 8

**ḥuat** filthy (of ) 100. 14

**ḥuau** filth, dung, offal 66. 1; 173. 12; 197. 14; 229. 7; 375. 5

**ḥui** = 27. 5

**ḥuia** to decree 113. 13; nay, but 399. 9

**ḥun**, **ḥunnu** boy, child, young man 7. 2; 8. 2; 9. 10; 185. 10; plur. 120. 14; 127. 3

**Ḥunt-Pe-χerṭet** (?) . . . . . . 506. 15

**ḥuḥu** watery abyss **459**. 8

**Ḥi-mu** one of the forty-two assessors **258**. 5

**Ḥit** a proper name **139**. 3

**ḥeb** festival **2**. 9; **52**. 8; **78**. 16; **179**. 11; **183**. 12; **197**. 3, 10; **318**. 2; **440**. 2; **480**. 5; **492**. 4; **497**. 1; **513**. 10; **316**. 2; **80**. 4; **497**. 1; **497**. 2; **147**. 2

**ḥebu** festivals **20**. 3; **198**. 4, 16; **223**. 10; **276**. 15; **278**. 6; **317**. 12; **347**. 9; **446**. 16; **492**. 4

**ḥebt** the book of the festival service **20**. 7

**ḥeb** to provide fish and fowl for the festival **167**. 2

**ḥebā** to play (at draughts) **51**. 1; to play **446**. 12

**ḥebebet** stream, flood **43**. 9; **212**. 7; **417**. 15; **420**. 12

**ḥebennut** a cake (?) **333**. 10

**ḥebs** to clothe, to dress, to deck out, to cover **19**. 12; **219**. 16; **220**. 1; **245**. 2; **246**. 12; **248**. 4; **339**. 1; **342**. 2, 9, 16; **343**. 9, 16; **344**. 7, 14; **345**. 6, 13; **346**. 4; **348**. 6, 12; **354**. 14; **355**. 5, 11; **356**. 2, 7, 13, 15; **357**. 5, 9, 11, 13; **370**. 9; **448**. 6; **469**. 10; **353**. 14; clothed, decked **430**. 8; clother **352**. 13

**ḥebs** garment, clothing, swathing **92.** 15; **136.** 2; **261.** 3; **516.** 8; plur. , **72.** 7; **147.** 1; **209.** 7; **267.** 15; **441.** 8; **497.** 11; **446.** 3

**Ḥebṭ-re-f** "Foamy Mouth", a proper name **378.** 3

**ḥept** **256.** 8; see

**ḥept** to embrace **1.** 9; **11.** 16; **36.** 6; **60.** 3; **139.** 12; **144.** 11; **452.** 2; **37.** 14; **9.** 5; breast (?) **49.** 10

**Ḥept-seśet** one of the forty-two assessors **252.** 14

**ḥeptu** the hold (?) of a boat **205.** 14

**ḥeptu** doorposts **265.** 6

**ḥept** , to walk, to traverse **10.** 8; **42.** 3; **140.** 2; advancing **42.** 11

**ḥeptet** a course, a place for walking **49.** 3

**ḥepṭ-re** to shut the mouth **104.** 14

**ḥefāu** serpent **100.** 10; **101.** 4, 11; **219.** 2, 5; **352.** 6; **370.** 5; **372.** 10; **380.** 2; plur. **24.** 1; **229.** 12; **302.** 15; **400.** 6, 11

**ḥefi χer reṭti** a serpent with two legs **413.** 13

**ḥefait**
**ḥefiu** . . . . . . **422.** 9; **424.** 11

**ḥefnu** one hundred thousand **137.** 1; plur. **10.** 9; **42.** 4

**ḥeft** to sit down **134.** 4; **162.** 12; **212.** 7, 8

**ḥem** . . . . . . **27.** 9

**ḥem** , to go back, to make to go back **68.** 2; **97.** 10; **109.** 10; **147.** 11; **168.** 6; **192.** 9, 10, 12; **193.** 9; **219.** 14; **220.** 1; **234.** 11; **243.** 2; **68.** 2

**ḥemu** , rudder **3.** 2; **134.** 13; **142.** 11; **207.** 7; **242.** 2; **318.** 16; **319.** 1, 3, 4; **364.** 9, 10, 12, 13; plur. **205.** 2

**ḥemi** ,
**ḥemit** } rudder **5.** 6; **130.** 5

**ḥem**
**ḥemu** } to steer a boat **10.** 10; **366.** 12

**Ḥemati** name of a chamber **171.** 4; **172.** 6

**Ḥemaḳ** name of a city **325.** 7

**ḥemen** slaughter **357.** 15

**Ḥemen** name of a god **505.** 12

**ḥement** forty **249.** 10

**ḥems** to sit, to dwell **20.** 16 *(bis)*; **22.** 10; **32.** 11; **51.** 2; **86.** 15; **88.** 12; **98.** 1; **114.** 3; **124.** 13; **129.** 4; **146.** 6, 12; **151.** 10; **152.** 7; **154.** 7; **165.** 2; **175.** 12; **180.** 5; **239.** 13, 14; **283.** 5; **376.** 14; **392.** 6; **395.** 1; **397.** 8; **430.** 7; **465.** 13; **479.** 7; **492.** 2; **493.** 8; **496.** 7;

215. 16; 447. 8; 439. 3; those who sit 269. 5

**ḥemt** woman 180. 9; wife 489. 8; plur. 142. 1; 146. 2; 248. 5; 312. 5; 427. 14; *ḥemt ṭai* woman belonging to a man, *i. e.*, wife 255. 6, 16; *suten ḥemt* queen 415. 8; an Asiatic woman 445. 14; 175. 11

**Ḥem-nu** (?) a proper name (?) 177. 7, 12

**ḥemt** cow, cow-goddess 303. 12; 318. 15; 333. 12; 439. 5; plur. 363. 8, 15; 364. 6

**ḥen** majesty 2. 12; 10. 1; 41. 12; 97. 1, 2; 141. 8; 145. 14; 248. 8, 11; 285. 6; 315. 3, 6, 7, 9, 10; 448. 1; 471. 7; 487. 9; 214. 1

**ḥen** servant 250. 8; 472. 2; 497. 10; plur. 250. 6; servant woman 180. 9

**ḥen**, **ḥenen** to advance, to move onwards 15. 13; 96. 6, 106. 16; 185. 16; 337. 11

**ḥenḥen** to move 287. 10

**ḥen**, **ḥeni** blossoms, flowers 139. 7; 144. 6

**ḥen** to bestow 388. 1

**ḥen** to rule 493. 12; 408. 7

**ḥen** to praise **471.** 2; **471.** 6, 10, 11

**ḥennu** offerings **107.** 1

**ḥeniu** offerings, gifts **47.** 13

**ḥennu** pillars **448.** 11

**ḥenā** with, and, along with, together **5.** 1; **12.** 15; **19.** 7; **34.** 4; **45.** 4; **52.** 6; **53.** 7, 12; **54.** 14; **56.** 10; **58.** 7; **60.** 7; **63.** 16; **69.** 15; **78.** 10; **98.** 10, 12; **108.** 2; **129.** 15; **141.** 11; **153.** 2; **154.** 9; **166.** 10, 11; **181.** 11; **184.** 8; **196.** 3; **210.** 7; **211.** 5; **232.** 12 *(bis)*; **234.** 2, 12, 13; **241.** 2; **244.** 11; **245.** 8; **261.** 10, 16; **268.** 8, 16; **276.** 16; **277.** 10; **280.** 8; **294.** 6; **296.** 6, 15; **297.** 13; **300.** 8; **301.** 6; **309.** 5; **312.** 1; **316.** 13, 16; **318.** 1; **335.** 9; **337.** 1; **361.** 13; **362.** 13; **363.** 8; **364.** 15; **377.** 14, 15; **380.** 4; **393.** 12; **398.** 1; **399.** 7; **409.** 14; **411.** 2; **414.** 4; **420.** 5; **424.** 7; **425.** 7; **426.** 2; **439.** 9; **464.** 10; **471.** 2; **478.** 17; **486.** 13; **496.** 6, 7; **507.** 8; **516.** 11, 16; **517.** 1, 2; **22.** 10; **20.** 14; **21.** 4; **166.** 3

**ḥenb**
**ḥenbeta** lands on which grows grain **254.** 10, 15; **474.** 8

**Ḥenbi** name of a god **474.** 8

**ḥenen** labourer **463.** 9

**ḥenen** phallus **52.** 16; **69.** 4, 5; **112.** 14; **118.** 17; **153.** 8; **196.** 13; **197.** 4, 16; **198.** 10; **505.** 9; **56.** 2

**ḥennu** to draw to oneself **144.** 14

**ḥennu** name of a sacred boat which was drawn round the sanctuary **20.** 9; **145.** 13; **336.** 6; **390.** 15; **513.** 7

**ḥennut**, **ḥennuit** fraud, deceit **254.** 8, 14

**ḥennuti** two horns **125.** 2; **171.** 14

**ḥenemnemu** devourers **375.** 4

**ḥens** to be blocked up (of a road) **204.** 16

**ḥenseki**, **ḥensekt**, **ḥensekit**, **ḥensekti** lock of hair, tress, hair **155.** 9; **182.** 13; **205.** 10; **237.** 1, 9; **302.** 15; **382.** 10; **386.** 13; **387.** 14; **501.** 10

**Ḥensek** name of a god **237.** 10; the hair gods **95.** 8

**Ḥenseket-menȧt-Ȧnpu-em-kat-utu** name of a rope **205.** 10

**ḥenk** to give, to offer up **489.** 11; **503.** 12; **504.** 13, 16; **505.** 2; **507.** 4, 9, 15; bestowed **386.** 16

**ḥenket** offerings **448.** 1

**Ḥenku-en-Ȧrp** a proper name **264.** 11

**Ḥenku-en-fat-Maāt** a proper name 264. 8

**ḥenku** balance 264. 8, 11

**ḥenket**
**ḥenkit** funeral bed or chamber 231. 16; 435. 12; 440. 14; 441. 15; 448. 15

**Ḥenket** name of a city 322. 9

**ḥent** pool, canal, stream 380. 9; 448. 5, 6

**ḥent** to be hostile to 137. 11

**ḥent** mistress 124. 7; 180. 2; 410. 11; 415. 8; 415. 4; 489. 9; 415. 4; 354. 12; 335. 6; 350. 8; 351. 5

**ḥent** to be hostile to 143. 10

**Ḥent** name of a place 150. 2

**ḥenti** crocodile 339. 4

**ḥennuti** crocodiles 339. 5

**Ḥenti** god of the two crocodiles, *i. e.*, Osiris 324. 3

**ḥentta** to fall into oblivion 268. 7

**ḥenti** double period of time 14. 3; 159. 14; 208. 11; 166. 14; 170. 7

**Ḥenti-requ** a proper name 351. 14

**Ḥent-śe** (?) a proper name 149. 8

**ḥer** in, at, upon, on, by means of, in addition to, by, from, for, with, because 3. 3; 5. 7; 10. 10, 15; 41. 14; 52. 14; 87. 6; 100. 1; 123. 10; 124. 2; 162. 11; 171. 2; 185. 5; 187. 2; 197. 5; 239. 4; 260. 3; 311. 1, 8; 352. 6; 370. 3, 5; 371. 3, 7; 373. 11; 375. 7; 423. 10, 13; 436. 1, 2; 468. 1; 491. 16; 494. 4; 495. 3; on behalf of 18. 10; 165. 14; 166. 9; 167. 1, 8; 304. 11; 305. 8; 456. 16; 507. 10; with infinitive 2. 11; 4. 7; 5. 9; 7. 6; 8. 9; 9. 16; 140. 8; and see *passim*; except 10. 3; *em ḥeru* (of labours) excessive 250. 4

**ḥer ā** straightway 485. 16

**ḥer áb**, **ḥer ábi**, **ḥer áb** in the middle, within, dweller in 7. 7; 13. 7; 39. 5; 45. 10; 59. 16; 60. 4, 8; 66. 5, 16; 67. 4; 86. 16; 99. 11; 106. 9; 127. 10; 131. 1; 158. 2, 3; 188. 11; 248. 7; 262. 9; 276. 11; 283. 5; 298. 5; 319. 2, 3; 311. 9; 317. 12; 318. 1; 321. 3; 323. 7, 8; 325. 10, 12; 326. 10; 364. 11, 13; 368. 5; 392. 11; 396. 16; 420. 4; 425. 8; 431. 6; 438. 10, 11; 461. 1; 493. 14; 496. 13; 508. 6; dear unto 471. 7; 107. 8

**Ḥer-áb-uáa-f** a proper name 292. 7

**Ḥer-áb-maat-f** a proper name 200. 16

**Ḥer-áb-kará-f** a proper name 292. 4

ḥer maā straightway, forthwith 263. 3; 265. 13

ḥer entet because 24. 3; 31. 12; 41. 4; 57. 10; 63. 5, [illegible]; 66. 1[illegible]; 91. 2; 138. 14; 160. 5; 171. 15; 214. 14; 216. [illegible]; 252. 3, [illegible]; 261. 9, 15; 262. 7; 265. 14; 394. 4; 430. [illegible]; because 44. 4

ḥer sa in addition to 137. 1; 259. 17

ḥer tep or ṭaṭa upon 14. 7; 23. 5; 295. 11; 409. 6; 452. [illegible]; 502. 6; 517. 3; 53. 13

ḥeri he who dwelleth above 6. 8; 445. 15, etc.

ḥerā, ḥert the upper regions, what is above, celestial 4. 5; 9. 6, 16; 27. 15; 35. 15; 135. 11; 146. 10; 185. 4; 190. 5; 293. 16; 355. [illegible]; 410. [illegible]; 420. 13; 431. 11; 436. 13; 456. 5; 475. [illegible]; 47[illegible]. [illegible]; 331. 14; 135. 4; 42. 13

ḥer, ḥeri, ḥer chief, governor, president 11. 12; 59. 12; 85. 5; 142. 9; 166. 8; 205. 2; 299. 10; 334. 12; 370. 2; 415. 5; 456. 6; 462. 2; 468. 5; 471. 9; 510. 5; 250. 8; 341. [illegible]; 350. 1; chief scribe 273. 16; 274. 15; 275. 8; 276. 4; 489. 12; chief of the altar 489. 12; 425. 11

ḥeru those who are on high, celestial beings, chiefs 2. 5; 63. 11, 15; 113. 12; 134. 16; 136. 10; 137. 13; 142. 14; 143. 12; 217. 8 *(bis)*; 230. 5, 6; 295. 5; 365. 6, 13, 15; 373. 13; 394. 5;

397. 10; 425. 3; 437. 7; 440. 2; 450. 10; 463. 16; 464. 3; 504. 8, 10; 8. 16; 485. 15; 137. 13; 143. 12; 338. 7; 426. 16; 474. 14; 160. 16

**Ḥeri-akebȧ-f** a proper name 136. 5

**Ḥer-uaṭ-f** a name of Horus 232. 14

**Ḥeri-uru** one of the forty-two assessors 255. 9

**Ḥertit** (?)-**ān** a proper name 106. 6

**Ḥeri-sep-f** a proper name 64. 14

**Ḥer-šāi-f** a title of Osiris 322. 3; 325. 2; 484. 8

**Ḥer-ta**, **Ḥer-taui** a proper name 64. 15; 434. 11

**ḥert** dominion 485. 6; 486. 2

**ḥer** to terrify 400. 9; 414. 15; 416. 7

**ḥeru** to strike fear into 255. 10

**ḥerit** terror 374. 6

**ḥeru** to strengthen 43. 13

**ḥeri**, **ḥeru** to go on, to go away, to depart 32. 4; 105. 7; 196. 7; 203. 2; 372. 9; 513. 16; begone, depart 101. 7; 102. 4; 493. 11

*ḥerset* crystal 447. 6, 12

*Ḥeru* Horus 3. 2; 5. 15; 52. 6; 56. 10; 62. 6, 9; 73. 2, 4; 82. 2, 3; 148. 10, 11; 154. 1; 224. 4; 387. 14; 388. 4; 395. 6; 441. 5; 446. 3, 5; 451. 3, 14; 455. 11; 458. 16; 459. 12, 15; 460. 8; 461. 11; 478. 9; 482. 15; 485. 5, 14; 492. 15; 504. 11; 505. 15

*Ḥerui* the pair of Horus gods 446. 12

*Ḥerui-senui* the two Horus brethren 485. 1

*Ḥeru-āā-ȧbu* "Horus, mighty of hearts" 512. 11

*Ḥeru-āi . . .* Horus . . . . . . 506. 12

*Ḥeru-ȧmi-ȧbu-ḥer-ȧb-ȧmi-χat* a title of Horus 93. 15

*Ḥeru-ȧmi-ȧθen* "Horus in the Disk" 260. 10

*Ḥeru-ur* "Horus the great" (*or* elder) *i. e.*, Haroeris 302. 11; 325. 16

*Ḥeru-Maat* the "Eye of Horus" 312. 14; 313. 4; 455. 1; 463. 9, 11; 464. 14; 466. 9; 503. 5; 504. 12

*Ḥeru-Maati* "Horus of two Eyes" 512. 12

*Ḥeru-em-χebit* "Horus of the South" 356. 9

*Ḥeru-em-χent-en-Maati* "Horus without Eyes" 60. 7

*Ḥeru-neb-ureret* a title of Horus 318. 7

***Ḥeru-nef-ḥrȧ-ȧtef-f*** 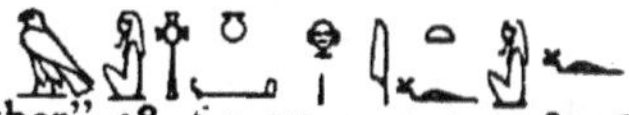 "Horus the avenger of his father" **48.** 6; **53.** 10; **59.** 13; **60.** 6; **72.** 4; **195.** 4; **306.** 9; **327.** 3; **435.** 14; **511.** 12

***Ḥeru-ḥer-neferu***  "Horus on the pilot's place in the boat" **44.** 16

***Ḥeru-χuti***  "Horus of the double horizon" **1.** 11; **4.** 8; **11.** 10; **15.** 4; **37.** 10; **38.** 7; **200.** 1; **222.** 6; **272.** 13; **325.** 13; **367.** 11; **381.** 3; **368.** 5; **443.** 10; with  **4.** 14; **5.** 15; **11.** 4

***Ḥeru-χuti-Χeperȧ*** 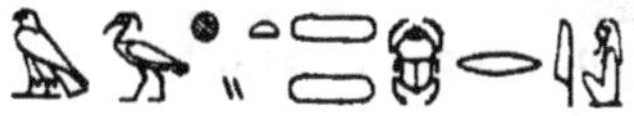 Harmachis-Kheperȧ **40.** 8

***Ḥeru-χent-ȧn-Maati*** 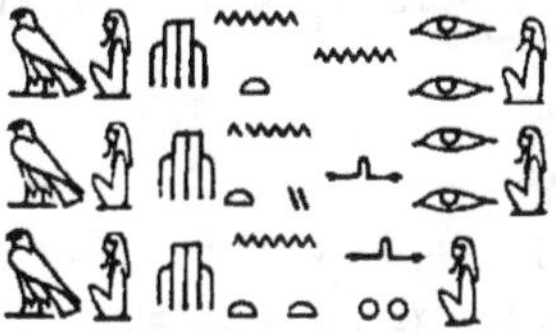 "Horus dweller in blindness" **59.** 4; **62.** 16; **72.** 11; **325.** 16

***Ḥeru-χent-χaṭθi***  a title of Horus **326.** 3

***Ḥeru-χenṭ-ḥeḥ***  "Horus, traveller of eternity" **114.** 4

***Ḥeru-χenti-ḥeḥ*** 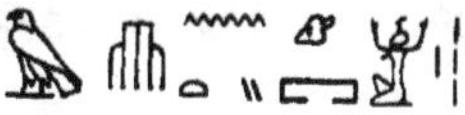 "Horus, president of eternity" **116.** 1

***Ḥeru-χenti-Seχem*** 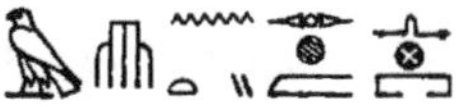 "Horus in Sekhem" **72.** 6

***Ḥeru-χesbeṭ-Maati*** 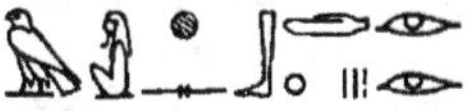 "Blue-eyed Horus" **462.** 6

***Ḥeru-sa-Ȧuset***  "Horus, son of Isis" **16.** 14; **65.** 9; **277.** 3; **403.** 11

***Ḥeru-sa-Ȧusȧr*** "Horus, son of Osiris" **77.** 16; **78.** 3, 6; **80.** 4; **102.** 14; **442.** 13

***Ḥeru-sa-Ḥet-Ḥeru*** "Horus, son of Hathor" **421.** 4

***Ḥeru-Seχai*** "Horus-Sekhai" **326.** 2

***Ḥeru-seśeṭ-ḥrȧ*** a title of Horus **512.** 11

***Ḥeru-Teḥuti*** Horus-Thoth **326.** 3

***Ḥeru-ṭeśer-Maati*** "Red-eyed Horus" **462.** 6

***Ḥeru-śesu*** "followers of Horus", a class of mythical beings **209.** 14; **213.** 12

***Ḥeru-ṭā-ṭā-f*** a son of king Cheops **97.** 3; **141.** 9; **309.** 12

***ḥrȧ*** face **4.** 4; **6.** 1; **40.** 2; **56.** 11; **64.** 3; **80.** 11; **93.** 8; **106.** 13; **112.** 8; **117.** 2; **136.** 11; **144.** 16; **192.** 6; **306.** 5, 6; **310.** 8; **311.** 2, 10; **332.** 8; **413.** 16; **445.** 15; **459.** 3, 4; **479.** 6; **484.** 13; **509.** 16; **280.** 4; **513.** 8; face to face **144.** 14; two faces **417.** 10; plur. , **10.** 1; **41.** 13; **116.** 2; **195.** 11; **262.** 7; **275.** 4; **291.** 14; **302.** 15; **369.** 10; **372.** 2; **417.** 3; **480.** 3; **134.** 14; **142.** 12

***ḥrȧ neb*** every one, everybody **9.** 16; **41.** 9

***ḥrȧ nebu*** , folk, all men, mankind, everybody **10.** 15; **11.** 14; **250.** 11; **291.** 9; **308.** 11; **400.** 9; **435.** 9

***Ḥrȧ-uā*** a proper name **156.** 8, 13; **157.** 3, 8, 13; **158.** 1, 5

*Ḥrȧ-nefer* "Beautiful Face", a name of Rā 320. 5; 386. 6; 387. 11; 387. 8

*Ḥrȧ-f-ḥa-f* one of the forty-two assessors 256. 8; 261. 12; 393. 13

*Ḥrȧ-k-en-Maāt* a proper name 97. 13

*ḥeḥ* million 64. 8; 136. 16;

*ḥeḥ* millions, millions of years 10. 6; 13. 8; 29. 14; 31. 12; 42. 4; 54. 13; 55. 1; 68. 9; 114. 4; 139. 1; 143. 3; 144. 1; 146. 7; 173. 6, 7; 180. 16; 196. 15; 198. 1; 282. 9; 287. 8; 292. 6; 312. 10; 339. 13; 458. 16; 459. 5 *(ter)*; 481. 12; 490. 12; 280. 10; 287. 8

*ḥeḥ en sep* a million times 77. 6; 152. 13; 294. 12; 312. 10; 159. 9; 162. 3; 334. 4; 402. 16; 80. 4

*ḥeḥ en sep* a million times 80. 16; 82. 18; 404. 13

*Ḥeḥ tet* (?) the land of millions of years 512. 5

*ḥeḥ* eternity, everlastingness 9. 11; 10. 13; 12. 3, 4; 19. 8; 39. 1; 63. 14; 65. 12; 78. 4, 5; 90. 11; 91. 11; 119. 5; 133. 1; 239. 12; 363. 14; 395. 16; 416. 8; 426. 12; 442. 4; 452. 5; 466. 5; 477. 2; 504. 14; 509. 13; 38. 3; 412. 7; 414. 10; 417. 13; 510. 2, 7; 514. 4, 8; 515. 1; 517. 3

*Ḥeḥi* name of a god 139. 1; 144. 1

*ḥeḥi* to hasten after 32. 13; 310. 2; 383. 8; 458. 10

**ḥes** will, pleasure **450.** 7

**ḥes** to be favoured, favourable to **273.** 10; **444.** 13 *(bis)*, 14 *(bis)*; **514.** 9; **516.** 11; favourable **349.** 7; **439.** 6, 15; **440.** 6

**ḥesu** favoured one **21.** 11; favoured one **17.** 8; **24.** 3; **466.** 16; **481.** 11; **490.** 13; **389.** 7, 14; plur. **17.** 7; **516.** 12; **4.** 16; **41.** 4; **42.** 14; **138.** 14; **270.** 9; **112.** 4, 6; favoured **461.** 9

**ḥest** favour **223.** 11

**ḥest** will **481.** 14

**ḥest** pleasure **213.** 12

**Ḥes-ḥrȧ** "Savage Face" **411.** 15; **416.** 9, 10

**Ḥes-fefef** "Savage Eye" **413.** 1

**ḥesu**, **ḥes** filth **67.** 3; **99.** 6; **123.** 7, 12, 15; **124.** 17; **179.** 13; **214.** 11; **238.** 15; **243.** 14; **465.** 9; **492.** 8, 10; **493.** 10; **494.** 1, 2

**ḥeseb** *faïence* (?) **291.** 2

**ḥeseb** to reckon up, to estimate, accountant **21.** 8; **159.** 4; **199.** 2; **211.** 12; **62.** 1; **61.** 14; **384.** 6, 12; **315.** 15

**ḥeseb ḥetep neter** computer of holy offerings **37.** 5; **74.** 6; **76.** 11; **248.** 15; plur. **85.** 12

**ḥeseb qeṭu** reckoner of dispositions 249. 13

**ḥeseb śes** a kind of priest (?) 339. 16

**ḥeseb** for *ḥebs* (?) clothed 25. 11

**Ḥesb-ent-Ȧuset** "Knife of Isis", a proper name 396. 13; a proper name 391. 6

**ḥespu** nomes 207. 4

**Ḥesepti** a king of the first dynasty 145. 14; 285. 7

**ḥesmen** natron 54. 14; 88. 16; 175. 1; 291. 3; 436. 16; 437. 2; 444. 6, 10; 508. 7

**Ḥesert** name of a city 324. 13

**ḥesq** to cut, to be cut, to wound, to make gashes, to mow 4. 10; 9. 8; 12. 11; 31. 2; 44. 2; 62. 14; 80. 6; 108. 12; 121. 17; 122. 11; 134. 5; 191. 7, 13, 16; 192. 16; 193. 6; 197. 5; 198. 11; 203. 2; 292. 16; 245. 5; 373. 3; 375. 10; 401. 16

**ḥesqet** knife 394. 15

**Ḥest** name of a city 323. 9

**ḥeset** libation vase 445. 4

*ḥeka*, *ḥeka*, *ḥekau*, *ḥekat* — charms, enchantments 31. 13; 86. 10; 87. 1, 5, 13; 88. 2; 97. 8, 11, 15, 16; 98. 2, 3, 6; 99. 16; 102. 13; 142. 4; 160. 1; 176. 11; 183. 6; 191. 9; 192. 1, 2; 193. 1, 8; 219. 13; 361. 11; 403. 5; 481. 12; 502. 3; 507. 5, 8

*ḥekennu* — to praise 77. 15; 79. 16; 80. 2; 272. 16; 273. 9; 275. 16; praise 316. 3, 4, 7, 8; 337. 9; 472. 12; 486. 5

*ḥekennu*, *ḥekeniu* — praises 6. 16; 44. 6; 272. 7, 8; 470. 10; 472. 12, 13; 495. 12; 431. 2

*ḥekennu* — unguent 294. 7; 336. 7; 339. 6

*Ḥekennut* — name of a city 324. 13

*ḥeq* — to rule 13. 1; 38. 10; 51. 7; 114. 4; 116. 2; 155. 7; 173. 13; 367. 10; 459. 2; 506. 10; 65. 6, 8

*ḥeqt* — rule 477. 4, 7

*ḥeq*, *ḥeqt* — sceptre 13. 11; 482. 10; 487. 5

*ḥeq* — ruler, governor 9. 12; 11. 12; 12. 3; 13. 13; 14. 5; 49. 14; 51. 7; 70. 13; 185. 2; 314. 2; 386. 6; 471. 8; 478. 4; 323. 7; plur. 14. 5

**ḥeq** 46. 14; 482. 9; 507. 11; 439. 2; 404. 8; 111. 10; 452. 5

**Ḥeq āṭ** the thirteenth nome of Lower Egypt, the capital of which was Heliopolis 504. 4; 256. 3

**(Ḥeq-Maāt-Rā-setep-en-Āmen)** the prenomen of Rameses IV. 271. 8, 15; 272. 8, 16; 273. 2, 6

**ḥeq** beer 510. 3; 514. 13

**ḥeq**, **ḥeqt** beer, ale 17. 2; 21. 1, 2; 124. 10; 151. 9; 161. 12; 179. 8; 209. 4; 231. 3; 244. 3; 267. 10; 333. 10; 363. 9, 16; 364. 7; 365. 1; 426. 2; 437. 2; 454. 8, 13; 464. 12; 465. 2; 477. 15; 493. 5; 494. 11

**ḥeqr** hunger 463. 1, 14; 466. 4; 462. 1

**ḥeqr**, **ḥeqrȧu** hungry man 261. 2; 516. 6

**Ḥeqtit** a goddess 326. 5

**ḥet** temple, house of a god, shrine 23. 7; 28. 11; 47. 11; 67. 13; 146. 8; 150. 7; 230. 3; 312. 13; 324. 1, 4, 5; 325. 5, 15; 348. 9; 349. 6; 388. 8, 14; 389. 4; 444. 10; 491. 15; 513. 3; 162. 10; plur. 163. 3, 4 *(bis)*; 491. 7

**ḥet** section of a book, chapter 445.

4; 445. 13; 446. 16; 447. 10; 448. 5; 448. 14; 450. 6; 451. 1; 451. 9

**ḥet āt** great house, palace, temple 64. 2; 85. 5; 242. 14; 290. 15; 285. 6; 299. 10; 325. 8; 331. 14; 345. 4; 349. 2; 357. 4; 443. 10; 449. 13; 477. 9

**Ḥet-āāḥ** Temple of the Moon 177. 3; 391. 16; 397. 6; 445. 15

**Ḥet-Ȧusȧr** Temple of Osiris 171. 12; 172. 2

**Ḥet-Ȧmen** Temple of Ȧmen 410. 11

**Ḥet-Ȧnes** Temple of the Ȧnes garment 59. 10

**Ḥet-āšemu** Temple of the gods in visible forms 319. 2; 364. 11

**Ḥet-ur** Temple of the Great or Aged One at Heliopolis 2. 8; 19. 5; 27. 12; 348. 10; 349. 6; 392. 11; 387. 2; 388. 3

**Ḥet-useχ-ḥrȧ** Temple of the Broad Face 92. 6

**Ḥet-ba** Temple of the Soul 1. 12

**Ḥet-Ptaḥ-ka** Temple of the *Ka* of Ptaḥ, *i. e.*, Memphis 37. 12. 89. 16; 257. 11; 478. 7

**Ḥet-ent-Ȧnpu** Temple of Anubis 130. 9

**Ḥet-ent-qem-ḥrȧu** Temple of Qem-ḥrȧu gods 130. 1

*Ḥet-nub* House of gold 444. 11

*Ḥet-nemmes* Temple of the Nemmes crown 168. 5

*Ḥet-nem-ḥrá* Temple of Nemḥrá 243. 5

*Ḥet-Ḥeru* Temple of Horus, *i. e.*, Hathor 11. 7; 15. 6; 101. 12; 107. 10; 108. 6; 112. 9; 117. 3; 124. 7; 151. 11; 180. 2; 194. 6; 215. 11; 220. 14; 266. 2; 315. 13; 331. 16; 383. 3; 393. 2; 421. 4; 443. 10; 493. 2

*Ḥet-χeperá* Temple of Kheperá 146. 8

*Ḥet-kau-Nebt-er-ṭer* Temple of the *Kas* of Nebt-er-tcher 318. 9; 364. 1

*Ḥet-ṭeśeru* Temple of the red gods 319. 4; 364. 13

*Ḥet-ur* name of a city 467. 7

*Ḥet-benbenet* part of a temple 314. 16

*Ḥet-net* palace of the king of the north 147. 1

*ḥeti* waste (?) 99. 6

*ḥeti* a kind of wood 335. 2

*ḥeti*, *ḥetit*, *ḥetet* throat 103. 12; 104. 13; 111. 6; 165. 5; 180. 7; 382. 13; 447. 2

**ḥetep** to be at peace, to rest, to set (of the sun), satisfied, content 1. 9; 2. 14; 7. 15; 8. 14; 9. 15; 21. 9; 35. 1, 10; 45. 9; 89. 5; 90. 4, 5; 106. 6, 7; 129. 2; 176. 13; 182. 5; 214. 1; 227. 4; 242. 10; 273. 8; 312. 15; 315. 6; 370. 15; 378. 11; 380. 9, 15; 383. 4; 384. 3; 401. 2; 406. 8, 11; 419. 5; 424. 3; 435. 7; 436. 6; 442. 4; 455. 11 *(bis)*, 12; 470. 14; 472. 1, 6; 474. 1, 13; 480. 13; 491. 9, 10; 509. 8; 226. 6, 11; 479. 10; 481. 6, 7; 76. 9; 411. 8, 13; 40. 7; 82. 3; 447. 16; 39. 3; 41. 9; 458. 10, 13

**ḥetep** peace, content 4. 9; 49. 8; 299. 1; 330. 5; 398. 7; 485. 3; things which satisfy 444. 15; those who are satisfied 471. 10; 472. 10; settings 139. 15; contentedly 4. 12; 5. 4; 7. 8; 35. 15

**ḥetep** table of offerings 39. 2, 5, 6; 393. 4; 394. 7, 14; 396. 11; 512. 3

**ḥetep** to make propitiatory offerings 155. 6

**ḥetep** an offering 93. 8; 379. 9

**ḥetepu**, **ḥetepet** offerings of cakes, ale, beasts, feathered fowl, unguents, linen, etc., 3. 8; 14. 13; 22. 11; 35. 2; 111. 8, 9; 123. 8, 16; 134. 12; 142. 11; 175. 13; 214. 12; 223. 1, 2; 243. 14; 284. 10; 299. 14; 303. 7; 331. 4 *(bis)*, 5; 332. 5; 364. 7; 365. 1; 372. 6; 375. 1; 380. 12; 415. 10; 424. 13, 14; 427. 9; 428. 2, 6; 434. 1;

449. 10; 466. 11; 472. 14; 479. 16; 492. 10; 514. 13; 516. 7; 347. 10; 227. 16

**ḥetep neter** divine offerings 199. 2; 486. 4; and see *passim*.

**Ḥetep** the god of offerings 225. 7, 13, 16; 226. 14; 227. 1, 16; 228. 3

**Ḥetepi** the god of offerings 474. 9; plur. 472. 12, 16; 473. 4; 319. 10

**ḥetepu** geese 154. 16

**Ḥetep** the city of the god Ḥetep 224. 13

**Ḥetep-mes** a proper name 346. 15

**Ḥetep-Ḥeru-ḥems-uāu** a proper name 392. 6

**Ḥetep-seχus** name of a goddess 57. 16; 58. 11, 13

**Ḥetep-ka** a proper name 502. 12

**Ḥetep-taui** a proper name 104. 2

**ḥetem** to destroy, to be destroyed 100. 3; 190. 14; 198. 14; 236. 16; 372. 12; 373. 15; 374. 7; 377. 9; 380. 13; 381. 14; 401. 12; 402. 3; 432. 1; 455. 3; 463. 2; 473. 15; 504. 1; 71. 9, 13; destroyers 271. 4; 272. 5; 274. 5; 275. 5; to be filled 461. 13

**Ḥetemt** name of a goddess **197**. 8

**Ḥetem-ur** "Great Destroyer", name of a god **80**. 8

**Ḥetem-ḥrȧ** "Destroying Face", name of a god **433**. 9

**ḥetrȧ** to bestow, to give, to pay tribute **125**. 3; **137**. 8

**ḥetertu**

**ḥetru** tribute **149**. 4

**ḥeṭeṭ** scorpion **186**. 5

**Ḥeṭeṭet** scorpion deity **105**. 12; **106**. 9

**ḥeθes** to be lord of **225**. 15

**ḥeț** to do evil, to plunder, to steal, to waste, to destroy, to make to diminish, calamity, wrong **16**. 4; **196**. 13; **197**. 17; **233**. 8; **250**. 12; **253**. 5; **336**. 13; **458**. 3, 5, 6; **459**. 7; **488**. 10; **351**. 6

**ḥeț** silver **96**. 15; **449**. 6

**ḥeț** , to illumine **2**. 12; **139**. 5; **144**. 5; **176**. 9; to shine **445**. 15; dawn, daybreak **72**. 14; **139**. 6; **144**. 6; **306**. 9; **307**. 2

**ḥețḥeț** light **177**. 15

**Ḥeț-re** a proper name **68**. 1

**Ḥeț-re-pesṭ-ṭep** a proper name **68**. 4

***Ḥef-âbeḥu*** "White teeth", one of the forty-two assessors **254.** 4, 14

***ḥefet*** white **151.** 9; **214.** 14; **244.** 3; **303.** 13; **312.** 14; **454.** 9; (of barley) **124.** 10; **493.** 4

***ḥefet*** the white crown, or crown of the south **13.** 10; **112.** 1; **164.** 3 *(bis)*; **230.** 5; **244.** 7; **294.** 3; **441.** 12; **482.** 10; **487.** 4; with *ṭešer* red crown **417.** 5

***ḥefeti*** white sandals **267.** 15

***ḥefau*** loaves **449.** 11

***ḥefas*** . . . . . . **506.** 14

---

# KH.

*χa* thousand 137. 1; 143. 3; 154. 13; 226. 1; 226. 2; plur. 189. 11; 478. 5; 296. 5, 14; 297. 11

*χa* chamber 416. 8, 15; 419. 7

*χa*, *χat* the material body, dead body 25. 11; 39. 6; 53. 4, 6; 64. 6; 90. 3; 187. 10; 189. 3; 190. 2, 13; 196. 7; 213. 14; 214. 2; 234. 15; 295. 1; 315. 14; 398. 15; 399. 8; 401. 1; 407. 1; 410. 8, 16; 411. 9; 412. 1; 418. 8; 419. 6; 422. 13; 425. 5, 7, 15; 436. 5; 438. 15; 471. 14; 409. 9; 411. 8, 13; 509. 15; 510. 1, 2; 512. 8; 514. 16; plur. 416. 14; dead fish 251. 9

*χaā* to set, to set aside, to forsake 183. 2; 356. 10; 412. 5; 413. 9

*χaāā* emissions 228. 12

*χaām* to hasten 204. 6

*χau* fire 337. 9

*χau-fet-f* a proper name **340.** 11

*χau* basins, bowls **449.** 6

*χau* abundant **379.** 15

*χaut* the dead, fiends **272.** 4

*χaut* / *χautet* altar for offerings **23.** 8; **70.** 5; **161.** 13; **209.** 13; **285.** 15; **347.** 9; **350.** 15; **441.** 4; **450.** 12; **464.** 16; **470.** 3; **480.** 5; **489.** 12; four altars **317.** 3, 4; plur. **175.** 13; **449.** 7

*χaut* . . . . . . **72.** 14

*χaui* darkness, night **71.** 7; **72.** 10; **81.** 9; **263.** 10; **380.** 7; **467.** 4; **478.** 7; **483.** 9

*χaibit* shade **195.** 12, 13, 16; **196.** 4; **375.** 9; **491.** 11, 16; with *ba* and *khu* **194.** 4; with *ba* **194.** 12; plur. **138.** 12; **253.** 2; **371.** 5; **375.** 4

*χaiti* slaughterers **372.** 5

*χabesu* stars **38.** 4

*χabet* fraud, deceit **253.** 9

*χapa* a portion of the body **54.** 6; *χap* navel (?) **447.** 16

*χam* to submit **440.** 16

*χames* ears of corn **222.** 1, 2, 3; **367.** 15; **368.** 2; **369.** 1

**χart** a kind of bird **440.** 9; 221. 5; 368. 8

**χarsaθȧ** a proper name **409.** 2

**χaχ** to seek **344.** 5; to extend to 353. 5

**χaχ**
**χaχet** swift (?) **87.** 10, 15; **88.** 3, 4

**χasu** lower eyelids **446.** 9

**χasi** bad, evil **5.** 10

**χast** territory (?) **149.** 3, 15

**χak-ȧbu** rebels **337.** 16

**χakeru** to be ornamented, ornaments **30.** 5; **327.** 2; **440.** 3; **441.** 9; **476.** 11 *(bis)*; **513.** 1; **447.** 1

**χati** a class of divine beings **348.** 9; 349. 5

**χat** body, belly, womb **13.** 9; **14.** 5; **58.** 1; **70.** 3; **90.** 14; **98.** 8, 14; **99.** 5, 7, 11; **112.** 16; **117.** 15; **123.** 16; **153.** 11; **179.** 14; **220.** 5; **232.** 11; **281.** 7; **335.** 7; **338.** 7; **339.** 2; **352.** 15; **370.** 12; **375.** 7; **376.** 2; **397.** 12; **436.** 5; **443.** 3; **447.** 15; **481.** 6; **482.** 11; **483.** 1; **487.** 5; **489.** 3; **492.** 12; **494.** 3; **153.** 6; plur. **114.** 15; **115.** 2; **137.** 13; **143.** 12; **191.** 9; **192.** 3; **260.** 8; **400.** 8; heart of sycamore **402.** 12; **403.** 8

**χat** (or **χar**) the sixteenth nome of Lower Egypt (?) **231.** 2

***Χat*** a proper name (?) 231. 1, 2

***χā***, ***χāā***, ***χāu***, ***χāt***, ***χāau*** to rise like the sun, rising, he who rises, he who is crowned 1. 6; 2. 4, 10; 9. 9; 11. 5; 31. 15; 42. 10; 51. 9; 163. 8; 164. 8; 194. 2; 216. 10; 283. 4; 314. 14, 15; 348. 14; 376. 9; 390. 15; 392. 8; 398. 3; 415. 6; 456. 6, 13; 473. 5; 482. 9; 486. 9, 11; 502. 9; 272. 3; one who rises 11. 9; 51. 7; 512. 16; 6. 10; 8. 15; 304. 4, 7, 16; 486. 16; 4. 3; 1. 7; 4. 8; 36. 5; 476. 3; 479. 5; 277. 8

***χāu***, ***χāā*** risings 4. 2; 8. 4; 43. 14; 125. 2. 154. 1; 180. 13; 286. 6; 471. 4; 472. 4; 476. 7 *(bis)*; 477. 10; 327. 2; 441. 5; 32. 8

***χāu*** crowns, diadems 470. 14

***χāi*** crown 348. 14

***χu*** to dress 448. 14

***χu***, ***χui***, ***χaui*** to protect, to strengthen, to be protected, to benefit, to be strong 66. 8; 159. 6; 244. 12; 266. 12; 267. 3; 334. 3; 373. 3; 414. 9; 428. 3; 440. 5; 478. 15; 482. 8; 510. 7; 511. 12; strengthened 480. 12; 261. 6

χu  the shining one, the divine being of light 26. 13; 125. 4; 127. 1; 131. 14; 134. 4; 149. 1, 14; 162. 12; 167. 3, 9; 168. 2; 170. 5; 178. 6; 185. 16; 187. 7; 202. 16; 319. 2; 364. 11; 369. 13; 442. 14

χu  the luminous, intangible, translucent form of the beatified dead in the world to come, the deceased 31. 5, 12; 34. 4; 37. 2; 61. 11; 96. 15; 143. 8; 160. 2; 167. 8; 272. 6, 14; 275. 6; 277. 12; 308. 6; 329. 16; 334. 2, 3; 362. 8; 364. 7; 365. 2; 366. 8; 395. 12; 402. 13; 403. 9; 404. 3, 12; 405. 1, 5, 10, 17; 408. 5; 409. 14; 410. 6; 433. 10; 491. 9, 10;  389. 4;  212. 1, 11, 14; 213. 2; 402. 15; 438. 8; 461. 4; 470. 11;  384. 4;  194. 4; 491. 10;  487. 15;  a name of Osiris 371. 8

χu  plur. of preceding 42. 14; 49. 4; 74. 3; 81. 15; 103. 3, 4; 113. 8; 119. 10; 136. 16; 138. 9; 143. 3; 167. 3; 191. 9; 192. 2; 222. 3; 225. 4, 6; 261. 5; 269. 9; 270. 2, 9; 298. 12; 308. 6, 15; 314. 16; 329. 16; 362. 10; 369. 8, 9, 10; 370. 7; 371. 3, 4, 8; 372. 12; 374. 3, 5; 375. 2, 3; 377. 9, 11; 378. 10; 379. 3; 380. 2; 442. 10; 462. 1; 470. 15; 475. 5, 6; 486. 6; 490. 2; 492. 14; 493. 1; 502. 10, 11; 516. 8; the four *Khu* 201. 3; the seven *Khu* 58. 3; 59. 2, 7; *Khu* nine cubits high 368. 3; 369. 4

χu  to be glorious 21. 14; 174. 16;  to glorify 293. 12; to glorify 37. 13; glorious 43. 10; 31. 5; being glorious or strong 11. 4; 85. 6; 479. 5

*χu* glory, splendour, honour 1. 10; 7. 11; 14. 9; 24. 9; 35. 12; 184. 11; 200. 14; 281. 11; 363. 9; 376. 11; 458. 12; 494. 10; 495. 5

*χu* splendours, glories, strength, powers 38. 5; 210. 15; 298. 3; 371. 9; 375. 8, 14; 403. 10; 461. 1; 473. 5; glorious 435. 15; 423. 4

*χui* words of power 405. 12; 479. 12; 481. 13; 482. 3; 485. 1

*χut* splendour 342. 8; glory 364. 16

*χut* splendid, glorious 18. 5; 50. 20; 51. 4; 108. 1; 240. 5

*χut* light 428. 15

*Χu-χeper-ur* a proper name 409. 9

*Χu-fet-f* a proper name 353. 7

*Χut* name of a goddess 49. 9; 315. 6

*χuu* evil things or deeds 249. 5; 266. 12; 267. 3; 509. 2

*Χiu* (?) name of a god 185. 16

*χunt* drink offerings **146.** 9

*χus* to dig out and stamp down clay to make a cistern **453.** 9

*Χut* the place where the sun shews himself on the horizon in rising or setting, the horizon **1.** 3; **3.** 13; **6.** 13; **31.** 11; **52.** 2; **54.** 3; **61.** 8; **103.** 14; **107.** 5; **110.** 6; **132.** 12; **167.** 13; **270.** 10; **278.** 16; **280.** 15; **281.** 4, 10; **288.** 10, 11; **305.** 11; **312.** 15; **314.** 15; **329.** 10, 14; **332.** 12; **363.** 6; **421.** 2; **441.** 2; **450.** 16; **456.** 14; **509.** 11; **175.** 16; **319.** 12; **462.** 13; **55.** 15; **46.** 4; **78.** 15; **208.** 16; **209.** 1; **384.** 3; **415.** 9; **36.** 1; **374.** 1; **441.** 16

*χut* fire **369.** 9; **378.** 6

*χi* babe, child **112.** 2; **114.** 11; **144.** 16

*χeb* to defraud, to pilfer **16.** 3; **250.** 11; **251.** 1, 2; iniquity **481.** 3

*χeb* weak **488.** 15

*χeb* to be defeated **94.** 5

*χebu* defeat **330.** 10

*χeba* to destroy **401.** 1

*χebu* steeped **402.** 12

*Χebent* a proper name **163.** 7

**χebent** evildoing 260. 13

**χebenti** evil, the wicked 279. 16

**χebχeb** torture chamber 460. 15

**χebχeb** to force a way 163. 3; 168. 16; 177. 13; destruction 334. 12; destruction 350. 1

**χebs** to plough 20. 11; 453. 9; 20. 11

**χebs-ta** the ceremony of ploughing the earth 74. 16; 75. 1, 3; 79. 8; 81. 16; 84. 5

**χebsu** devourer 356. 11

**χebs**
**χebsu** star, lamp 213. 13; 296. 11; plur. 296. 2; 297. 7; 446. 14

**χebt** to suffer hurt 237. 4

**χebt** little 238. 13

**χebt** dancer 355. 16

**χebt**
**χebti** destroyer 343. 14; 344. 12; 356. 14

**χebt** torture chamber, slaughter house 80. 6; 184. 1, 10; 255. 5; 347. 15; 416. 14; 171. 10

**χep** to travel, to journey 163. 12; 209. 1; 273. 11; 371. 7; 464. 14; 478. 14; *χept* journey 163. 11

**χep** a part of the body 99. 9

**χepen** fat 417. 11

**χeper** to come into being, to become, to be, to turn into 3. 1, 16; 9. 1; 44. 11; 51. 4, 6, 10, 14; 55. 16; 56. 4; 60. 4, 16; 74. 3; 114. 8; 163. 15; 174. 3; 181. 5; 283. 7; 346. 12; 358. 14; 362. 5; 363. 12; 364. 14; 379. 7; 400. 2; 401. 7, 9; 402. 1; 414. 16; 426. 7; 430. 10; 431. 9; 434. 7; 457. 3; 473. 11, 15; 476. 1; 477. 1, 2; 47. 2; 48. 8; , non existent 13. 15; 167. 16; when taketh place 35. 9; to become satisfied 9. 7; what is thy name? 129. 14; 241. 19

**χeper ṭesef** self-created 8. 3; 12. 14; 40. 9; 49. 1; 51. 12; 174. 6; 398. 1

**χepert** what hath become, what exists 36. 14; 126. 6; 438. 6; 439. 10; 455. 12; 457. 10

**Χeperá** the god Kheperá 1. 5 *(bis)*; 2. 2; 5. 15; 66. 5, 16; 103. 5; 107. 8; 111. 2; 113. 14; 138. 3; 145. 3; 181. 5; 184. 8; 197. 7; 198. 13; 236. 11; 283. 6; 292. 7; 316. 5; 443. 10; 87. 6

**χeperu** form, transformation, phase of being, evolution 320. 15; 511. 3; 517. 1; 316. 5; change 75. 5

*χeperu* forms, transformations **15**. 10; **23**. 3; **36**. 12; **37**. 11; **42**. 10; **45**. 15; **51**. 1; **63**. 13; **82**. 17; **96**. 2; **134**. 15; **145**. 2, 3; **161**. 4; **163**. 15; **164**. 7; **165**. 9; **167**. 10, 14; **168**. 7; **176**. 7; **178**. 3, 11; **179**. 7; **181**. 3; **182**. 4, 11; **183**. 16; **185**. 2; **186**. 3; **187**. 14; **188**. 3, 10; **209**. 8; **210**. 2; **243**. 9; **268**. 15; **273**. 4; **276**. 2; **290**. 15, 17; **400**. 14; **408**. 9, 12; **419**. 2; **423**. 6; **429**. 15; **442**. 9; **459**. 9; **469**. 12; **470**. 5 *(bis)*, 13; **473**. 11, 15; **475**. 4, 6; **477**. 7; **480**. 12; **490**. 4; **502**. 4; those who become **90**. 17

*χeperut*

*χeper*, *χeprer* scarab, beetle **96**. 14; **142**. 1; **413**. 1; **420**. 4; **502**. 1

*χepeś* thigh **132**. 14; **136**. 5; **142**. 15; **333**. 7; **449**. 4; plur. , **435**. 16; **448**. 16

*χepeś* the constellation of the Thigh **58**. 10; **75**. 16

*χept* to happen **122**. 1

*χeptet* buttock, top of the thigh **57**. 5; **113** 1; **136**. 16; **142**. 16; **340**. 13; **364**. 14; **447**. 6; plur. **118**. 16; **190**. 11; **292**. 12; **363**. 12; **371**. 4

*χefa* food **507**. 1, 2

*χefā* fist, grasp **92**. 11; **99**. 15; **113**. 6; **115**. 16; **155**. 9, 10; **439**. 16; to take by handfuls **464**. 4; plur. **158**. 13

**χefāt** grasp 415. 10

**χeft** in front of, according to, conformably to, when 1. 3; 3. 13; 6. 13; 22. 3; 39. 14; 44. 11; 52. 10; 55. 8, 14; 110. 4; 141. 10, 13; 153. 10; 183. 7; 211. 16; 212. 2; 249. 3; 259. 14, 16; 270. 14; 294. 15; 308. 6; 309. 11; 314. 14; 316. 13; 344. 6; 349. 13; 350. 5, 12; 351. 2, 9, 16; 352. 10, 16; 353. 8; 354. 1, 8, 15; 355. 6, 13; 357. 1, 6, 9, 13; 358. 12; 362. 8; 366. 4; 451. 14, 15; 213. 13; 487. 11; 488. 9

**χeft** enemy, fiend 2. 16; 4. 11; 44. 15; 89. 10; 190. 8; 513. 15; 32. 3

**χefti** foes, enemies 5. 5; 7. 7; 18. 12; 31. 9; 52. 5; 58. 15; 60. 13; 62. 11; 66. 8; 68. 10; 71. 3, 4, 5, 9, 15, 16; 72. 8, 9, 15, 16; 73. 8, 9, 15, 16; 74. 6, 7, 14, 15; 75. 2, 9, 10; 76. 2, 3, 6, 10, 12, 15; 77. 14; 78. 1, 7, 8, 15; 79. 15, 16; 80. 3, 5, 13; 81. 3, 4; 82. 2, 5; 83. 2, 3; 84. 2; 108. 16; 147. 12; 187. 10; 304. 12; 305. 8; 306. 14; 307. 7; 310. 10; 313. 15; 314. 5; 316. 6; 336. 14; 341. 6; 347. 5, 14; 351. 6; 366. 13; 382. 14; 387. 1; 385. 4; 388. 2; 421. 3; 430. 15; 431. 8; 438. 3; 445. 9, 10; 451. 12; 452. 11; 453. 1; 454. 2, 3; 460. 6; 467. 5, 6, 16; 468. 2; 469. 7, 16; 475. 7; 476. 16 *(bis)*; 480. 2, 11; 481. 16; 482. 4; 486. 14; 493. 9; 502. 7, 12

**χem** to be extinguished 232. 13

**χem** shrine 331. 14

**χem** to put an end to 299. 9; 331. 12; 366. 13; 298. 6; and see 31. 15; 361. 11; 469. 4

**χem** to be unknown 109. 9; 113. 11;

135. 12; 346. 10; to be ignorant of 128. 7; 172. 12; 359. 5; 409. 6; 183. 9; 131. 14

*χem* an ignorant man 119. 14; 145. 4; 238. 8

*χem* to overthrow, to destroy 100. 7; 184. 16; 292. 9, 13; 293. 5; 300. 5

*χemi* one of the forty-two assessors 254. 12; 255. 11

*χemi*, *χemit* overthrowing, destroying, destroyer, destroyed 123. 8; 214. 12; 244. 1; 293. 5; 292. 9; 293. 4; 429. 11

*χemā* to do away with 187. 3; 270. 4

*χemāu* those who carry away 269. 12

*χemu* wind, air 152. 8

*χemennu* eight 16. 7; 98. 11; 219. 3; 333. 9, 10 *(ter)*, 11; 508. 11; eight 339. 9; 353. 1; 425. 1

*Χemennu* the eight gods of Hermopolis 416. 4

*Χemennu* Hermopolis, the city of the eight gods 51. 11; 92. 7; 96. 16; 135. 8; 140. 14; 141. 6; 235. 7, 15; 236. 2, 6; 238. 3, 10; 253. 1; 386. 12; 510. 9; 515. 5

*χemt* three 116. 5; 143. 3; 212. 14; 222. 2; 417. 3; 464. 6; third 262. 14; 328. 1; 335. 15; 350. 12; 359. 10

*χemt* copper 346. 13

*χen*, *χenen*, *χennu* to perch upon, to alight, to hover over 148. 11; 160. 9; 164. 10, 13; 179. 11; 237. 8; 370. 3; 493. 13, 14; 140. 2

*χenit* the divine beings who alight on the sycamore in heaven 124. 8; 493. 2

*χen* to be dressed in 136. 2; garment 136. 10

*χen* , interior, inner part of a house 11. 6; 100. 2; 195. 7; 196. 8; 244. 8; 227. 2; 229. 4; and see

*Χennu* name of a city in the Elysian Fields 227. 5

*χen* to stir up strife or storm 256. 5

*χennu* baleful things, storm, strife, breakers, opposition 68. 7; 107. 4; 114. 9; 122. 1. 14; 196. 14; 197. 17; 225. 3; 232. 13; 415. 10; 457. 12; 481. 14; 483. 8; 485. 2

*χen*, *χenen* to decay, to rot, to wither 399. 15; 401. 9, 12, 13

*χen* to ferry across, to transport, to travel by water, to row, to paddle 5. 6; 9. 14; 29. 2; 46. 8; 133. 8; 134. 1, 2; 224. 9, 12; 225. 5; 227. 11; 358. 12; 368. 11; a journey,

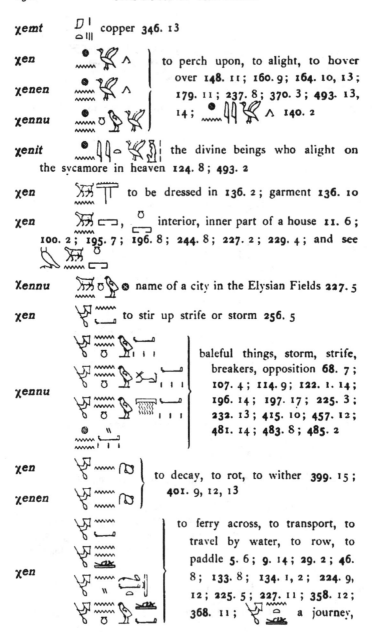

that in which a journey is made, boat 125. 10; 215. 1; 282. 10; 368. 10; 384. 9

*χenen* sailor 221. 8

*χenȧ* to deprive some one of something to make or to keep in captivity, to shut in 41. 2; 74. 12; 195. 11; 196. 5; 90. 3; 194. 8

*χenp* to draw out, to pluck out 64. 6; 92. 6; 36. 15; tearers, renders 158. 8

*χenf* cake 223. 9; 333. 9

*χenem* jasper, carnelian 316. 14; 403. 3, 7

*χnem* to make, to form, to join or be joined together 2. 12; 7. 8; 15. 12; 37. 12; 39. 3; 41. 6; 44. 2; 46. 6; 139. 12; 179. 1; 212. 10; 213. 12; 223. 1, 15; 276. 16; 478. 17; 483. 2; 513. 14; 511. 14

*Χnem*, *Χnemu* the god Khnemu 96. 5; 102. 5; 129. 3; 134. 4; 504. 4; Khnem-Ḥeru-ḥetep 326. 2

*Χnem-ȧmentet-en-Qemt* a proper name 414. 4

*Χnemet-urt* a proper name 468. 4

*Χnemet-em-ānχ-ȧnnuit* name of a cow 318. 13; 364. 3

*χenem* to snuff up, to smell 6. 6; 8. 5; 446. 5

**χenemu** to scent out **136.** 11

**χenem** to nurse **101.** 12; nurse, companion **136.** 13; **483.** 14

**χenemem** to feed upon **22.** 9

**χenemes** protector **239.** 12; **246.** 12

**χenememti** / **χenemtet** the two nurses, *i. e.*, Isis and Nephthys **23.** 1; **449.** 11

**χenemu** nursery **495.** 8

**χennu** those who cry out **414.** 9

**χenrȧ** shut in **19.** 1; **193.** 15; **437.** 12

**χenrȧ** fiends **234.** 9

**χenrit** prison (?) **504.** 5

**χens** to walk about, to travel **227.** 15; **466.** 3; **471.** 5; **472.** 5; **475.** 1; **446.** 15

**Χensu** the god Khonsu **181.** 13; **398.** 10

**χent** what is in front, the nose or face, before, in front of **137.** 5; **442.** 6; **446.** 2, etc.

***χent***, ***χenti*** dweller at the head **116.** 6, 7; **134.** 4; **138.** 16; **143.** 16; **153.** 14; **169.** 11; **201.** 8; **388.** 16; **457.** 5; **458.** 16; **489.** 14; **506.** 10; **507.** 15; plur. **172.** 1; **147.** 1; **151.** 11; ..... **433.** 13

***Χent-Àmentet*** Governor of Àmentet, a title of Osiris **22.** 13; **70.** 2; **207.** 15; **246.** 6; **276.** 12; **303.** 15; **304.** 3, 6, 10; **305.** 3; **306.** 1, 5, 7, 10; **307.** 8; **308.** 10, 16; **330.** 16; **469.** 11; **475.** 10; **476.** 3; **496.** 15; **501.** 9; plur. (of the gods) **110.** 15; **452.** 4; **466.** 10; **482.** 13; **513.** 10

***Χenti Āba*** (?) ...... **504.** 15

***Χenti āt Àment*** a title of Osiris **272.** 13

***Χentet-Un*** a title of Osiris **323.** 3

***Χenti-Peku*** a title of Osiris **320.** 10

***Χenti-menàtu-f*** a title of Osiris (?) **149.** 4

***Χentet-nep*** a title of Osiris **323.** 4

***Χent-Naàref-f*** a title of Osiris **39.** 1

***Χent-nut-f*** a title of Osiris **324.** 3

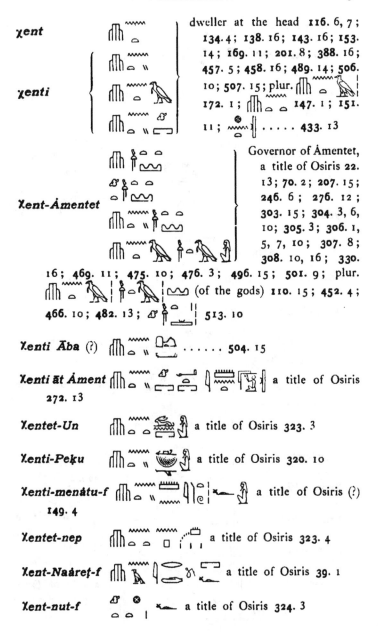

*Xenṭ-ȧn-maati*  a title of Horus 170. 13

*Xenti-neter-ḥet* 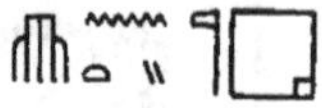 "dweller in the divine house" 247. 15

*Xenti-neter-seḥ* 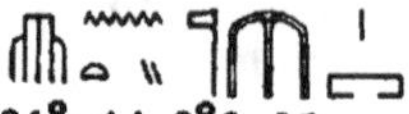 "dweller in the divine hall" 326. 3; 348. 4; 383. 15

*Xenti-Re-stau*  a title of Osiris 321. 3; 323. 7; 377. 7

*χenti-ḥenseketiti*  "dwellers in their tresses" 95. 8; 501. 10

*χent ḥeḥ* 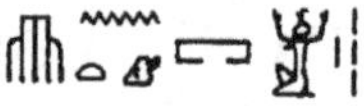 a title of Osiris 146. 6

*Xenti-ḥeq-āṭ* 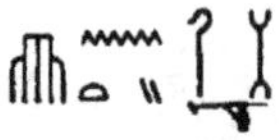 a title of Osiris 504. 4

*χenti ḥet-āt* 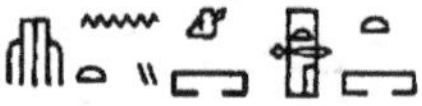 "dweller in the great house" 85. 5

*χentet ḥespu* 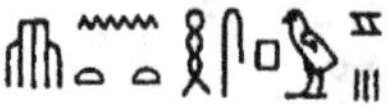 name of the bows of the boat 207. 3

*χentet-χas* 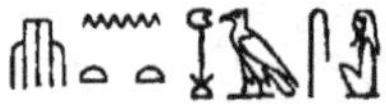 a name of a god 112. 10

*Xenti-χati*
*Xent-χaṭθi* 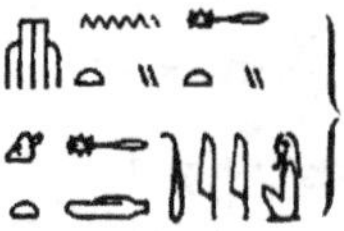 a title of Horus 90. 14; 91. 4; 326. 3

*Xent Seχem*
*Xenti Seχem*  a title of Horus 62. 9; 181. 11

*Xenti-seḥ-ḥemt*
*Xent-seḥt-kaut-f*  a title of Osiris 322. 4; 325. 2

**Χent Suten-ḥenen** a title of Osiris **65.** 4, 6

**Χent-śet-āati** a title of Osiris **325.** 5

**Χenti-θenent** a title of Osiris **323.** 5

**χent** abode, shrine **115.** 3; **146.** 13; **304.** 7; **313.** 13; **462.** 14; **243.** 10; plur. **128.** 5; **320.** 12; **506.** 15

**χent**, **χentet** to sail against the stream **87.** 12; **161.** 5; **224.** 13; **309.** 14; **336.** 3, 6; **348.** 7, 13; **350.** 16; **490.** 6; boat **112.** 2; **456.** 4; **89.** 7; **14.** 10; those who advance **202.** 5

**χenti** a mineral colour **268.** 4; **284.** 12; **291.** 5; **294.** 5; **332.** 15

**χenṭ**, **χenṭu** to travel **64.** 10; **93.** 7; **114.** 4; **115.** 13; **123.** 9; **124.** 1; **138.** 7; **208.** 5; **214.** 13; **244.** 2; **265.** 12; **268.** 5; **359.** 9; **464.** 16; **494.** 3; **495.** 2; **506.** 5; **265.** 15

**χenṭ** thigh **80.** 7; **92.** 15; **205.** 8; **218.** 2; **263.** 4; haunch **466.** 14; **478.** 7

**Χenṭ-Ḥāpiu** name of the steering pole **205.** 8

**χer** with, before **1.** 12; **4.** 13; **16.** 9; **23.** 10; **44.** 2; **54.** 7; **63.** 10 *(bis)*; **67.** 16; **69.** 12, 14; **70.** 2, 13; **76.**

3; 85. 6; 92. 3; 95. 16; 124. 3; 125. 7, 8; 146. 14; 173. 6; 175. 9; 209. 15, 16; 216. 10; 240. 13; 249. 7; 260. 13; 277. 4; 286. 11; 306. 8, 16; 358. 7; 362. 2; 366. 8; 374. 14; 375. 13; 379. 4; 384. 5; 386. 11; 414. 14; 427. 12; 433. 2, 6; 437. 7, 8; 452. 9; 456. 16; 463. 2, 3; 464. 7 *(bis)*; 479. 1, 14; 482. 4; 484. 10; 491. 2; 492. 15, 16; 496. 14, 15, 16; 497. 16; 510. 1 *(bis)*; 516. 2, 3; 87. 14; 501. 14; in the reign of 285. 6; = 70. 13

χert course 456. 5

χert , things of, property of, affairs, matters 137. 14; 138. 2; 144. 10; 167. 6; 168. 4; 170. 4; 266. 11; 267. 2; 469. 14; 471. 5; 472. 5; 373. 12; 329. 7

χer under, beneath, with 24. 13; 25. 2; 41. 12; 70. 2; 80. 9; 96. 16; 100. 1; 124. 7; 140. 15; 141. 7; 151. 13; 180. 1; 186. 12; 190. 7, 8; 195. 1; 201. 14; 230. 5; 233. 14; 244. 5; 277. 15; 278. 1; 289. 9; 310. 9; 316. 1; 330. 3; 349. 1; 363. 12; 364. 14; 382. 15; 385. 4, 8; 387. 1; 402. 9; 408. 5; 409. 4; 436. 5; 452. 10; 457. 1; 469. 9; 470. 2; 493. 1, 15; 495. 10; 507. 1; χer 511. 6; 234. 13; under the favour of 223. 11; 301. 14; 338. 8; 352. 7; 486. 9

χer , to have, to possess, having, possessing 62. 6, 7, 9; 67. 5; 342. 2, 9, 16; 343. 8, 15; 344. 7, 13; 345. 6, 13; 346. 4; 354. 14; 355. 5, 11; 356. 2, 7; 357. 5, 8, 13, 16; 413. 13, 14, 16; 414. 2; 417. 3; 446. 9; 482. 6; 488. 7; 490. 5; 412. 9; 59. 4; 169. 11; 263. 2; 282. 8; 289. 8; 459. 14

***χeru*** things or beings who are below, *i. e.*, terrestrial **2.** 5; **437.** 7; **447.** 15; **154.** 11; **136.** 10; **151.** 10; **230.** 6; **9.** 1; **213.** 14; those who have **424.** 5

***χert*** under, beneath **140.** 13; **143.** 3; **206.** 1; **294.** 1; **371.** 10; possessions **5.** 12; **28.** 16; **114.** 7; **199.** 12; **245.** 3; **259.** 2; **367.** 13; **442.** 16; **488.** 11; **384.** 8, 14; **407.** 13; **136.** 16

***χert hru*** things which the day hath, *i. e.*, times and seasons, or hours **106.** 10; **159.** 8; **223.** 8; **366.** 3; **482.** 7; **56.** 5; **211.** 12; **285.** 15; **330.** 16; **510.** 4; **494.** 13

***χer***, ***χerui*** testicles **56.** 11; **192.** 6; **503.** 6

***χer*** to fall down **2.** 7; **4.** 10, 11; **5.** 5; **6.** 7; **64.** 11; **80.** 1, 3, 5; **93.** 8; **98.** 8; **101.** 16; **105.** 10, 14; **106.** 3, 7; **119.** 9; **123.** 16; **169.** 7; **176.** 12; **198.** 6; **204.** 14; **246.** 13; **260.** 1; **280.** 2; **288.** 11; **291.** 14; **293.** 11, 14; **295.** 12; **371.** 12; **372.** 16; **373.** 2; **445.** 9; **480.** 3; **493.** 11; **503.** 6; **144.** 4; **304.** 13; **305.** 2, 4, 6, 9; **306.** 14; **307.** 7

***χerit*** the dead, the damned **62.** 2; **64.** 5; **217.** 7; sacrifices **232.** 7; victims for sacrifice **453.** 11, 13

***Χer*** name of a god **84.** 6

**Xerá** a proper name **222.** 6

**χeru** sound, voice, word, speech **2.** 9; **36.** 12; **105.** 15; **166.** 2; **230.** 12; **276.** 2; **288.** 12; **289.** 5; **314.** 4; **315.** 1; **342.** 8; **354.** 4, 5; **355.** 4; **377.** 4; **405.** 11; **408.** 14; **481.** 3, 14; **516.** 1; loud-voiced **258.** 6, 13; **341.** 5; plur. **24.** 11; **346.** 9; **503.** 17; with **271.** 11, 12, 14; **278.** 4; **285.** 14; **445.** 12; man's voice **246.** 16; **257.** 10, 14

**χerui** enemies **131.** 11; battle **457.** 11; hostile attacks **200.** 7, 9

**χer-āba** the name of a city near Memphis **22.** 7; **38.** 4; **68.** 12; **112.** 15; **118.** 13; **252.** 14, 18; **296.** 3, 11; **297.** 7; **379.** 12, 13; **380.** 7, 12; **382.** 1; **388.** 15; **439.** 6; **478.** 5; **483.** 15; **515.** 4

**χerp**, **χerpu** to be chief or master **185.** 5; **214.** 8; **234.** 9; **250.** 5; **281.** 12; **287.** 5; **92.** 3; offered, presented **463.** 8

**Xerp** Prince, Chief **186.** 11; plur. **166.** 2

**χerpu** a steering pole **205.** 8

**χerefu** lion-gods **301.** 7

**χer ḥeb** he who hath the service book **22.** 11; **337.** 13; **339.** 16; **497.** 9

**χerserȧu** a proper name 409. 2

**χersek** to destroy 54. 5; 177. 15; 210. 10; 280. 10; 283. 1; 295. 3; 437. 2; 481. 3; 488. 16; 269. 13; 270. 5; 274. 6

**χersek-Śu** a proper name 248. 10

**χerṭ** (?) child 109. 13; 247. 9

**χerṭ en seśeṭ** (sic) a title of the scribe Nebseni, child of the *seshet* chamber 139. 11; 387. 15

**χeχ** to run 340. 9; 408. 12

**χeχ** throat 96. 15; 213. 10, 11; 216. 15; 402. 13, 14; 403. 9; 404. 3, 16; 405. 5, 9, 16; 409. 14; 410. 6; 436. 6

**χeχu** darkness 195. 11

**χes** to slay 506. 9

**χesbeṭ** lapis-lazuli 14. 7; 126. 12; 140. 15; 177. 6; 228. 14; 229. 16; 316. 10; 420. 5; 446. 2, 3, 5; 447. 12; real lapis-lazuli 141. 7; 446. 8; 445. 16; 7. 10; blue-eyed 462. 6

**χesef** to meet, to meet hostilely, to drive back, to repulse, he who drives back 15. 11; 47. 15; 62. 11; 96. 3; 97. 7; 100. 10; 102. 3, 10; 105. 3; 107. 6, 11, 13; 108. 10; 109. 6; 110. 9;

111. 16; 169. 10; 210. 16; 211. 2; 229. 16; 241. 4; 251. 9; 279. 12; 284. 5; 286. 15; 293. 9; 296. 7, 16; 297. 15; 299. 4; 302. 8; 307. 11; 310. 5, 11, 13; 311. 5; 328. 7; 329. 3; 330. 13; 333. 2; 334. 12; 358. 14; 361. 1; 362. 6; 429. 5, 8; 437. 16; 480. 11; 497. 15; 501. 6; 504. 10; repulsed 21. 10; 85. 16; 86. 11; 95. 15; 128. 14; 283. 12; 491. 3; 501. 3; irresistible 51. 15; 63. 2; 350. 2; 379. 13; 383. 8; 383. 12

*χesefu* those who meet, adversaries 12. 2; 46. 12; 47. 14; 98. 6; 137. 12; 143. 11; 203. 3; 299. 7; 313. 12; 331. 10; 367. 6; 372. 3; bowings 40. 16; faces that repel 171. 2

*Χesef-aṭ* a proper name 360. 6

*Χesef-ḥrȧ-āś-χeru* a proper name 328. 5; 360. 4

*Χesef-ḥrȧ-χemiu* the herald of the seventh Ārit 329. 3

*Χesef-χemiu* a proper name 362. 1

*χesṭeḥ* to destroy 271. 5

*χet* steps 86. 3; 432. 16

*χet* fire, flame 77. 4; 82. 17; 192. 7; 251. 11; 287. 12, 13; 301. 1, 2; 302. 11 *(bis)*; 320. 8; 351. 12; 378. 5, 6; 381. 5; 515. 14

*χet* to follow (see also ) 193. 9; 475. 7; 479. 13

***χet*** to retreat, to go back **192**. 3; **487**. 8

***χetχet*** to go backwards **59**. 11; **226**. 10

***χetita*** fiends **390**. 12; **394**. 3

***χet*** board, list **3**. 7; wood, sceptre, staff **112**. 1; **128**. 12; **203**. 8; **504**. 10; branch **439**. 2; measure **218**. 14 *(bis)*; **353**. 12; **370**. 4 *(bis)*; **505**. 8; planks of a ship **206**. 15

***χet*** mast **205**. 15

***χetu*** . . . . . . **10**. 7

***χetu*** inscribed **141**. 7; **310**. 7; **311**. 8, 16; **440**. 5; graven **485**. 9

***χet*** things, affairs, cases, goods, property, offerings, possessions **3**. 7; **5**. 13; **62**. 11; **66**. 13; **135**. 1; **137**. 2; **142**. 1; **250**. 7; **314**. 6; **449**. 12; **451**. 1, 7; **476**. 12, 13; **515**. 9; things of every class and kind **226**. 6, 12; **479**. 2; all sorts of bad things **77**. 5; **226**. 9, 13; **366**. 9; **468**. 3; **477**. 1, 2, 14; **483**. 8; all kinds of beautiful and holy things **161**. 3; **316**. 12; **451**. 12; **464**. 13; **477**. 16; **514**. 14; **437**. 5; **365**. 10; **198**. 1; **71**. 7; **72**. 10; **81**. 9; **478**. 7; **483**. 9; **72**. 13; **76**. 5; **73**. 3; **81**. 11; **83**. 7; **79**. 4; **83**. 6; **168**. 10;

464. 14; 464. 14; 464. 4; their personal affairs **261. 14**

*χetem* to shut in, shut 30. 4; 139. 3; 142. 2; 153. 15; 160. 13; 192. 1; 193. 6; 194. 15; 195. 1

*χetemiu* those shut in 195. 16

*χetemit* closed place, prison 143. 14

*χeṭ* to float down stream 14. 10; 89. 7; 161. 5; 488. 1; 490. 6; 507. 2, 14; rippling like water 445. 14

*χeṭebet* 230. 2; =

# S.

**s** . . . . . . 440. 2

**s** her, she, its 1. 8; 3. 1; 4. 6; and see *passim*. 153. 1

**s** they, them, their 29. 15

**sa** person, man, one 5. 12 *(bis)*; 28. 9; 31. 9; 80. 11; 82. 15; 87. 10; 90. 8, 17; 93. 3; 116. 17; 132. 3; 156. 3; 178. 13; 270. 14; 308. 4; 316. 14; 317. 11, 15; 366. 4; 384. 8, 14; 410. 16; 414. 5; 488. 10; 492. 7; 501. 3; 502. 2; everybody, all folk 49. 5; 286. 5

**sa** son 13. 8; 52. 6; 97. 3; 116. 18; 119. 1, 16; 121. 6; 153. 2; 156. 10 *(bis)*; 161. 2; 233. 8; 291. 10; 308. 13; 314. 7; 317. 11; 337. 4; 360. 7; 379. 10; 407. 16; 417. 2; 452. 8, 13, 16; 455. 8; 458. 16; 459. 12; 460. 7; 471. 3; 481. 10; 482. 15; 484. 10; 485. 5, 14; 486. 10; firstborn son 276. 10; son of Rā 271. 8, 15; 272. 8, 16; 273. 2, 6; 449. 15; 471. 6; 472. 6

**sat** daughter 186. 5; 383. 3; 384. 16; 437. 3; the two daughters 175. 12; 495. 16

**Sa-mer-f** "son loving him", title of a priest 70. 3; 337. 13

**Sa-pa-nemmȧ** a proper name 416. 12

**Sa-ta** name of a serpent 188. 3, 4, 5

**sa** see

**sa** side, back 134. 6; 372. 5, 6; 494. 13; with 136. 2; following 466. 15

**sa** chamber (?) 144. 3

**sa** to know, to recognize 45. 16; 49. 5; 236. 3; 400. 8; 497. 15; knowledge 275. 12; 266. 6

**Sa** the god of knowledge 15. 7; 56. 5; 60. 15; 238. 14; 302. 10; 439. 4; 455. 10

**Sa-Ȧmenti-Rā** a proper name 457. 1, 5

**sa** protection, to protect, things which protect, amulets 273. 2; 439. 4; 479. 12; 482. 6, 7; 12. 16; 46. 6; 59. 5; 113. 5; 140. 7; 143. 8; 304. 10, 11, 13, 14; 305. 3, 7; 306. 4, 5, 12; 310. 5, 14; 311. 6, 5; 386. 10; 403. 5; 411. 9; 434. 13; 510. 8; 511. 9; 143. 8; with 382. 12; 383. 1, 7, 10, 14, 16

**saa** — to watch, to keep guard over, to protect, to keep in restraint, to fetter, to bind, **66.** 8, 10; **68.** 3; **86.** 11; **126.** 6; **127.** 10; **150.** 8; **183.** 9; **200.** 7; **234.** 12; **373.** 9; **375.** 5; **379.** 1; **403.** 6; **438.** 12; **460.** 1; **462.** 6; **495.** 15; **504.** 15; **505.** 1; **512.** 13; , , guarded **101.** 15; **333.** 16; **437.** 13, 15, 16; **440.** 16; **291.** 11

**saau**, **saautu** — ward, restraint **80.** 9; **457.** 15; **359.** 3; **360.** 5, 13; **361.** 7, 15

**saa**, **saau**, **saai**, **saaiti** — warden, warder, guard, guardian, he who fetters, he who is fettered **64.** 13; **65.** 1; **164.** 3; **186.** 7; **327.** 13, 16; **328.** 3, 7, 11, 15; **329.** 3; **334.** 11, 14; **335.** 6, 8; **336.** 1, 4, 13, 16; **337.** 9, 11; **338.** 4, 8, 16; **339.** 3, 11, 14; **340.** 7, 11; **341.** 4, 7; **343.** 12; **346.** 9, 11; **347.** 16; **349.** 16; **350.** 8; **351.** 5, 12; **352.** 3, 13; **353.** 3, 11; **354.** 3; **358.** 4; **456.** 12; **464.** 6; plur. **329.** 6; **195.** 11, 15; **224.** 15; **225.** 1; **429.** 6; **195.** 12; **71.** 8; **249.** 11; **475.** 14; **275.** 4;

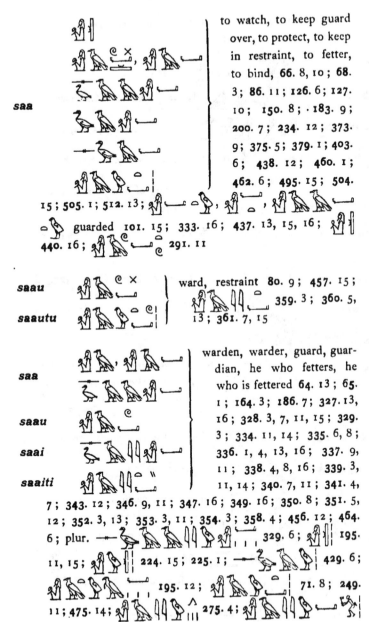

71. 12; and see 86. 12; 172. 5; 195. 16; 196. 4, 8; 271. 2; 272. 2; 274. 4; 320. 4

***saatu*** fetters 147. 4

***Saa*** a name of Osiris 320. 11

***Saau-ur*** a proper name 457. 1, 2

***Sau*** the god Sa or Saa, *q. v.* 348. 8

***Saau*** the city of Saïs 111. 13; 117. 11; 257. 3; 323. 10; 413. 12; 496. 3

***Saau ḥeri*** Upper Saïs 322. 7; 323. 14

***Saau χeri*** Lower Saïs 321. 7; 323. 13

***Sabes*** the herald of the second Ārit 327. 17

***sam*** loins 447. 5

***sam*** (or ***sma***), ***samt*** to join, to unite with, to be united to, union, assembly 42. 14; 115. 6; 125. 10; 176. 10; 210. 13; 215. 2; 226. 5, 10; 377. 8

***Samti uati*** uniter of the two ways 438. 11

***samt åuset*** burial place (?) 67. 12

***sam ta***, ***samt ta*** union with earth, *i. e.*, burial 23. 14; 95. 11; 137. 10; 213. 10; 390. 6; 402. 13; 403. 10; 488. 6; 501. 13; with 65. 7, 10; 461. 2; day of the funeral 404. 13; 405. 6

***samau*** darkness 35. 1; 85. 5; 245. 7

***sami***, ***samai***, ***samaiu***, ***sami*** fiends 68. 11; 71. 13; 75. 4; 78. 10

***samait*** fiends 146. 12; 293. 10; 382. 11; 388. 2; 453. 4; 496. 6

***samatu*** torture chamber 66. 13

***samait*** tresses 122. 12; 171. 9

***samt*** bows of a boat (?) 207. 3

***samau*** branches 180. 1; 495. 10

***Samait*** two goddesses 144. 4

***Samti*** a proper name 338. 8

***samau*** . . . . . . 289. 8

***samet*** to burn up 58. 14

***samut*** hair 121. 17

***sanehemu*** grasshoppers 262. 12

***Sanehem*** city of grasshoppers 508. 10

***saru*** order for dismissal 351. 7; restrained speech (?) 443. 4

***sariu*** a class of divine beings 144. 11

***Saḥ*** Orion 22. 8; 118; 20; 137. 3; 153. 9; 323. 4; 449. 14, 15; 473. 3; a name of Osiris 320. 11; 86. 16

***saḥ*** to journey, to travel 23. 8; 46. 7; 153. 10; 451. 6

***saḥu*** fingers 113. 3; 118. 21; 492. 13; toes (?) 448. 9

***Saḥ-en-mut-f*** a proper name 264. 15

***saḥ*** an estate, homestead 14. 13; 16. 11; 70. 9, 15; 434. 11

***saqa*** to collect, to gather together 130. 2; 138. 15; 140. 1; 173. 10; 241. 20; 289. 6; 361. 5; 385. 10

***Saq-baiu*** "Gatherer of souls", the name of a boat 130. 2; 241. 20

***Saqenaqat*** a proper name 415. 15

***sat*** apparel, robe, garment 163. 2; 176. 9; 229. 4

[illegible] to think scorn of the god () 250. [illegible] 250. 4

[illegible] evil one 64. 11

**satu** wall **310.** 8, 11; **311.** 2, 3, 10, 11; **312.** 3

**sat** earth, ground **36.** 14; **208.** 5; **246.** 10; **268.** 4; **436.** 5; the floor of a chamber **265.** 12; **267.** 7

**sati** threshold **264.** 12

**Satiu** name of a city **257.** 9

**sati** to burn **308.** 6

**sat**, **satu**, **satet** to shoot forth something, to shoot at, to be shot **63.** 7; **68.** 14; **150.** 9; **288.** 2; **353.** 13; **463.** 16; **494.** 4

**satetu**, **satetiu**, **sateti** to illumine, to shine, light, rays **2.** 11; **7.** 11; **8.** 4; **10.** 1, 14; **11.** 10; **12.** 6; **37.** 4; **40.** 1, 10; **134.** 14; **142.** 12; **291.** 15; **476.** 6 *(bis)*; **511.** 6, 10

**satet** to sow seed **227.** 10; sprinkled **486.** 7

**satetit** seed, progeny **174.** 5

**satet** adversaries **480.** 3

**Satet** name of a goddess **247.** 9

**satet** an Asiatic woman **445.** 14

***Satet-ṭemui*** (?) a proper name 370. 5; (var. )

***saṭu*** terrors 108. 6

***Sȧ*** name of a city 325. 3

***Sȧa*** the god Sa 457. 1, 3

***Sȧa*** name of a city 505. 14

***sȧat*** to encroach, to attack 251. 3

***sȧati*** slaughterers 191. 12; 192. 12

***sȧu*** to drink 414. 7; 417. 14; 420. 12; 510. 5

***sȧbit*** animals for sacrifice 154. 14

***sȧbkui***, ***sȧbt*** to weep 25. 2; 339. 1

***sȧp*** to judge, to decide, to pass sentence, to compute, to decree, to inspect, to examine, to award 13. 3; 22. 2; 79. 3; 84. 4; 92. 5; 106. 15; 128. 17; 158. 14; 186. 13; 235. 14; 275. 5; 313. 12; 485. 7; 491. 12; 492. 1; judged, computed 41. 15; 244. 14; 245. 1; judges 113. 12; 232. 12; to acquit 444. 1

***sȧp*** judgment 342. 2, 9, 16; 343. 8, 15; 344. 7, 13; 345. 6, 13; 346. 4; 354. 14; 355. 5; 356. 2, 7, 13; 357. 5, 13; 476. 11, 12; 66. 7; 67. 2; 355. 11; 75. 8

**sȧpu**
**sȧpt** account, reckoning, examination, judgment 53. 3; 74. 2, 9, 12; 97. 4; 141. 10; 186. 15; 275. 5; 309. 15
**sȧpti**

**sȧm** to be gracious 485. 2

**sȧn** length, extent 370. 6

**sȧn** to do good to, to benefit, to nourish 209. 16; 496. 9; things which benefit 462. 8

**sȧn** clay 303. 11; 310. 7, 15; 311. 1, 7, 16; 333. 11, 14

**sȧn** to pass 199. 10

**sȧn** to pull, to draw 69. 7; safe 99. 9

**sȧs** (?) six 20. 3; 137. 1; 147. 2; sixth 137. 5; 328. 13; 338. 2; 361. 5; 143. 5; sixth day of the festival 496. 16

**Sȧsȧ** name of a city 203. 6, 7

**sȧka** to relieve 53. 14

**sȧqer** to make strong or perfect 45. 10; 210. 6; 278. 11; 288. 8; 291. 7, 11; 292. 3; 294. 7; 309. 10; 317. 12, 13; 320. 14; 496. 13

**Sȧti** name of a city 322. 5; 325. 3

**sȧtia** executioners (?) 193. 5

*sāṭi* headsman, executioner **62.** 4

*sāṭen* to transfer **404.** 10

*sāa* to magnify **25.** 3; **42.** 11; **45.** 11; **496.** 14

*sāu* to provision **275.** 11

*sāui* journeyings **138.** 5

*sāb* . . . . . . . **392.** 1

*sāb* jackal **126.** 17; plur. **126.** 17

*sāba* to make an entrance into **45.** 13; **497.** 7

*sāb* to purify, to wash, to cleanse **142.** 2; **463.** 10; **502.** 1; **508.** 10; plated, washed **316.** 11; **509.** 6, 7; **291.** 3; **216.** 12; **369.** 11

*sām* to devour, to consume **24.** 10; **260.** 15; **418.** 8; **516.** 4

*sāmiu* devourers **249.** 12; **260.** 9, 15; **269.** 10

*sām* flowers **101.** 14

sāma . . . . . . **483.** 8

**sānᵡ** to vivify, to keep alive 7. 16; 9. 3; 138. 10; 173. 14; 252. 4; 278. 12; 332. 4; 333. 1; 461. 8; 481. 8; 511. 14; 513. 4; ⟨hieroglyphs⟩ 369. 13; ⟨hieroglyphs⟩ 489. 4; ⟨hieroglyphs⟩ 45. 3

**sār** to make to advance 4. 14; 156. 15; 175. 4; 245. 11; 260. 2; 279. 9; 332. 1, 4; 426. 7; ⟨hieroglyphs⟩ 203. 1; ⟨hieroglyphs⟩ 458. 4

**sāriu** ⟨hieroglyphs⟩ those who make to advance 269. 6; 271. 3; 274. 4; 438. 4; ⟨hieroglyphs⟩ 440. 7

**Sāḥ** ⟨hieroglyphs⟩ the divine spiritual body 23. 13; 175. 16; 190. 13

**sāḥ** ⟨hieroglyphs⟩ to become or to endow with a divine spiritual body 31. 5; 163. 10; 168. 3; 170. 1; 171. 7; ⟨hieroglyphs⟩ 168. 7

**sāḥ** ⟨hieroglyphs⟩ the spiritual body 278. 3; 284. 4; 303. 2; 362. 5; 405. 13; 425. 7; 451. 7; 475. 3 ; 509. 15; plur. 190. 6; 240. 5; 245. 14; 247. 12; 261. 10; 407. 8; 496. 8; 513. 11; ⟨hieroglyphs⟩ of **sāḥu** the god ⟨hieroglyph⟩ 241. 3; 358. 14; with ⟨hieroglyphs⟩ 167. 5; with ⟨hieroglyphs⟩ 449. 1

**sāḥ** ⟨hieroglyphs⟩ honour 281. 8; 329. 11

**Sāḥā** to set up, to make to stand up 22. 3; 177. 10; 211. 15; 212. 1; 213. 2; 414. 8; 435. 12; 441. 5; ⟨hieroglyphs⟩ 73. 2, 5, 7; ⟨hieroglyphs⟩ 412. 6; ⟨hieroglyphs⟩ 72. 1, 5; 79. 1; 81. 8; 83. 5

*su* he, him, it 4. 6; 5. 4; 11. 11; 24. 1; 25. 3; 26. 3; 42. 12; 53. 13; 56. 16; 68. 2; 81. 16; 92. 3; 97. 3; 98. 9; 106. 5, 6; 111. 5; 123. 8, 16; 141. 12 *(bis)*; 151. 8; 226. 16; 227. 14; 231. 16; 243. 14; 279. 3; 284. 2; 291. 9; 294. 10; 306. 11; 316. 13; 361. 4; 379. 15; 385. 8; 401. 15; 403. 12; 406. 9; 408. 14; 418. 3; 438. 5; 444. 1; 452. 1; 456. 2; 461. 13; 466. 4; 468. 15; 476. 4; 479. 9; 481. 6; 487. 4; 491. 11; 497. 16; 501. 12; 505. 6; = 492. 9, 10; them 10. 9, 11

*su ṭesef* he himself 92. 4; 100. 7; 119. 14

*sua* to pass 163. 16; 216. 1; 203. 3

*suaś*, *suauś* to adore, to praise 6. 4; 7. 15; 10. 4; 40. 7; 138. 7; 274. 5; 419. 8, 15; 473. 14

*suaṭ* to make vigorous, to make to flourish 95. 10; 158. 12; 174. 6; 230. 6; 315. 5; 363. 15; 482. 5; 483. 15; 485. 13; 501. 12; 513. 5

*suȧs* (?) decay 112. 4

*sui* crocodile 97. 10

*sun* to open 186. 10

*sun* destroyed 109. 12

**sun** / **sunen** 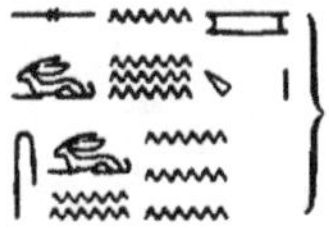 pool, lake **130**. 6; **242**. 5

**sunȧt** 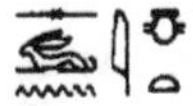 unguent **337**. 3

**Sunnu**  the city called by the Greeks Syene **321**. 8; **323**. 15

**surȧ**  to drink **103**. 7; **124**. 17; **125**. 5; **132**. 9; **133**. 5; **175**. 14; **179**. 8; **224**. 2; **225**. 9; **238**. 16; **300**. 7, 9; **378**. 7, 15; **379**. 2, 5; **425**. 4; **436**. 11; **440**. 6; **465**. 12, 13; **466**. 13

**suriu**  drinkers **146**. 9

**surṭ**  **485**. 12 see *seruṭ* 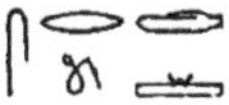

**suha**  to supplicate **348**. 9

**suḥ**  a garment **449**. 1

**suḥt**  egg **61**. 7; **85**. 14; **116**. 1; **126**. 5, 9; **127**. 11; **131**. 2; **157**. 14; **164**. 9; **185**. 14; **211**. 5; **374**. 5, 10, 13; **441**. 1;  double egg **113**. 15; **447**. 6, 11

**suχa**  evil recollection (?) **191**. 5, 8, 15; **192**. 4

**suχeṭ**  to mummify (?) **497**. 5

**suser** 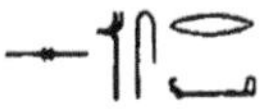 to strengthen **210**. 12, 15

**suseχ**  to make broad **135**. 10; **320**. 15; **334**. 1; **497**. 5; to make wide (*i. e.*, long) the steps **470**. 12; **487**. 1

**Suḳaṭi**  name of a god **420**. 11

*sut* it, himself, they, them 177. 15; 305. 12; 313. 1; 399. 15

*sut* hair 136. 3

*Sut*
*Suti* the god Sut or Set 31. 2; 66. 3; 92. 13; 112. 14; 122. 13; 126. 10; 146. 12, 15; 171. 15; 172. 10; 181. 10; 192. 5; 201. 1; 206. 7; 219. 10; 231. 14, 16; 235. 1; 293. 10; 294. 4; 305. 11; 306. 8; 315. 11; 376. 8; 395. 6; 414. 13; 496. 4

*Suti-mes* a proper name 489. 13

*suten* king 1. 7; 4. 3; 8. 16; 9. 12; 11. 12; 13. 7; 14. 4; 19. 9; 36. 5; 40. 11; 51. 9; 70. 12; 141. 13; 257. 16; 258. 2; 268. 8; 276. 11; 471. 8; 478. 4; the reigning king 260. 6; plur. 14. 4; sovereignty 485. 6; 487. 2; 120. 1

*suten net* King of the South and North 97. 2; 141. 8; 145. 14; 214. 1; 271. 8, 15; 272. 8; 273. 6; plur. 398. 10; and 268. 12; 300. 8

*suten net Ȧusȧr* a title of Osiris 39. 7

*suten ḥeḥ* king of eternity, a title of Osiris 452. 5

*suten Ṭuat* king of the underworld, a title of Osiris 482. 8

*suten sa* royal son, *i. e.*, prince 97. 3; 141. 9; 309. 12

***suten ḥemt*** royal wife, *i. e.*, queen **415.** 8

***suten ān*** royal scribe **11.** 3; **23.** 16; **24.** 4; **25.** 12; **37.** 6

***suten śes*** linen of kings **213.** 8

***suten ṭā ḥetep*** "give a royal oblation" **223.** 6; **514.** 11

***Suten-ḥenen*** Heracleopolis **20.** 11; **39.** 2; **51.** 9; **54.** 10; **65.** 4, 6, 11; **67.** 10; **111.** 16; **245.** 14; **252.** 3; **253.** 12; **276.** 14; **307.** 9; **490.** 3

***sutennu*** stretched out **420.** 7

***suṭeχ*** to embalm **45.** 13; **483.** 13

***sufa*** to make to set out **226.** 16; **227.** 4; **228.** 13; **230.** 7; **295.** 13; **479.** 9

***sufa*** to make strong, to preserve **12.** 8; **15.** 13; **96.** 5; **106.** 7; **122.** 1; **136.** 13; **156.** 3, 4, 10; **157.** 1, 5, 11, 15; **212.** 14; **277.** 2; **295.** 2; **338.** 7; **410.** 8; **416.** 7, 8, 14; **486.** 12; **122.** 14

***si*** it, its, them **12.** 13; **62.** 8; **114.** 4; **163.** 6; **184.** 5; **225.** 4; **235.** 9, 15; **327.** 13, 17; 328. [illegible], 7, 11, 15; **329.** 3; **373.** 9; **379.** 1; **391.** 10, 12; 393. 9; 421. 12, 13, 14, 15; **457.** 16; **504.** 11, 12, 16; **505.** 1, 6, 12, 13

***sia*** (?) (for [illegible]) to cut 357. 15

***Seb*** the god of the earth 13. 9; 15. 5; 33. 5; **61.** 2; **66.** 4; **77.** 15; **80.** 9; **94.** 3; 100. 12; 103. 8; **107.** 7; **108.** 5; **110.** 13; **125.** 8; **126.** 7; 146. 15, 16; 150. 7; **151.** 7; **154.** 1; **166.** 15; **180.** 9, 12, 13; 201. [illegible]; 264

13; 265. 11; 276. 11; 292. 8; 294. 4; 298. 1; 315. 11; 318. 8; 325. 16; 347. 16; 388. 9; 393. 10, 12; 405. 3; 425. 12; 436. 2; 437. 8; 438. 8; 443. 9; 478. 13; 479. 8; 485. 7; 487. 2; 89. 11; 509. 7; 509. 13

**seb** to pass by 10. 13; 13. 8; 19. 3; 103. 10; 113. 12; 128. 5, 6, 7, 17; 131. 12, 13, 15; 218. 5; 301. 7; 307. 14; 129. 14; 241. 18; 460. 10

**seb** star, star-god 471. 5; 472. 4; plur. 44. 6; 204. 15; 224. 11; 291. 3; 292. 16; 420. 13; 439. 14; 461. 14; 497. 11; 447. 15

**sba**
**sba**
**sbaut**
**seb**
**sbat** door, gate 55. 5, 6, 11; 110. 13; 114. 10; 187. 1; 221. 4, 12; 264. 2, 4, 7, 10, 12, 14; 265. 1, 4, 7, 10; 268. 11; 273. 7; 312. 8; 333. 4; 368. 5, 14; 409. 5; 432. 14; 456. 4; 456. 7; 478. 14

**sbau** doors, gates, 14. 12; 33. 4; 90. 4; 103. 8; 105. 16; 160. 12; 187. 8; 203. 13; 272. 3, 9; 273. 5, 7; 275. 9; 278. 16; 279. 1; 307. 12; 319. 16; 320. 2, 3; 410. 4; 475. 14; 492. 3; 514. 6; 274. 13; divine double door 272. 11

**sbaut** to rebel (?) 515. 16

**sebaķi** helpless one **455.** 15

**Sebȧ** a goddess **7.** 6

**Sebȧu**, **sebȧ** fiend **2.** 6, 15; **12.** 10; **47.** 15; **78.** 12; **137.** 6; **143.** 6; **38.** 14; **105.** 9; plur. **19.** 1; **20.** 1; **71.** 8, 13; **81.** 7; **160.** 12; **197.** 3, 10; **198.** 4, 9, 16; **209.** 3; **325.** 11; **341.** 16; **343.** 6; **344.** 5; **345.** 5; **354.** 12; **356.** 5; **357.** 4; **437.** 14; **453.** 3, 11; **457.** 13; **36.** 8; **88.** 4

**seben** to retreat, to depart **105.** 4, 14

**sebeḥ** for to make festival **6.** 1

**sebeḥ**, **sebḥu**, **sebḥet** to praise, to supplicate **341.** 5; **354.** 4; **471.** 12; praised **428.** 14; **320.** 5*

**sebeχ** to become master of **301.** 14

**sebeχbeχet** to scatter **68.** 9

**sebχet** pylon **194.** 8; **248.** 8, 10; **334.** 9; **335.** 4, 15; **336.** 11; **337.** 7; **338.** 2, 14; **339.** 9; **340.** 5; **341.** 2, 13; **342.** 1, 5, 12; **343.** 3, 11; **344.** 2, 9, 16; **345.** 8, 15; **346.** 5, 14; **349.** 14; **350.** 6, 12; **351.** 2, 10, 16; **353.** 1, 9; **354.** 1, 9, 16; **355.** 7, 13; **356.** 3, 8; **424.** 16; **428.** 13; **474.** 5; **422.** 12

**sebχet** 〔hieroglyphs〕 pylons 46. 1; 246. 16; 270. 1, 7; 309. 5; 320. 1; 333. 3; 334. 7; 336. 1; 349. 11; 362. 9; 475. 16; 514. 8; 〔hieroglyphs〕 431. 4, 5

**Sebek** 〔hieroglyphs〕 a form of the Sun-god 58. 12; 158. 2; 188. 10, 11, 12; 218. 15; 220. 14; 233. 10, 12; 234. 2; 265. 2; 390. 16; 〔hieroglyphs〕 of the 〔hieroglyphs〕 443. 12; 〔hieroglyphs〕 443. 13

**sebeq** 〔hieroglyphs〕 thigh 391. 3; 394. 12

**Sebeq-en-Nemu** 〔hieroglyphs〕 a proper name 391. 3

**Sebeq-en-Tem** 〔hieroglyphs〕 a proper name 396. 8

**Sebek̆** 〔hieroglyphs〕

**Sebk̆a** 〔hieroglyphs〕 name of a god 296. 8; 297. 2; 298. 1

**Sebak̆u** 〔hieroglyphs〕

**sebt** 〔hieroglyphs〕 satisfied (?) 135. 7

**sebt** 〔hieroglyphs〕 walls 350. 1

**sep** 〔hieroglyphs〕 time, season, occasion, opportunity 3. 1, 16; 5. 7; 122. 3; 148. 3; 260. 3; 405. 14, 15; 415. 13; 443. 5; 482. 1; plur. 〔hieroglyphs〕 39. 8; 124. 8; 183. 9; 〔hieroglyphs〕 224. 14; 〔hieroglyphs〕 493. 2; 〔hieroglyphs〕 fate 〔hieroglyphs〕 459. 9; 〔hieroglyphs〕 126. 11; 〔hieroglyphs〕 evil hap, ill luck 260. 6; case, trial, matter, affair 21. 16; 〔hieroglyphs〕 a right case 16. 2; 286. 16; 467. 8; 〔hieroglyphs〕

unlucky time 5. 10; at no time, never 146. 11; 285. 13; 289. 16; the occasion of the night 467. 4; another time 134. 11; 142. 10; first time, primeval time 9. 1; 315. 10; 338. 6; 487. 14

***sep sen*** twice 4. 2 *(bis)*, 7; 8. 1; 95. 2; 96. 1; 106. 1, 2; 107. 1; 112. 3; 123. 6, 14; 383. 2; 419. 9, 13, 14, 15; 428. 1; 443. 2; 458. 9, 10; 482. 8; 492. 9; 501. 5; 502. 4; 505. 9; 517. 4; duplicity, a double motive 17. 7; 39. 10; 70. 4; four times 79. 15; 80. 2; 109. 3; 112. 2, 6; 180. 7; 252. 1; millions of times 152. 13; 182. 8; 187. 15; 210. 3; 308. 10; 402. 16

***sep*** to pass sentence on some one 309. 8

***sep*** crown (?) 323. 4

***sep***, ***sept*** lip, edge 494. 7; 505. 15; edge of the water 233. 14

***septi***, ***seputi*** the two lips 102. 5; 112. 11; 117. 5; 373. 1; 446. 10

***Sepa*** name of a god 58. 4; 153. 13; 154. 2

***sper*** to come forth 48. 5; 158. 11 *(bis)*; 201. 15; 224. 12; 225. 5; 227. 11, 14; 240. 3; 249. 3; 259. 16; 270. 14; 333. 4; 349. 13; 350. 5, 12; 351. 2, 9, 16; 352. 10; 353. 1, 8; 354. 1, 8, 15; 355. 6, 13; 356. 9; 357. 1, 6, 9, 14; 362. 8; 341. 5; 49. 16

***sepeḥ*** to advance 183. 1

***sepḫu*** to fetter **383**. 4, 5, 6; **416**. 16; **419**. 7; **454**. 1

***Sepes*** a proper name **469**. 2; and see **311**. 12 *(bis)*, 14

***sept*** nome **230**. 8; plur. **227**. 5; **486**. 3; **22**. 5

***Sept*** the star Sothis **62**. 11; **99**. 8; **280**. 5; **456**. 4; **502**. 15; *Septet* **213**. 13; **228**. 15; **377**. 4; **381**. 13

***sept*** a kind of wood **338**. 12

***sept*** to be provided or equipped with **9**. 10; **11**. 4; **152**. 9; **171**. 14; **219**. 14; **225**. 6; **263**. 2; **271**. 3; **298**. 7; **340**. 8; *septu, septet* provided **62**. 13; **353**. 4; **182**. 14; **227**. 12; **229**. 14; **463**. 7

***Sept-χeri-neḥait-ȧmi-beq*** a proper name **263**. 2

***sept*** leg **391**. 8

***Sept-mast-en-Rerti*** a proper name **391**. 9

***sef*** yesterday **8**. 2; **27**. 9; **52**. 2, 3; **57**. 5; **113**. 11; **114**. 12; **115**. 14; **134**. 10; **142**. 9; **181**. 7; **190**. 12; **212**. 9; **236**. 11; **468**. 14; **469**. 1; **2**. 14; **183**. 11

***sef*** be ye gracious (with ) **183**. 8

***sefi*** babe **416.** 9

***sefeχ*** to untie, to withdraw, to unloose, to undress **147.** 5; **150.** 8; **156.** 7, 12; **157.** 1, 6, 12, 16; **158.** 3; **175.** 3; **179.** 8; **224.** 5; **380.** 14; **448.** 14; **405.** 2; **405.** 3

***seft*** to slay **75.** 6

***seft*** knife **392.** 13

***seft*** unguent **340.** 1; pitch **311.** 9

***sem*** a priest **20.** 8; **238.** 7

***sem*** image, figure **40.** 16; **412.** 9; plur. **407.** 8

***sem*** figure, design, drawing, form, similitude **145.** 14; **211.** 6; **268.** 3; **332.** 14; **333.** 14

***sem*** to lead, to guide, guide **5.** 9; **37.** 13; **85.** 8; **92.** 13; **103.** 9; **111.** 1; **169.** 12; **197.** 5; **203.** 11; **230.** 5; **240.** 7, 8; **244.** 12; **247.** 8; **271.** 7; **272.** 8; **278.** 1; **280.** 7; **282.** 9; **284.** 4; **326.** 10; **329.** 13, 15; **336.** 2; **347.** 8, 10, 13; **385.** 7; **386.** 15; **388.** 1; **448.** 9; **474.** 3; **482.** 1; **483.** 10; **504.** 12; **506.** 11; **512.** 5; to guide **243.** 6; divine guide **505.** 13; plur. guides, leaders **45.** 12; **135.** 2; **178.** 16; **226.** 15; **275.** 8; **273.** 16;

274. 9; and see 279. 9; 317. 15; 472. 11; 473. 4; 474. 4; 475. 13; 365. 13, 15

***semu*** to lead, leader 125. 2; 152. 9; 319. 1; 373. 16

***sem*** guidance 224. 14; 438. 12; 440. 1

***semt*** advance, journey 379. 15; 464. 13

***sem*** a name of Rā 65. 12; 94. 9; to direct affairs 220. 12

***Semu-ta***, ***Semu-taui*** a proper name 205. 1; 364. 10; 392. 9

***Semu-ḥeḥ*** a proper name 54. 15

***semt åb*** gratification (?) 213. 6

***sma*** to join, to unite 137. 4; 143. 4

***sma*** to slay 93. 14; 340. 9

***sma*** . . . . . . 442. 8

***smaiu*** renewal 389. 1

***smaår*** to oppress 250. 1; escape 336. 14

***smam*** to slay 250. 10 *(bis)*; 253. 5; 254. 6; 353. 5; 400. 16; 401. 2; 453. 2, 15; 480. 2

***smamiu*** slaughterers, slaughtered things 122. 14; 399. 16; 400. 15

***smamu*** victims **453.** 12

***Smam*** name of a god **132.** 14; **462.** 3

***Smam-ur*** the soul of Seb **66.** 4

***smam*** a bull **183.** 6

***Smam*** name of a lake **230.** 4

***Smamti*** a proper name **352.** 8

***smamu*** foliage or branches of a tree **151.** 11; **244.** 5, 9, 15

***smamu*** clouds **202.** 14

***smat*(?) *ent* *ḥeb*** half-monthly festival **177.** 1, 4; **234.** 6, 10; **236.** 3. 5; **238.** 13; **330.** 2; **366.** 2; **371.** 10; **391.** 16

***smaā*** to pay what is due **486.** 3

***smaāiu*** slayers **18.** 14

***smaā-χeru*** to justify, to make triumphant **18.** 11; **19.** 3; **48.** 3; **71.** 3, 4, 5, 14, 15; **72.** 7, 8, 15, 16; **73.** 7, 8, 14, 15; **74.** 5, 6, 14; **75.** 2, 8, 9; **76.** 1, 2, 5, 10, 11; **77.** 13; **78.** 6, 10, 13; **81.** 3; **82.** 2, 4; **83.** 3; **84.** 1, 2; **140.** 10; **141.** 3; **145.** 9; **272.** 1, 10; **273.** 4; **274.** 14, 16; **275.** 10, 15; **347.** 14; **348.** 1; **481.** 3, 15; **488.** 15; **504.** 12

***smȧ*** to report, to announce, to bear a message, report, message **25.** 2; **63.** 8; **102.** 7; **108.** 1; **186.** 9, 16; **261.** 6; **266.** 4, 6, 14; **267.** 5; **271.** 3; **274.** 4; **516.** 8;

266. 10; 267. 2; 267. 9; 329. 7

***smȧ*** herald 327. 14, 17; 328. 4, 8, 12, 16; 329. 4; 330. 2; 358. 5; 359. 4, 13; 360. 6, 14; 361. 8, 16; plur. 475. 15; report 24. 13

***smȧ*** leather 439. 16; plur. 221. 8; 368. 10

***smu*** (or ***uasmu***) refined copper 14. 6; 41. 13

***semu*** herbs, pastures, grass land 251. 7; 268. 3; 333. 12; 379. 7

***semiu*** devourers 24. 3

***semi*** to entreat 261. 13

***[illegible]*** to stablish 12. 4; 79. 5; 107. 7; 111. 8, 9; 121. 16; 122. 10; 128. 19; 160. 16; 169. 6; 172. 6; 195. 2; 204. 10; 211. 15; 212. 2; 225. 13; [illegible]; 282. 9; 283. 3; 310. 16; 311. 8; 367. 7, 8, 9, 10; [illegible]; 453. 6; 454. 16; 472. 13; 473. 2; 479. 5; 486. [illegible]; 505. 10; 81. 11; 235. 13; 310. 6; 487. 4; 73. 2; 173. 3; 213. 13; 463. 7

***[illegible]*** a kind of goose 63. 14; 179. 10; 202. 13; 376. 12; 377. 3; 438. 7; 493. 13; plur. 506. 9

***[illegible]*** to perfect 275. 11; 359. 16; 481. 11; [illegible]. 12

**smert** eyelids **446.** 8

**smer** to inflict pain **250.** 9

**smeḥ** to fill full **348.** 14

**smeḥ**
**smeḥ** to flood out, to submerge **29.** 1; **247.** 10; **349.** 1; **453.** 8; **384.** 13; **384.** 9

**semχeṭ** to stumble(?) **436.** 12

**smes** to produce **9.** 11; made to be born **338.** 7

**sems**
**semsu** firstborn, eldest **25.** 7; **104.** 7; **153.** 6; **154.** 1, 3; **184.** 16; **206.** 10; **330.** 12; **393.** 6; plur. **135.** 9; **224.** 15

**smet** to pry into something **254.** 11

**Smetu** the warder of the first Ārit **327.** 12

**smet** woven with, or shot with (of cloth) **440.** 4

**Smet āqa** name of a rudder **130.** 5

**Smeti-āqa** name of the *mātchabet* of a boat **242.** 3

**Smetti** a proper name **358.** 2

**smetru** to put right or straight, to adjust **137.** 3; **262.** 1

**sen** they, their, them 2. 8; 7. 10; 49. 15; 50. 1. 7; 53. 13, 15; 58. 3; 61. 4; 63. 6; 66. 11, 12, 13; 80. 7, 9; 86. 12; 93. 8, 9; 106. 5; 153. 4; 171. 12; 314. 6; 331. 13; 339. 4; 347. 16; 359. 8; 366. 5; 371. 5; 374. 9; 382. 11; 395. 3; 416. 8; 421. 1; 423. 15; 425. 3; 431. 2; 434. 14; 443. 17; 445. 10; 446. 11; 447. 14; 451. 3; 452. 3, 11; 458. 2, 3, 6; 460. 7; 461. 8; 464. 4; 471. 12, 13; 475. 14; 478. 1; 479. 2; 487. 8, 9; 492. 14; 497. 15; 501. 11; 506. 9, 11, 12, 14, 15; 507. 1

**sen**
**sent** two 192. 3; 222. 1; 304. 4; 361. 9; 413. 14; 416. 12; 464. 7

**sen**
**sent** second, fellow, equal, companion, counterpart, like, equal 10. 2; 49. 5; 57. 3; 138. 3; 210. 15; 262. 13; 327. 15; 335. 4; 350. 6; 359. 2, 6; 443. 2; 459. 3; 450. 1; 420. 10

**sen** to smell, to snuff the air, to breathe 155. 8; 279. 2; 289. 3

**sen ta** to smell the earth, *i. e.*, to pay homage to someone 110. 14; 223. 2; 484. 3, 7; 489. 10

**sensen** breathings, breaths 508. 3; 510. 2, 10, 11; 511. 7, 8, 9, 16; 512. 6; 513. 2, 4, 13, 14; 514. 14; 516. 15, 16

**sen** house, abode (?) 68. 14

**sen** brother 73. 11; 79. 13; 81. 13; 152. 16; 153. 1; 205. 4; 405. 2; 485. 11; 83. 9; 276. 16

***senui***, ***senti*** — the two divine brethren **237.** 6; **485.** 1; of **232.** 11; of **232.** 11

***sennu*** — brethren, see

***sent*** — sister **163.** 7; **102.** 12; **304.** 4; **313.** 3; **478.** 17; **485.** 3; **446.** 4

***seni*** — companion, fellow **340.** 8

***sensen*** — to fraternize, to act or become as a brother to someone, to be at peace with, to be reconciled **44.** 6; **446.** 4; **479.** 6; **485.** 4; to smell **247.** 2

***sensen*** — to become corrupt, to decay **401.** 6

***Sennu*** — a city near Åpu (Panopolis, Akhmîm) **245.** 15

***senå*** — adoration **315.** 2

***senåha*** — injury **340.** 16

***senāāt*** — to be gratified (?) **262.** 14

***sen***, ***seni***, ***sent*** — to pass away, to depart **101.** 14; **115.** 6, 11; **116.** 3; **173.** 10; **482.** 12

**seni** to slit, to cut 191. 8, 13, 16; 192. 16; 193. 6

**senb** to be well, to get well, health 231. 16; 232. 4; 460. 5

**senbȧ** to be healthy 426. 12; health 513. 2

**senb** wall 334. 12; plur. 129. 3

**senbet** libation vessel 203. 9; 450. 11

**senpu** slaughterings 137. 10

**snef** blood 24. 3; 56. 1; 137. 9; 143. 9; 206. 12; 207. 11; 249. 12; 254. 5; 293. 3; 333. 8; 344. 12; 356. 14; 403. 4; 75. 1, 7

**Sen-nefer** a proper name 169. 8

**senfeχfeχ** to be unloosed 149. 1, 13

**senem** abundance, to be full 5. 13; 464. 3

**senem** adoration 50. 4

**snemȧi** to make to advance 4. 5

**Senemti** a proper name 504. 16

**senemem** hair 79. 9

**sennu** to sever 106. 13

***seneniu*** those who cut off (?) **158**. 7

***senen*** image, statue **159**. 2

***senenit*** . . . . . . **423**. 3

***senenȧu*** to fail **115**. 6

***sennu*** to gather **135**. 16

***sennu*** cakes **16**. 11; **70**. 16; **159**. 7; **223**. 9; **244**, 16; **510**. 7

***sennuṭ*** carrier **138**. 12

***seneh*** to be in servitude **225**. 11

***senehep*** to be strong **108**. 4

***Senehaqareha*** name of a city **411**. 10

***Senehaparḳana*** name of a city **411**. 13

***seneḥem*** to deliver **173**. 11

***senχa*** to disembark (?) **101**. 13

***senχeχ*** to grow old **168**. 1

***senes***
***sensi*** to praise **12**. 14; **46**. 12

***sensu*** to cry out, to invoke **135**. 9

**Sensenb** name of the mother of Nu 178. 5

**seneś**, **senśu** to unbolt, to unbar, to be opened 89. 11; 103. 8; 132. 11; 150. 7, 10; 278. 15; 279. 1; 298. 5; 380. 9; 474. 2; 210. 10; 377. 1; 438. 7

**senśu** chambers (?) 163. 5

**seneśni** storm, thunder 301. 4

**Senk** a proper name 426. 13

**senket** light 24. 9; 352. 3; 484. 16

**senkti** light 513. 4

**senket** name of a city 234. 14

**senk áb** strong-willed 457. 5

**senq**, **senqet** to suckle 25. 7; 462. 4

**sent** labourers (?) 203. 14

**sent** to found 67. 12

**sentet** foundation 145. 12; 388. 14; 407. 8

**sent** the game of draughts 51. 2

**sent** to pass over or away 236. 15; 237. 7

**sent** decay 400. 12

**Sent-Rā** a proper name 237. 7

***sentu*** enemies **281.** 13

***sentrá*** incense **347.** 13; (and see with fresh incense (?) **417.** 7

***sentrát re*** to perfume the mouth with incense **465.** 7

***senteḫ*** to have power **225.** 12

***Sent . . . .*** the brother gods Horus and Set **103.** 10

***sent***, ***sentu***, ***sent*** to fear, to be afraid of, fear **14.** 2; **66.** 2; **68.** 13; **114.** 15; **165.** 13 *(bis)*; **167.** 6; **168.** 14; **301.** 4; **353.** 6; **374.** 3, 5; **376.** 3; **378.** 9; **379.** 2; **389.** 6; **392.** 7; **404.** 9; **460.** 3; **477.** 8, 12; **505.** 1, 16; fear **24.** 6; **487.** 8; *sent áb* timid **449.** 10

***senθetet*** . . . . . . **422.** 11

***senefem*** to be glad, to rejoice, to gratify, to relieve pain **135.** 10; **139.** 4; **239.** 7; **280.** 13; **336.** 2; **360.** 1; **439.** 11; **483.** 13; **350.** 15; most pleasant smell **186.** 5; ease **358.** 16

***senefem*** to sit **359.** 5; **433.** 7; **434.** 10

***senfert*** restraint **356.** 5

***ser*** prince, chief **397.** 8; **471.** 8; plur. **280.** 7; everlasting prince **489.** 14

***Ser-āa-ḥems-ḥer-ḳes-ȧbt-en-pet*** a proper name **397**. 8

***ser*** / ***ser*** to order, to arrange **44**. 12; **167**. 12; **228**. 3; **281**. 14, 16; **299**. 5; **304**. 2; **331**. 8; **345**. 11; **350**. 2; **448**. 1; **304**. 6; **449**. 12; **334**. 12

***ser*** / ***sert*** to set in order, disposer **356**. 11; **357**. 7; **389**. 11; **481**. 16

***Ser-χeru*** one of the forty-two assessors **256**. 5

***Serȧt-beqet*** name of a cow **462**. 4

***seru*** grain, barley **367**. 16

***seru*** birds **454**. 1

***serui*** (?) flame **415**. 15

***seruχeṭ*** to embalm **399**. 1, 2

***seruṭ*** to grow, to flourish, to make to flourish, to make to germinate **29**. 1; **89**. 13; **167**. 16; **200**. 10; **202**. 16; **233**. 11; **238**. 11; **308**. 9; **384**. 8, 13; **385**. 1; **418**. 8; **441**. 7; **213**. 15; **429**. 12

***seref*** flame, fire **88**. 1; **398**. 12

***serem*** to make to weep **250**. 9

*serer* designer, draughtsman, artist **28.** 4, 10; **110.** 10; **138.** 4; **222.** 10; **223.** 4, 11; **309.** 11; **312.** 13; **385.** 16; **387.** 5; **450.** 2; **461.** 9; **463.** 11; **139.** 11

*serer* to make to revolve **302.** 15

*serḫu* (?) to overthrow **62.** 2

*sereχ* to make to know, to inform **496.** 9; **507.** 6, 7

*sereχ* throne **459.** 15; **460.** 9

*Sereχi* one of the forty-two assessors **257.** 7

*seres* to be vigilant, to watch **282.** 4; **439.** 11; **503.** 8, 11, 12; **504.** 2, 3, 13; **507.** 3, 9, 15; **383.** 4; **420.** 16; **421.** 1; **439.** 14

*Seres-ḥrá* a proper name **359.** 12

*Serqet* the goddess Serqet or Selqet **99.** 13; **112.** 11; **117.** 6; **326.** 6; **460.** 7

*Sert* a city in the seventh Áat **281.** 11

*Sert* "Goad", name of a part of a ship **130.** 4

*serṭ* see

*sehep* lawgiver **8.** 7

**seher** to make quiet 483. 6, 7

**seherer** subduer (of the world ) 481. 13

**sehert** carnelian 94. 8

**seḥ** hall 51. 2; 189. 5; 465. 15; 104. 8; a name of Osiris 325. 12; 497. 11

**seḥap** to hide 352. 14

**seḥaptet** name of a boat (?) 216. 2

**seḥuā** to confuse, to disarrange 458. 1

**seḥurȧ** to curse 68. 14

**seḥui** . . . . . . 233. 10

**seḥui** to collect 228. 11

**seḥeb** to keep a feast, to make festival 43. 10; 488. 2

**seḥem** to turn back 211. 1

**seḥen** . . . . . . 5. 2

**seḥer**, **seḥeru**, **seḥeri** to drive away, to make to depart 37. 14; 379. 2; 432. 8; 54. 7; 215. 7; 190. 5

**seḥeset** (?) beset (?) 198. 5

***seḥes*** to turn back (?) 462. 7

***seḥeq*** to cut off, to hack in pieces 36. 9

***seḥeq*** to appoint as prince 65. 9; made governor of 52. 6

***seḥeqer*** to make hungry, to keep hungry 250. 9

***seḥetep*** , to propitiate with offerings, to make to rest, to pacify 40. 3; 44. 8; 156. 14; 163. 11; 169. 8; 201. 1; 216. 7, 9; 224. 15, 16; 228. 1; 261. 1; 421. 12, 14; 438. 13; 446. 11; 450. 10; 467. 13; 483. 6; 485. 1; 489. 10; to put oneself to rest (of the Sun) 434. 16; to quiet the heart 184. 11; to propitiate with offerings the *ka* 290. 13; pacifiers 269. 8

***seḥetep*** pacification 201. 13

***seḥetepet*** the offerings which bring peace 35. 3

***Seḥetep-taui*** a proper name 244. 8

***seḥetem*** to destroy 2. 16; 52. 5; 467. 5

***Seḥetem-āu-ā-em-ābet*** name of the banks of the river 208. 3

***Seḥtet*** a proper name 321. 4

***seḥef***, ***seḥefet*** , to illumine 6. 15; 7. 12; 8. 4; 37. 16; 40. 10; 43. 6; 164. 2; 181. 9; 271. 5; 274. 6; 280. 16; 310. 2, 3; 342. 15; 355. 10; 383. 8; 413. 7; 442. 14; 484. 15; 491. 15; 509. 16; 235. 9

**seḥef ur** great luminary, *i. e.*, the Sun **43.** 8; **125.** 3

**seχ** see **49.** 4

**seχ** to stir or break up **183.** 2

**seχ** to cut **448.** 16

**seχa**, **seχau** to remember, to make mention of **88.** 10; **180.** 8; **227.** 3; **228.** 5; **404.** 8; **450.** 3; memory **88.** 7; **192.** 15; **176.** 13; remembrance for good **477.** 9

**seχau** remembrance of evil **193.** 11

**seχa** , to be deaf **256.** 3, 12

**seχai** a proper name **326.** 2

**seχabui** eaters (?) **272.** 3

**seχap** to swallow **219.** 9

**seχar** to give milk **439.** 4

**seχaru** to shape, to be moulded **268.** 4

**seχakeru** to ornament **195.** 10

**[illegible]** a form of Isis or Hathor **439.** 5

**[illegible]** to make to rise **12.** 15

**[illegible]** name of a double serpent **144.** 12 (var.

**seχu** to glorify, to praise 37. 2; 43. 15; 167. 11; 277. 11; 450. 2; 454. 11; 478. 5; 110. 12; endowed with power 449. 5

**seχu**, **seχut** praise, songs of praise, glorifyings 18. 5; 50. 19; 244. 6; 277. 1; 303. 10; 348. 7, 13; 444. 8, 10; praised 445. 6

**seχun**, **seχunennu** to revile, to curse 254. 13; 515. 12; 255. 4

**seχuṭ** to fortify 373. 12

**seχep** to make to advance 107. 1 *(bis)*, 2

**seχeper** to make to become 9. 4; 140. 4; 167. 10; 174. 5; 239. 8; 316. 5; 487. 3; let not things be brought up against me 95. 5

**seχeperu**, **seχeperiu** those who cause something to happen 91. 1; 262. 6

**seχef** seven 58. 3; 59. 2, 7; 124. 4; 143. 7; 158. 5; 181. 8; 212. 13; 218. 16; 219. 9; 222. 2; 309. 3; 312. 1; 346. 14; 362. 8; 363. 8, 15; 492. 15; 494. 5; seventh 329. 1; 338. 14; 352. 10; 361. 14

**seχem**, **seχmet** to forget, forgetfulness 227. 3; 228. 5

**Seχem** the shrine of the city Letopolis 90. 18; 181. 11; 186. 14; 279. 5; 299. 11; 478. 8; 483. 9

**Seχem** — the city of Letopolis 19. 16; 20. 2; 62. 10; 72. 6, 10, 11; 79. 4, 5; 81. 9, 10; 83. 6 *(bis)*; 138. 1; 188. 15; 203. 13; 253. 8; 388. 16; 439. 12; 515. 15; — the gods of the shrine 373. 13

**seχem** — to have power, to gain the mastery over, to prevail over, power, might, victor, conqueror 34. 2, 8; 62. 15; 63. 3; 89. 16; 90. 1, 2; 91. 6, 7; 100. 1; 103. 6; 120. 17; 127. 16; 128. 3; 129. 12; 130. 14; 131. 10; 132. 6, 13; 146. 5; 150. 12, 16; 151. 2, 14, 15; 160. 1; 170. 6; 171. 16; 179. 15; 180. 1; 182. 12; 196. 15, 198. 2; 224. 1; 226. 16; 227. 1; 275. 14; 291. 12; 306. 9; 307. 10; 308. 6, 16; 309. 4; 314. 5; 333. 1; 336. 13; 344. 13; 362. 11; 372. 4; 374. 16; 378. 14; 379. 10; 380. 9; 399. 4; 401. 3; 411. 15; 423. 1; 426. 15; 428. 2, 6; 431. 8; 432. 14; 435. 6; 437. 10 *(bis)*, 11; 445. 10; 462. 14; 463. 1, 6; 464. 15; 469. 8, 16; 470. 4; 472. 7; 477. 13; 496. 14; 497. 14; 502. 7; 512. 10; 479. 5; 373. 6; 375. 8; victor 204. 8; 462. 12; brave of heart 427. 5; unconquerable 182. 7

**seχemu**

**Seχem** — Power, Form 9. 9; 43. 12; 46. 1; 170. 14; 205. 2; 235. 15; 247. 13; 287. 5; 314. 15; 364. 9; 462. 1; 469. 3; plur. 172. 3, 5; 305. 11; 358. 10; 480. 6; 477. 11; 312. 16; 43. 13; 240. 15; 196. 16; 198.

3; **381.** 15; **378.** 5; the double Power **272.** 14; **447.** 14

***seχmet*** possessor, prevailer over **351.** 5; **375.** 3; **376.** 2

***Seχem-ur*** a proper name **456.** 10

***Seχem-em-áb-f*** a proper name **390.** 5; **393.** 13

***Seχem-nefer-*** .... .... a proper name **318.** 15

***Seχemet-ren-s-em-ābut-s*** name of a cow **318.** 14; **364.** 4

***seχen*** to direct **297.** 9

***seχen*** to embrace **127.** 9; **131.** 1; **358.** 16; **398.** 11; **139.** 13; with **359.** 9; **398.** 5

***seχni*** to alight **139.** 9; **144.** 8; **376.** 13

***Seχen-ur*** a proper name **341.** 7; **354.** 7

***seχenen*** to make to rot **400.** 16

***seχenś*** to make to stink **96.** 6

***seχent***, ***seχenti*** to make to advance **92.** 8; **111.** 8, 9; **442.** 12; **444.** 16

***seχent*** pillars **450.** 13

***seχer*** to offend **15.** 14; **16.** 9

plans, devices, counsels, arrangements 24. 7; 70. 13; 172. 12; 486. 8; celestial existence 93. 12

to overthrow 7. 6; 35. 15; 49. 8; 78. 1; 80. 2, 3, 5; 83. 4; 89. 10; 105. 13; 106. 5; 108. 16; 137. 6; 139. 3; 143. 6; 177. 9; 187. 9; 292. 7, 8; 304. 11; 305. 307. 6; 316. 4; 347. 5; 387. 1; 388. 2; 452. 11, 14; 453. 7; 486. 14; fallen

overthrow 81. 7; 332. 12; 445. 9

the god of the sixth Åat 371. 16; 372. 4

a proper name 381. 8

straighten 360. 2

penetrate 163. 2

...sten 136. 9

to make to go back, to repulse 94. 17; 106. 11

...ct, to snare, snare 81. 4; 251. 7; 438. 14; 465. 16

...ers 147. 2

***seχtit*** }
***seχti*** } snarers, hunters, fowlers **231.** 2; **393.** 16; **396.** 1

***seχettu*** rushes **397.** 1

***Seχet*** the goddess Sekhet **86.** 15; **89.** 15; **113.** 1; **118.** 5; **128.** 3; **148.** 9; **348.** 9; **349.** 6; **456.** 4; **470.** 4; **512.** 11

***Seχet-Bast-Rā*** three forms of the Sun-god **415.** 3

***seχet*** field, meadow **46.** 4; **153.** 14; **177.** 6; **178.** 8; plain **185.** 10; **226.** 10; plur. **29.** 1; **201.** 5; **223.** 14; **225.** 7; **309.** 15; **384.** 8, 13; **453.** 7

***Seχti*** divine fields, or gods of the divine fields **319.** 13

***Seχet-āat*** Great Field **470.** 3

***Seχet-Áanru*** the Elysian Fields **23.** 9; **334.** 7; **417.** 16; **434.** 9

***Seχet-Áaru*** the Elysian Fields **14.** 14; **44.** 3; **55.** 9; **132.** 16; **161.** 6, 14; **187.** 9; **208.** 7; **209.** 10, 12; **210.** 2; **218.** 3; **221.** 14; **223.** 15; **349.** 12; **367.** 13, 14; **368.** 6, 16; **381.** 3; **434.** 1; **454.** 10; **474.** 16; **495.** 14

***Seχet-em-ārāt*** . . . . . . **346.** 2

***Seχet-neḥeḥ*** Field of Eternity **169.** 12

***Seχti-neter*** Field of the gods **462.** 10, 12

***Seχet-Rā*** Field of Rā **474.** 15

***Seχet-ḥetep***, ***Seχet-ḥetepet*** the Elysian Fields **16.** 12; **70.** 9, 16; **92.** 9; **222.** 13; **223.** 7, 14, 16; **224.** 5; **230.** 13; **303.** 5; **422.** 6; **423.** 13; **434.** 4; **437.** 9; **227.** 6; **434.** 12; **466.** 1; **508.** 9

***Seχti-ḥetep*** the god of the Elysian Fields (?) **165.** 3; **227.** 15; **331.** 1; **376.** 15; **494.** 12

***Seχet-sanehemu*** Field of the Grasshoppers **262.** 12; **508.** 10

***Seχet-Sȧsȧ*** Field of Sȧsȧ **203.** 6, 7

***seχet*** to overturn **114.** 6; **125.** 6; **204.** 14; **213.** 1; **327.** 11; **358.** 3; **494.** 8; **123.** 5

***Seχet-ḥrȧ-āś-ȧru*** porter of the first Ārit **327.** 11; **358.** 3

***seχtu*** to hunger **492.** 7

***sesu*** (?) seasons (?) **251.** 12

***sesunt*** to destroy **40.** 15

***seseb-θȧ*** to slay **504.** 4

***sesen***, ***sesenet*** to snuff the air **126.** 8; **127.** 7, 13, 16; **130.** 14; **131.** 3; **374.** 9, 16; **438.** 16

**seska** [hieroglyphs] body, skin **155.** 10

**seset** [hieroglyphs] legs **113.** 2

**seset** [hieroglyphs] to light up **383.** 13

**seś** [hieroglyphs] to pass, to journey, to travel **24.** 8; **27.** 15; **29.** 6; **50.** 2; **67.** 4; **143.** 15; **163.** 5; **164.** 4; **171.** 16; **186.** 16; **212.** 13; **213.** 1; **215.** 12; **248.** 14; **262.** 15; **263.** 3 *(bis)*; **264.** 11; **265.** 11; **270.** 1, 7; **273.** 8; **281.** 12; **288.** 3; **298.** 16; **301.** 1; **302.** 9 ([hieroglyphs]); **303.** 1; **330.** 4; **332.** 8; **359.** 9; **360.** 11; **407.** 6; **428.** 13; **460.** 16; **468.** 6; **491.** 3; [hieroglyphs] **482.** 11; [hieroglyphs] impassable **353.** 5

**seśt** [hieroglyphs] passage **371.** 7; **375.** 7; **376.** 7

**seś** [hieroglyphs], [hieroglyphs] to open, to unbolt **19.** 13; **131.** 8; **462.** 13

**seś** [hieroglyphs] knowledge **476.** 13 *(bis)*

**seś** [hieroglyphs] skilled one (?) **9.** 13

**seś** [hieroglyphs] = [hieroglyphs] (?) **46.** 16

**seś** [hieroglyphs] nest **126.** 12; plur. [hieroglyphs] **448.** 8

**seś** [hieroglyphs] birthplace **185.** 13

**seśui-āat-urt** [hieroglyphs] the great and mighty double nest **54.** 10

**Seśet** [hieroglyphs] a proper name **324.** 11

**seśai** [hieroglyphs] man of understanding (?) **141.** 12; [hieroglyphs] skilful **446.** 13

**seśu-θà** [hieroglyphs] empty of, free from **21.** 15

*seśep* palm **218.** 16; **220.** 2

*seśep*
*seśept* to shine, be bright, light **85.** 4; **105.** 9; **136.** 14; **138.** 8; **170.** 7; **176.** 7, 9; **177.** 7, 14; **184.** 9; **240.** 12; **301.** 13; **358.** 7; **359.** 1; **360.** 3; **398.** 3; **448.** 1; white **494.** 16

*seśep* (?) to shine upon, to illumine **176.** 10; **177.** 8, 9; **428.** 15

*seśep* to receive **1.** 8; **3.** 3, 9; **20.** 10; **23.** 1; **70.** 16; **79.** 11; **83.** 8; **103.** 2; **107.** 9, 10; **149.** 3; **162.** 17; **163.** 2; **165.** 5; **175.** 13; **179.** 2; **222.** 15; **227.** 1. **228.** 8; **237.** 5; **239.** 3; **240.** 6; **277.** 16; **279.** 5; **282.** 5; **283.** 10; **284.** 4; **286.** 10, 15; **329.** 12; **348.** 14; **392.** 4; **405.** 13; **430.** 1; **438.** 1; **449.** 1; **451.** 7; **455.** 17; **456.** 9; **472.** 9; **473.** 5, 10; **479.** 8; **509.** 11; **510.** 6; **514.** 10; **516.** 14, 15; to take in the hands, to grasp **47.** 14

*seśepiu* receivers **428.** 4, 15; with **423.** 1

*seśep ȧb* the heart's desire **153.** 12

*seśen* to spread oneself out **287.** 3

*seśen* to defend (?) **140.** 8

*seśen*
*seśennu* lily **178.** 3, 6, 11, 12; **456.** 8; **468.** 9; **456.** 14; **104.** 1

*seśeru* garments **456.** 12 (var.

*seśert* cakes **218.** 3

*seśet* fire, flame **2.** 6; **13.** 3; **64.** 9; **80.** 12; **133.** 6;

252. 14; 263. 8, 13, 16; 267. 6; 294. 8; 311. 10; 312. 6; 318. 3; 320. 8; 333. 13; 372. 10; 374. 7; 377. 8; 382. 2; 412. 2; plur. 340. 8; 320. 6

***Seśeta*** name of a goddess 129. 2; 388. 13; 439. 3

***seśeta*** hidden one or thing, mystery 376. 6; 470. 15; hidden things, mysteries 24. 6; 141. 14; 213. 4; 233. 4; 344. 6; 346. 11; 403. 12; 285. 5; 407. 14; 19. 14; hidden of fire 75. 11, 15; hidden of name 29. 14; it is indeed a very great mystery 408. 1; 498. 2; 426. 4; 497. 3; 308. 13

***seśeṭ*** to break up, to dig out, to tear open 31. 10; 105. 11; 107. 4; 263. 15; 496. 8; division 185. 7

***seśeṭ*** to recite 20. 7; 104. 12; 230. 11; recited 77. 3; 141. 15; 145. 16

***seśet*** to deliver 30. 5; 176. 16; 228. 11; 243. 1; 296. 5; 297. 10; 359. 9; 361. 12; 398. 7; 399. 11; 504. 5, 6; 296. 13; deliverers 465. 11

***seśeṭ*** to tie, to bind up, to strengthen 169. 2, 5; 171. 9; 172. 3; 195. 2, 9; 279. 8; 457. 12; 375. 9

***seśeṭ*** bandage, bandlet, girdle, head-binding or tiara **34.** 5; **120.** 15, 17; **170.** 6; **213.** 8; **296.** 3, 12; **297.** 8; **335.** 12

***seśeṭet*** a chamber **156.** 9; **387.** 15

***seśeṭet***, ***seśeṭit*** a pool or excavated place **262.** 10. 11; **496.** 4; plur. **494.** 7

***seśeṭu*** leather straps **206.** 6

***Seśeṭ-χeru*** one of the forty-two assessors **256.** 1

***Seku*** starry gods **376.** 16

***sek*** to decay, to perish **120.** 13; **152.** 12; **184.** 1; **185.** 11; **190.** 14; **300.** 4; **308.** 8; **377.** 12, 13; **402.** 2; **410.** 16; **503.** 17; to perish (of the name) **155.** 16; incorruptible **399.** 9

***sek*** to break through **282.** 14; to constrain **180.** 9; to diminish **243.** 1; **463.** 1 *(bis)*; to slay **63.** 14

***sek*** to fight **225.** 10; *sek* battle (?) **321.** 16

***sek*** to draw onwards, to advance **4.** 6; **12.** 12; **13.** 16; **36.** 10; **44.** 13; **389.** 12, 14

***seksek*** to destroy **342.** 7; **355.** 3

***sek re*** to direct **478.** 13

***seka*** to plough 224. 1; 225. 9; 227. 4, 9; 229. 15; 243. 11; 434. 4; 454. 9; 495. 13; 496. 1

***Seker*** the bark of the god Seker 14. 2; 20. 9; 38. 13; 66. 2

***Seker***, ***Sekri*** the god Seker 162. 9; 210. 11; 321. 10, 15; 391. 2; 394. 13; 449. 6; 324. 7

***Sekri*** the festival of Seker 497. 2

***Seker***, ***Sekri*** the city of Seker 324. 1, 14

***Sek-ḥrá*** a proper name 301. 6

***Seksek*** name of a fiend 101. 14

***sektiu*** to fetter 106. 3

***Sektet*** the boat of the setting sun 3. 3, 9; 4. 6; 5. 3; 9. 8, 15; 12. 12; 35. 13; 36. 10; 40. 6; 102. 13; 125. 8; 164. 12; 201. 3; 207. 11; 214. 15; 244. 4; 279. 1; 284. 13; 319. 7; 324. 9; 335. 9; 362. 4; 382. 8; 386. 8; 387. 11; 395. 13; 489. 15

***seq*** to collect, to gather together, to assemble 98. 9; 278. 4; 382. 13; 440. 16; 478. 10; heaped up 437. 15

***seqa*** to exalt 7. 4; 42. 10; 165. 12; 172. 14; 276. 15; 277. 8; 282. 16; 386. 5; 387. 10; 445. 1, 6; 484. 8; 487. 1; 489. 16;

9. 14; 37. 4; exalted ones **20. 5; 471. 16**

***seqeb*** image (?) **325.** 15

***seqebeb*** to pour out cold water, to refresh oneself **180.** 12; **200.** 8; **201.** 15

***Seqebet*** a proper name **326. 8**

***seqer*** to injure, to lead captive **231.** 13; defaced **406.** 6, 7

***seqrȧ*** injury **232.** 2

***seqeṭ***, ***seqṭet***, ***seqṭu*** to sail round about, to voyage, to journey **10.** 1; **46.** 11; **136.** 8, 12; **142.** 2; **295.** 5; **316.** 3; **367.** 8

***seqṭet*** to go or sail round about, the boat in which the sun performs his daily course **10.** 1; **22.** 7; **41.** 12; **44.** 3; **48.** 12; **61.** 9; **203.** 12; **204.** 9; **211.** 15; **212.** 2; **221.** 6; **287.** 6; **294.** 10; **299.** 2; **330.** 5; **349.** 2; **368.** 9; **465.** 14. 15; to sail **369.** 8; **370.** 8; to embark **291.** 7; boat **219.** 9; **296.** 15, 16; **298.** 14; voyagings, sailings **214.** 8; **215.** 7

***seqeṭtu*** boatmen **204.** 9

***seqeṭet*** encircled **502.** 1

***seqeṭ*** dispositions **166.** 6

***Seqeṭ-ḥrá*** warder of the second Ārit **327.** 16; **359.** 3

***seḳeneni*** inert mass **400.** 1

***seḳer*** to put to silence **314.** 2; **415.** 7; silence **36.** 13

***seḳeru*** to be silent **88.** 1; **247.** 13

***seḳert*** silence **380.** 6; **467.** 14

***set*** she, it, its **16.** 7; **41.** 7; **59.** 16; **86.** 12; **95.** 4; **334.** 3; **356.** 7; **365.** 11; **368.** 4; **374.** 11; **376.** 4; **384.** 6, 11; **400.** 7; **448.** 6; **454.** 11; **457.** 11; **485.** 16; **504.** 10

***set*** , they, them, their **98.** 11; **120.** 7 *(bis)*; **174.** 10; **183.** 10; **209.** 15; **214.** 16; **222.** 5; **231.** 5; **234.** 12; **266.** 1; **292.** 16; **416.** 8, 14; **446.** 3, 5; **447.** 12; **485.** 16; **495.** 8, 9

***set*** (or ***seṭet***) to break **180.** 9

***set*** , mountain **42.** 14; **52.** 12; **321.** 3; **346.** 13; **383.** 13 *(bis)*; **487.** 14; **512.** 8; plur. **43.** 10; **41.** 15; **323.** 8; **485.** 12

***set ent ḥeḥ*** mountain of eternity, *i. e.*, the grave **91.** 10

***set ṭesert*** holy mountain, *i. e.*, the grave **23.** 15

**set** ground 219. 1

**Set** *i. e.*, Suti, the opponent of Horus 56. 10, 12; 67. 14; 71. 13; 73. 6; 75. 4; 86. 10; 92. 2; 121. 18; 131. 11; 132. 13; 177. 2; 186. 12; 193. 12; 199. 11; 219. 12; 224. 5, 6, 7; 312. 16; 382. 11; 388. 2; 443. 9; 453. 4; 456. 1; 459. 16; 465. 10; 496. 6; 503. 5, 7; 504. 10; 505. 4; 246. 12; 118. 12; 78. 10; 98. 15; 341. 9; 107. 4; 337. 2

**stau**, **stat** to kindle 311. 9; 312. 13; flame 357. 2; 317. 3. 4

**stat** filth, beastliness 53. 5; 56. 11; 64. 7

**Sta** a proper name 426. 9

**sta** to tow along, to carry, to draw, to bring, to flow along, led 11. 13; 13. 15; 210. 11; 238. 5; 240. 14; 268. 12; 307. 13; 342. 14; 355. 9; 358. 8; 474. 5; 487. 16; 12. 13; 36. 11; 440. 8; 300. 8; 316. 16

**stau**, **staiu** leaders, bearers, carriers 62. 13; 135. 3; 171. 3; 190. 4; 474. 5; 475. 9; 183. 5

**stau** see 19. 14, and *passim.*

**statet** a piece of land 209. 14; 251. 2

**setut** to run to meet 5. 6

**setut** to typify, to be a symbol of 130. 6; 242. 4

**sti** smell, odour 247. 2; 314. 15; 377. 13; 483. 13; 513. 10; 8. 5; 476. 9 *(bis)*

**sti** unguent 335. 11

**seteb** captives 438. 4

**setep** to cut 80. 7

**setep** to choose 503. 6

**setepu**, **setepet** choice pieces of meat for offerings 229. 1; 251. 12, 15, 16; 478. 6

**setep sa** to protect 383. 16; 480. 12; plur. 46. 6; 304. 11, 14; 305. 4, 7; 306. 4, 5, 12

**setem**, **setemu** to hear, to obey 15. 15, 17; 20. 14; 22. 11; 24. 10; 50. 4; 91. 7, 9; 93. 7; 96. 8; 111. 11; 140. 9; 165. 1; 177. 13; 217. 6; 235. 1; 261. 9, 15; 278. 4; 281. 2, 10; 342. 1; 345. 3; 355. 4; 383. 2; 391. 15; 409. 3; 426. 9; 427. 11; 450. 4; 511. 1; 516. 1; 377. 3; a hearing, what is heard, listener 10. 5; 282. 1; 290. 10; 356. 1; 445. 11

**setemiu** hearers, listeners 135. 1; 142. 14; 166. 1; 290. 6; *setemu* . . . . . 439. 11

**setem ḥeri**, **setemet ḥeri** the upper hinges of the door 248. 12, 13

**[illegible]** the lower hinge of the door 248. [illegible]

**Se[illegible]** a proper name 237. 7

**[illegible]** distinctions 258. 16

**[illegible]** to traverse 383. 14

**[illegible]** [illegible] 440. 5

**set-[illegible]** woman 237. 9

**[illegible]** to make to enter 20. 13

**[illegible]** those who make to enter 20. [illegible]

**[illegible]** to invade 458. 2

**setet** trembling 334. 11

**set** [illegible] 504. 10 [illegible]

**set** to break, to split open 106. 14; 263. 16; 281. 15; 372. 14; 394. 10; 406. 15; 457. 4; 185. 13

**Set-qesu** "Bone-breaker", one of the forty-two assessors 253. 12

**seṭ** to clothe 99. 15; 335. 12; 336. 8; 337. 3; 338. 11; 339. 6; 340. 1, 15; those who clothe 92. 2

**seṭ** a garment 340. 2

**seṭ** to dress 181. 6

***seṭa***, ***seṭau*** trembling, terror 105. 8; 289. 9; 350. 1; 455. 8

***seṭuiu*** to defame 250. 8

***seṭu*** regions (?) 138. 11

***seṭeb*** garment 438. 1; hangings (of a shrine) 156. 9

***seṭeb*** obstacle, opposition 28. 15; 107. 2; 299. 12; 306. 7, 15; 307. 14; plur. 201. 11; 243. 4; 269. 14; 271. 11; 274. 11; 281. 3; 365. 8; 384. 14; 35. 2; 384. 7

***seṭeb*** . . . . . 504. 16

***seṭebḥu*** zealous (?) 141. 11

***seṭem*** edicts for slaughter 504. 9

***Seṭeḳ*** a proper name 426. 1

***seṭeḳa*** to cover over 305. 11

***seṭeḳaut*** sleep 219. 8

***seṭeṭ*** to travel 153. 10

***seθ*** scent 186. 6

***seθi*** drink 175. 14

***seθen*** distinctions 258. 12

***seθenem*** to make to walk 311. 5

**seθes** to lift up, to raise 22. 7; 244. 7; 461. 8; of the and 463. 6; 386. 6; 436. 1; 441. 1, 7, 14, 15; 442. 2, 7, 16; 360. 5

**seθes** exaltation 317. 1

**seθes**
**seθesu** praisings, exaltings 18. 4; 50. 19; 387. 10; 444. 5

**seθesu** exalted ones 134. 15; 142. 13; 368. 14; supports 51. 10; 221. 11

**seθes Śu** what Shu supports, *i. e.*, the sky 485. 11

**seθesu Śu** the props of Shu, the four cardinal points 55. 12; 61. 10

**seθesu** to knit together 9. 3

**seθesu** libations 225. 13

**sefa** to make to set out 280. 16; 441. 2

**sefami** (?) to protect 166. 12

**sefit** a mineral (?) substance or grain 506. 4

**sefeb** to be opposed by some one or something 228. 11

***sefefa***
***sefefaiu*** — to be provided with *tchefa* food, those who are so provided **288**. 11; **363**. 3, 10, 11; **366**. 8, 15; **453**. 13

***sefer*** — to lie down in sleep or death **6**. 5; **73**. 10; **76**. 4; **79**. 13; **111**. 6; **169**. 11; **188**. 5, 6; **189**. 10 *(bis)*; **243**. 3; **372**. 16; **412**. 1; **465**. 3; **503**. 11; dead one **183**. 12; **194**. 16; **421**. 1; those who lie down **189**. 11; slain **37**. 16; **506**. 8

***sefer*** bier **25**. 11

***sefeser*** to sanctify **11**. 13

***sefeṭfu*** to wound or snare **288**. 3

## Sh.

**śe** pool, lake, laver 202. 10; 292. 12; 301. 6; 303. 11; 333. 11; 376. 13; 434. 8; plur. 111. 11; 132. 15; 201. 6; 224. 12; 225. 5; 226. 4; 227. 5, 11, 14; ..... 203. 9

**śe asbiu** pool of fire 134. 3

**śe Aḳeb** pool of Aḳeb 493. 14

**śe åqer** pool of perfection 450. 9

**śe ur** great pool 239. 9

**śe Maāti** pool of Maāti 55. 4, 6

**śe em māfket** emerald pools 107. 14

**śe Nu** pool of Nu 105. 5

**śe en amu** pool of fire 203. 5, 6

**śe en Åusår** pool of Osiris 242. 10; 496. 8

**śe en Maāti** pool of Maāti 433. 15

**śe en Māāat** pool of Mäāat 54. 15

**śe nesert** (?) pool of two-fold fire **86.** 4; **87.** 13; **226.** 8, 12; **459.** 3, 13; **186.** 8; **382.** 2; **158.** 9; **456.** 10

**śe neter** pool of the god **450.** 13

**Śe en Ḥeru** pool of Horus **33.** 14; **36.** 16

**śe ḥeru** celestial lakes **230.** 11

**śe ḥeḥ** pool of millions of years **287.** 9

**śe en ḥesmen** pool of natron **54.** 14

**śe-ḥetep** pool of Ḥetep **224.** 10

**śe ent ḥeṭet** pool of light **340.** 15

**śe en χeben** pool of the wicked **279.** 16

**śe en χaru** pool of the *kharu* geese **368.** 8

**śe en seḥetep** pool of pacification **201.** 13

**śe en seśet** pool of fire **64.** 5

**śet Ṭesṭes** (?) pool of Ṭesṭes **395.** 2

**śeu Ṭesert** lakes of Tchesert **229.** 7

**śa** food **182.** 5

**śa** plants **504.** 9

**śa** to go on to **279.** 6

**śaȧ** pig 232. 1, 4, 5; 268. 5; plur. 232. 8

**śaȧs** to advance 99. 3

**śaā** one hundred 137. 1; 143. 3; 218. 14; two hundred 370. 4; three hundred 218. 14; 300. 12; 370. 4

**śaā** to begin, beginning, origin, source 51. 7, 9; 352. 6; 416. 6; for ever 412. 7

**Śau** name of a city 322. 10; 324. 14

**Śabu** name of a god 360. 14

**śabu** water plants 448. 8

**śabti** funeral statuette 28. 9, 11; 384. 6, 11

**Śapuneterȧrika** name of an Utchat 413. 4

**śam** damned 280. 1

**śamt** the first of the three seasons of the year 448. 6

**Śareśareśapuneterȧrika** a proper name 412. 13

**Śareśareχet** name of an Utchat 413. 4

**Śareśaθȧkaθȧ** a proper name 419. 14

**śas** to pass on, to journey 31. 11; 134. 6; 138. 6; 171. 10, 11; 286. 11; 292. 15; 302. 14; 458. 8; 474. 14; 389. 3

**Śakanasa** a proper name 413. 6

**Śaka** ..... ..... a name of Åmen **413**. 5—7

**śāi, śāt** sand **29**. 2; **89**. 6; **92**. 7; **311**. 4; **325**. 2; **383**. 11; **384**. 9; **437**. 15; **484**. 8; a kind of grain or fruit **317**. 6

**śāmu** decorated **446**. 1

**śāt**, **śātet** book, writing **23**. 5; **151**. 13; **152**. 10; **155**. 14; **210**. 6; **268**. 6; **288**. 8; **309**. 10; **314**. 13; **317**. 11, 13; **320**. 14; **333**. 16; **366**. 11; **410**. 9, 11, 15; **414**. 10; **477**. 13; **480**. 10; **496**. 13, 16; **497**. 12; **498**. 1; Book of praise **270**. 13; Book of holy words **441**. 10; Book of Thoth **151**. 13; **199**. 8

**śāit en sensen** Book of Breathings **508**. 3; **510**. 10; **511**. 8; **513**. 6, 13, 14; **514**. 14; **516**. 15

**śāt**, **śāṭ** to wound, to cut, wound, gash, slaughter **56**. 3; **57**. 15; **58**. 11; **64**. 11; **65**. 3; **66**. 9; **94**. 2; **105**. 6; **108**. 14; **110**. 9; **111**. 16; **116**. 17; **119**. 2; **153**. 16; **158**. 9; **182**. 15; **197**. 11; **198**. 5; **199**. 1; **207**. 10; **269**. 13; **270**. 5; **292**. 10; **293**. 3; **310**. 5; **345**. 4; **357**. 3; **376**. 5; **388**. 10; **414**. 13; **421**. 5; **457**. 14; **502**. 14; **356**. 12; cut off **54**. 6; **128**. 15; knives **260**. 1; **392**. 12; **438**. 3; **455**. 9

**Śāṭ** the god of slaughter **200**. 8

**śu** light, day 15. 5; 39. 6; 135. 12; 214. 1; 480. 13; 484. 15; 498. 1; light

**śu** 87. 11, 15; 88. 3; 88. 4

**Śu** the god Shu 51. 10; 55. 12; 60. 9; 61. 1, 10; 67. 10; 71. 12; 75. 14; 86. 13; 100. 12; 120. 14; 126. 17; 137. 8; 138. 6; 139. 7; 144. 6; 149. 2, 14; 169. 7; 170. 3; 191. 12; 193. 5; 202. 6; 221. 12; 224. 11; 225. 14; 227. 13; 229. 2; 237. 15; 286. 11; 294. 4; 315. 11; 318. 8; 368. 14; 386. 5; 387. 10; 398. 8, 9; 406. 9; 443. 8; 464. 10; 465. 1; 485. 11; 509. 8; 511. 14; 516. 4

**śu** to be in want of, needy 5. 13; 115. 10; 243. 4; 336. 14; 351. 7; without 113. 4; 159. 13; 262. 10; sinless 43. 1; *śut-θà* empty 288. 15

**śu** plants, papyrus 211. 7; 504. 7

**śut** feather, flight 127. 2

**suti** the two plumes on the head of a god 4. 3; 6. 1; 53. 9, 12; 413. 16; 414. 2; 417. 4, 5; 420. 3; 454. 15; 461. 12; 54. 1

[illegible] feathers (of a hawk ) 397. 1

[illegible] merchant 3. 14; 4. 12; 5. 14; 6. 14; 8. 9

[illegible] lands (?) 231. 2

[illegible] cakes 16. 3; 228. 16; 250. 12

**śebeb** throat 206. 3; 447. 10

**Śebeb en Mesθi** name of a part of a boat 206. 3

**śeben** cakes 440. 1

**śebennu** mixed 211. 8

**śep** palm of 4 fingers 116. 5

**śep** blind 436. 2

**śepent** vessel 333. 10

**śeps**, **śepsi**, **śeps** holy, sacred, venerable, worshipful 2. 12; 22. 8; 42. 14; 97. 1; 128. 7; 176. 2; 203. 8; 323. 4; 386. 11; 452. 5; 487. 16; 489. 14; 511. 5; 49. 12; 41. 5

**śept áb** wrath, loathing 34. 10, 13; 35. 4; 485. 4

**śefu** insolence 258. 10, 15

**śeft** ram 420. 7; *śeft ḥrá* terrible 341. 4

**śeft**, **śefit**, **śef-śeft** terror, strength, power 30. 14; 45. 12; 68. 8, 13; 112. 16; 165. 13; 167. 7; 171. 5; 172. 13; 184. 13; 194. 1; 287. 1; 293. 3; 354. 6; 373. 14; 378. 9; 404. 9; 416. 5; 454. 14; 476. 8; 477. 5; 487. 9; 490. 1, 3; 496. 15

**Śefit** the ram-god 118. 14

**śem**, **śemt**, **śemt**, **śemi** to walk, to journey 21. 13; 32. 12; 41. 10; 42. 1, 2; 53. 12; 55. 3, 8; 89. 9; 100. 12; 123. 5; 125. 4; 152. 11; 162. 13, 17; 169. 11; 183. 1; 226. 3; 239. 12, 13; 279. 14; 283. 15; 288. 14; 320. 14; 334. 1; 356. 7; 361. 10; 370. 12, 13; 406. 8; 436. 11, 12; 447. 7; 462. 9; 468. 14; 475. 2; 492. 7; 493. 10; 506. 12; 511. 2; 513. 2; 517. 2; 366. 14

**śem re** to set the mouth in motion against any one 16. 5; 254. 15; 255. 1

**śemiu**, **śemt** to travel, journeys, goings about, steps 116. 2; 221. 11; 332. 7; 368. 13; 456. 5; 470. 12; 492. 4; 497. 6

**śemem**, **śememt** flame, fire 295. 13; 345. 12; 357. 7

**śememet** poison 373. 1

**śen** circuit 388. 15

**Śenȧt-pet-uθeset-neter** name of a cow-goddess 318. 10; 364. 5

**śenā** body, breast 112. 13; 117. 11

**śenā** whirlwind, storm 489. 1; plur. 283. 14

**śenā** to turn back, to be repulsed 160. 12; 179. 4; 187. 13; 251. 12; 268. 11; 279. 13; 307. 12; 309. 6, 7; 312. 8; 333. 2; 70. 6; 281. 4; 477. 14; 430. 3

**śenār** to turn back, to be repulsed **14.** 11 ; **41.** 2 ; **362.** 9

**śenrā** to turn back, to be repulsed **509.** 15; **510.** 8; **516.** 10; repulsed **21.** 10; **22.** 8, 12; **23.** 7; **410.** 4; **414.** 6; **417.** 13

**śenu** to be powerful **97.** 15 *(bis)*; **97.** 14

**śenu** to load **479.** 2

**śeni** wickedness **429.** 5

**śeni** hair, locks **56.** 13, 16; **68.** 5; **69.** 6, 8; **112.** 8; **117.** 1; **130.** 3; **145.** 3; **229.** 14; **242.** 1; **401.** 16; **445.** 16; **446.** 1

**śenit** storm **481.** 4

**śeniu** chamber **63.** 3; **64.** 10

**śenit** princes, chiefs **15.** 14; **96.** 7; **173.** 4; **268.** 8; **282.** 9; **286.** 9; **329.** 14

**śenit** circle **301.** 1; **302.** 14

**śenbet** body, breast **6.** 1; **14.** 8; **35.** 13; **37.** 5; **112.** 15; **118.** 13; **191.** 2; **211.** 9; **213.** 16; **417.** 11; **440.** 5; **510.** 6; **463.** 10; **484.** 15

**Śenmu** name of a city **406.** 9

**śenen** orbit, circuit **43.** 7

**śennu** orbit, circuit **174.** 12

**śennu** hair **349.** 4

*śennu* powder of some sort (?) **248.** 5

*śennu* snares **394.** 2

*śennu* acacia trees **346.** 13

*Śennu* name of a city **322.** 8; **324.** 13

*śens* cakes **130.** 7; **208.** 13; **209.** 12; **215.** 2; **242.** 6; **268.** 9; **270.** 2, 8; **333.** 9; **367.** 5, 16; **382.** 5; **449.** 7; shewbread **449.** 7

*śent* flesh **305.** 13

*śentu* to curse (god) **258.** 8, 14; **260.** 5; to curse (the king) **257.** 16; **258.** 1; blasphemer **257.** 2

*śenti* granary **37.** 6

*śenti* heron **182.** 11

*śenti* a garment **347.** 13

*śentet* evil deeds **266.** 12; **267.** 4

*śenṭet* a tree with thick foliage **247.** 8, 9

*śen-θȧ* read 6. 7

*Śenθit* name of a goddess **326.** 5

*Śerem* a proper name **426.** 7

*śerȧt* little **42.** 4

**śereriu** lesser gods 243. 6; 301. 11

**śererȧu** helpless ones 225. 3

**śerśeru** breaths 511. 4

**śert** little 10. 11

**śertet** what is of no value 236. 3

**śert** nostrils 126. 5; 128. 8; 129. 1, 9; 178. 7; 436. 6; 451. 11; 456. 10, 14; 468. 9; 484. 14; 446. 6

**śert** grain 454. 9

**śert** cake 464. 16; 494. 14

**Śeret-Ȧmsu** (?) the mother of Ȧuf-ānkh 34. 6; 77. 10; 80. 12; 413. 3; 419. 4; 501. 5; 349. 8

**śes**, **śesi** to follow 12. 16; 62. 9; 190. 12; 229. 2; 279. 3, 4; 286. 5, 6; 303. 4; 313. 8; 330. 15; 363. 12; 371. 11; 388. 11; 422. 5; 439. 1; 485. 14; 487. 12; 512. 6; 513. 6; 514. 3; 516. 10

**śesu**, **śesut**, **śesi** those who follow or who are in the train of some one 121. 6; 135. 3; 289. 4; 290. 8; 378. 2; 389. 3; 409. 12; 422. 7, 15; 424. 3; 439. 5; 486. 7; 490. 7; 80. 14; 279. 3; 312. 9; 315. 3; 433. 11; 468. 2; 468. 9; 63. 12; 103.

13; 229. 4, 5; 422. 3; 491. 2; 3. 8; 16. 12; 17. 3; 70. 10; 433. 6; 215. 13; 484. 11; 245. 4; 362. 11; 365. 15

*śes* (?) beings 410. 3

*śes* / *śesȧ* name of a garment 213. 8; 336. 8; 337. 4

*śes* . . . . . . 228. 1

*śesu* to be hurt or injured 406. 12; injury (?) 406. 4

*śes-ui* (?) the two eyes (?) 144. 15; var.

*śes maāt* cord of law, *i. e.*, unfailing regularity 77. 5; 80. 16; 82. 18; 152. 13; 162. 2; 194. 9; 210. 3; 211. 13; 268. 13; 308. 10; 334. 4; 402. 16; 403. 13; 410. 5

*Śes-χentet* a proper name 456. 4

*śessau* intelligence, mental faculties 491. 13

*śes ṭepi* linen of the first quality 449. 1

*śeta* turtle 181. 6

**śeta**
**śetai**
**śetat** — to be hidden, to hide, hidden one or thing, secret mystery **38.** 5; **45.** 8; **370.** 2;. **371.** 15; **374.** 3; **474.** 12; **481.** 8; hidden goddess **429.** 11; hidden one **359.** 14; **425.** 14

**śetait** hidden place **135.** 2; **254.** 11; **325.** 10; **423.** 4; **428.** 10

**śetait** hidden city **256.** 6

**śetau**
**śetait** — hidden things, mysteries, secret things or persons or places **20.** 6; **33.** 4; **34.** 12; **46.** 1; **137.** 12; **143.** 11; **145.** 15; **169.** 15; **174.** 9; **187.** 8; **199.** 13; **270.** 1, 7; **271.** 9; **274.** 10; **280.** 6; **285.** 5; **290.** 10; **309.** 6; **310.** 1, 2; **349.** 12; **359.** 7; **482.** 3; **497.** 3; **428.** 5; hidden of **195.** 15; of **61.** 12; **69.** 1; of **134.** 12; **142.** 10; of **146.** 7, 16; **320.** 3; **331.** 14; of **418.** 12; **475.** 3

**Śetau-ā** a proper name **427.** 5, 8

**Śetet-pet** a proper name **468.** 1

**Śeta-ḥrá** a proper name **299.** 10

**śeṭ** tied up in **335.** 1

**śeṭentet** bound, tied **89.** 12

**śeθit** hidden place (?) **37.** 12

# K.

**k** thee, thou, thy 1. 6; 2. 6; 4. 1, 5; and see *passim.*

**k** *k* with sign of dual thy two hands 85. 6; and see 92. 11; 370. 13; 373. 1; 386. 9; 387. 12; 436. 3, 12; 437. 10; 438. 1; 446. 6, 8; 447. 8, 11, 13; 448. 5, 6, 9, 10; 449. 5, 13

**ka**
**kai** } to call, to proclaim, to cry out 29. 2; 184. 5; 194. 3; 197. 6, 7; 270. 1; 272. 11; 315. 4; 384. 10, 15

**kaiu** shouts, acclamations 329. 13

**ka** verily, prithee 147. 15; 148. 1, 2; 197. 3; 198. 13; 212. 14; 213. 6; 234. 15; 399. 11

**ka** bull 125. 2; 153. 14; 169. 10; 173. 5; 217. 7; 228. 14, 15; 230. 6, 7; 325. 13; 360. 7; 363. 8, 16; 375. 12; 397. 16; 405. 13; 413. 1; 493. 11; divine bull 254. 6; plur. 232. 7

**Ka Ȧmentet** Bull of Ȧmentet, a name of Osiris 18. 8; 133. 6; 482. 5; 483. 1

**Ka-ur** a proper name 464. 5; red bull 333. 7

***Ka-tai-kaut*** "Bull, husband of cows", a name of the Bull of the Seven Cows 318. 15; 364. 6

***kaut*** cows 325. 2

***ka*** the double of a man or god 1. 11; 3. 10; 90. 3; 94. 12; 179. 13; 216. 7; 217. 2; 223. 1, 11; 277. 10; 303. 15; 304. 1; 305. 2, 6; 306. 1, 2, 11; 307. 5; 373. 2; 395. 3; 399. 10; 438. 13; 439. 9; 441. 11; 448. 16; 482. 8; 486. 6; 494. 2; 513. 5; 514. 9, 14; plur. , 123. 8, 16; 159. 13; 229. 1; 318. 9; 456. 16; 462. 12; with and 487. 15; with 196. 3; 96. 4; of Osiris 326. 15; of Rā 43. 11

***Ka-Ḥetep*** a proper name 277. 11

***ka*** , food 1. 13; 65. 12; 92. 10; 244. 1; 278. 1; 479. 3; 493. 10

***Kaa*** name of a god 203. 8

***Kaȧrik*** a proper name 418. 13

***kaui*** a class of fiends (?) 412. 11

***kabit*** lamentation 73. 11

***Kaharesapusaremkaḥerremt*** a proper name 415. 13

***Kasaika*** a proper name 418. 14

***karȧ*** shrine, 9. 8; 13. 2; 44. 8; 82. 8; 107. 12; 169. 1; 195. 14; 259. 11; 279. 7; 289. 1; 422. 10; 425. 3; 442. 3, 6; 481. 15; plur. 55. 10; 103. 10; 107. 16; 183. 2

***kari***
***karȧut*** shrine 135. 4 *(bis)*; 315. 1

***kat*** work, labours 28. 3, 9, 14; 205. 11; 384. 6, 12; 447. 14

***kuȧ*** I 4. 15; 22. 2, 4, 5; 52. 2; 58. 1; 63. 5, 6; 135. 15 *(bis)*; 147. 5, 6; 247. 2; 336. 5, 16; 337. 12; 338. 9; 339. 10; 340. 12; 343. 12; 344. 3, 4; 345. 1; 346. 7; 347. 13; 349. 15; 350. 7; 351. 3; 419. 1; 472. 11; 483. 16; 484. 11; 488. 9; 493. 10; 504. 3, 14; 505. 2; 506. 4; 507. 4, 6

***ki*** verily 412. 7

***ki*** another, the other 5. 12; 256. 13; .... the one .... the other 54. 14, 16; 55. 1; 97. 13; 346. 15, 16; 347. 1, 2; 413. 4, 5; 417. 3; another person 60. 3; 495. 13; another chapter 27. 3; 31. 9; 83. 1; 278. 11; 294. 15; 295. 16; 415. 3; another person 497. 9; another time 134. 11; 142. 10

***ki ṭeṭ*** another reading, a variant 22. 2, 9; 52. 1, 7, 16; 53. 4, 6, 15, 16; 54. 15, 16; 55. 7, 13; 56. 2; 57. 2, 7; 58. 13; 59. 6, 7; 61. 1; 62. 5, 6, 9, 10; 63. 1, 2; 64. 12, 13, 14; 68. 2; 69. 3, 5; 79. 8; 98. 8; 101. 6; 129. 1; 131. 9; 152. 15; 155. 5; 197. 2; 217. 8; 242. 7;

294. 16; 315. 4; 323. 9; 324. 13; 339. 12, 16; 340. 3; 346. 14, 15; 502. 9; 512. 13

**kep** a hidden place 383. 9

**kep** to hide 310. 3; compounded (?) 375. 10

**Kep-ḥrá** a proper name 383. 8

**kefa** strong 237. 10, 11; seized 414. 11

**kefa** to carry away, to remove, to strip off from, to put off, to clothe (?) 68. 10; 133. 11; 154. 10; 165. 16; 247. 16; 251. 6; 334. 16; 338. 4; 481. 4; 489. 1; take off (your wigs) 367. 5; 372. 2; 348. 1

**Kemkem** name of a god 163. 6

**kená** to speak evil 254. 3

**Kenemet** name of a city 257. 13

**kenemet** night, darkness 257. 1

**Kenemti** one of the forty-two assessors 257. 1

**kenḥu** night 446. 1; 448. 1

**Kenset** Nubia 412. 15

**Ker** a proper name = 106. 15

**kerit** habitation, abode 136. 11

***Keḥkeḥet*** a proper name 163. 8

***kes*** to pay homage to 11. 8; 487. 8

***kesu*** homage 46. 9; 164. 15; 188. 14

***Kesemu-enenet*** a class of divine beings 172. 4

***keku*** darkness, night 24. 8; 30. 16; 66. 1; 85. 5; 119. 10; 165. 16; 169. 12; 176. 7, 10; 177. 8, 9, 10, 14, 15; 185. 3; 236. 12; 245. 6; 271. 5; 274. 7; 392. 7; 428. 10; 429. 1; 439. 1; 481. 4; 489. 1; darkness 279. 15; being dark 458. 9

***ket*** another 34. 4; 316. 13; 407. 10, 11

***ketuit*** abode, habitation 423. 6

***ketut*** weapons, knives 62. 15; 63. 5

***keteχu*** other or various things 459. 9; 506. 6, 8, 12

***ketet*** little, bad 42. 3

#  Q.

qa  ground (?) 158. 2

qa  to be high, exalted, height 13. 10; 100. 1; 163. 9; 169. 2, 4; 173. 1; 176. 1; 184. 14; 193. 16; 217. 3; 221. 15; 282. 12; 312. 2; 334. 11; 337. 9; 338. 5; 339. 13; 350. 1; 367. 15; 369. 1; 373. 7; 473. 14; 477. 3; 483. 16; 486. 16;  with  352. 5;  exalted one 185. 9;  exalted 471. 14;  doubly high 368. 15;   exceedingly high 370. 2; 381. 6;  height of heaven 182. 17; 
 lord or high of voice 258. 6, 13; 354. 5; 
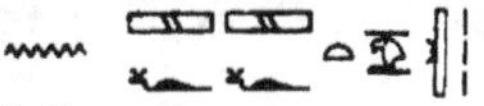 most terrible 378. 9; 
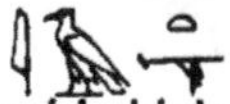 exalted of station 262. 3;  god with high plumes 408. 6

**Qa-ha-ḥetep**  a proper name 373. 5, 8

**Qa-ḥrá**  a proper name 484. 1

qaa  to putrefy 139. 6; 144. 6

**qaat** bolts, fastenings 136. 9

**qaȧ** / **Qaȧu** form, divine form 465. 3; 510. 12; 512. 16

**qai** fire 342. 8

**qab** bend, bight, fold 27. 6; 125. 10; 146. 12; 186. 7; 301. 6; 356. 5; 24. 7

**qabt** knees 448. 8

**Qabt-ent-Śu-erṭā-nef-em-Sa-Ȧusȧr** a proper name 265. 5

**qamȧi** incense (?) 420. 5

**qart** part of the underworld 471. 16

**qart** bolts, fastenings 150. 7; 474. 3

**Qaḫu** a proper name 375. 3; 381. 12

**qaḫit** fire 355. 3

**qasu** to bind, to fetter, tied up in something 2. 7; 12. 11; 36. 8; 106. 5; 153. 3; 228. 14; 279. 10

**qases-tu** tied 225. 14

**qasu** fetters 105. 12; 453. 4; 460. 7

**qaqa** hill 51. 11

**qā** to be provided 349. 1

**qāḥu** arm and shoulder 19. 15; 68. 8; 131. 13; 215. 5, 6; 238. 5; 308. 5; 420. 7, 8; 483. 12; 507. 8; the two shoulders 447. 12; plur. 111. 11; 131. 15; 155. 11; 72. 5

**qāḥ** to stretch out 186. 14

**qu** . . . . . . 407. 6

**qeb** fold, bend (see ) 64. 5, 14; 65. 1; 109. 12; 423. 13; 435. 4

**qebḥ**, **qebḥu** cool, cold, refreshment, to cool or refresh oneself, cold water, to pour out cold water, water flood 14. 13; 132. 11; 137. 10; 143. 9; 220. 2; 422. 6; 430. 5; 435. 6; 437. 1; 439. 2; 486. 6; 510. 3; place of refreshing 430. 5; the cool stream of Elephantine 454. 4

**Qebḥu** the land of cool water 174. 12; 377. 1

**Qebḥ-sennu-f** one of the four children of Horus 57. 14; 58. 9; 59. 3; 232. 9; 235. 4; 306. 4; 319. 6; 326. 10; 385. 8, 9; 407. 5; 505. 5

**Qebti** Coptos 442. 3

*qefen* baked cake 208. 13

*Qefennu* name of a city 321. 9; 323. 16

*qefṭennu* ape, Ape 116. 4, 7; 397. 3

*qem* to make an end of, to finish 10. 11; 42. 5, 6; 148. 4; 469. 9; 470. 2

*qem*, *qemt* black 231. 11; 232. 1; 445. 16; 462. 4; 494. 11; 502. 12; strong (?) 236. 1

*Qem-ur* name of a city and lake 136. 1; 145. 2; 188. 14; 247. 12

*qem* to find, to discover 3. 7; 60. 2; 68. 4; 92. 16; 97. 3; 108. 3; 115. 4; 141. 9; 176. 14; 189. 8; 190. 2; 204. 15; 229. 8; 233. 11, 13; 248. 2; 285. 6; 309. 13; 348. 5; 406. 9, 14; a find 234. 2; 263. 11; 466. 9; , found 16. 3; 21. 14; 96. 16; 140. 13; 145. 12; 273. 11; 288. 15; 352. 5; 487. 13; things found 309. 12

*Qem-ḥrȧu* a class of divine beings 130. 2

*qemqem* to discover 233. 8

*qemtu* evil one, evil 29. 12

*qema* to create, to fashion, to form 12. 4; 48. 8; 278. 3; 326. 16; 343. 7; 346. 3; 404. 9; 442. 9, 14; 455. 10; 484. 3; 487. 2; 515. 7

**qemam** to create, to fashion, to form, to produce, form, qualities, creator, created thing 1. 6; 7. 9; 9. 2 *(bis)*; 51. 12, 14; 68. 12; 87. 16; 90. 14; 115. 13; 165. 13; 167. 6, 9, 15; 174. 4; 184. 4, 13; 185. 3, 12; 224. 16; 246. 10; 264. 1; 279. 2; 308. 1; 343. 7; 344. 6; 346. 13; 356. 12; 357. 11; 361. 10; 397. 13; 457. 13, 14; 461. 10; 467. 11; 477. 5; 491. 13; to create by a word 233. 6; creatress 138. 3; those who make themselves to be 137. 12; 143. 11

**Qemamu** god of creation 469. 2

**qemā** to praise 210. 12; a singer 489. 9

**qemā** south 12. 13; southern 97. 1

**qemā**, **qemā ta**, **qemāt** south, south land 141. 7; 278. 14; 453. 5, 7; 488. 1; 512. 4; southern stones 164. 11; 353. 13; South and North 298. 8

**Qemāt** goddess of the South (?) 40. 12

**qemḥ** to see, sight 439. 7; 481. 16

**qemḥet** eye 155. 12

**Qemḥusu** a proper name 461. 12

**qemḥut** hair (?) 356. 4

*qemt* lasting, enduring 238. 11

*Qemt* Egypt 173. 13; 313. 14; 325. 12; 414. 5; 486. 1

*qemtu* overturned 338. 5

*qemṭu* to say, to repeat 96. 9

*qen* to do evil 71. 14

*qen* to fortify, strength 298. 11; 313. 15

*qenȧ* to embrace 50. 8

*qenȧt* a kind of incense 374. 1; 379. 11

*qeni* a kind of linen 375. 1

*qenbet*, *qenbit* a class of beings, human and divine 135. 1; 142. 14; 414. 14

*Qenna* a proper name 3. 14; 4. 13; 5. 14; 6. 14; 8. 9; 476. 2

*qennu* strong 413. 11

*qenret* a kind of grain or fruit 49. 14

*qenqen* to strengthen (?) 67. 9

*qenqen* to feed 229. 10

*Qentqet* name of a lake in the Elysian Fields 229. 10

*qer* wind 456. 1

**qerȧ** / **qerȧu** storm, thunder **105**. 15; **107**. 4; **439**. 1; a proper name **69**. 3

**qerȧs** sepulture, burial, funeral rites **34**. 7; **417**. 2

**qerfiu** tied, fastened **89**. 13; (?) tied, bound **436**. 3

**qeres** / **qereset** to bury, tomb, burial, funeral **18**. 6; **23**. 6; dead body **52**. 8; **59**. 6; and see **92**. 16; **130**. 6; **168**. 12; **263**. 9, 14; **399**. 6; buried **187**. 10; a happy burial **488**. 6; coffin, bier **65**. 11; **72**. 14; **75**. 16; **101**. 16; **159**. 6; **161**. 10; **437**. 5; plur. **436**. 7

**qert** cave, cavern **285**. 7

**qerti** double cavern **317**. 14; **326**. 11

**qerti** caverns of the source of the Nile at Elephantine **380**. 3

**Qerti** one of the forty-two assessors **254**. 3

**qerti** the caverns of the underworld **270**. 13; **271**. 1; **515**. 8; **516**. 11

**qerert** a division of the underworld 253. 2, 14; 272. 9; 274. 2; 425. 1; 428. 14; 430. 8; 433. 13; plur. 275. 10; *qerert* 428. 14; 430. 8; 433. 13

**qert** fastening 264. 14

**qeḥeḥtum** (?) castrated animals for sacrifice 453. 16; 510. 3

**qesu** bones 100. 14; 106. 14; 253. 12; 289. 6; 361. 4; 367. 7, 8; 372. 14; 385. 10; 399. 16; 400. 1; 407. 1; 411. 4; 416. 7; 417. 13; 440. 15; 478. 11; 510. 5

**qesu** preserves (of birds) 251. 8

**Qesi** Cusae, the capital of the fourteenth nome of Upper Egypt 235. 11

**qesen** bad 29. 6; 204. 5, 14; baleful 371. 15; 412. 11

**qeq** see *ām* to eat 31. 13, etc.

**Qetetbu** a proper name 225. 13

**qeṭ** to build 67. 12; 129. 2; 224. 5; 243. 10; 388. 8, 14; 389. 4; 491. 7

**qeṭáu** to build 514. 8

**qeṭ** draughtsman's work (?) 222. 11; 223. 12; 444. 11; 445. 3

**qeṭu** sailors, mariners 4. 11; 7. 8; 27. 7; 44. 14; 49. 8; 106. 16; 111. 3; 211. 2; 212. 11, 15; 262. 13; 282. 11; 283. 11; 316. 3; 332. 4; 373. 12; 431. 2

***Qețu*** a fiend 415. 11

***qețu*** work of the artist or draughtsman 274. 1, 15; 275. 8; 276. 4

***qeț*** orbit 236. 12

***qeț*** character, disposition 249. 13; 467. 1; 110. 11

***qeț*** with *md*, like 242. 8; 313. 11; 314. 17; 352. 5

***qețet*** with , throughout (?) 409. 16

***qețet*** slumber 455. 15

## ⚘ Ḳ

ḳa     [hieroglyphs] to go forward 214. 7

ḳa     [hieroglyphs] dung 99. 7

ḳa     [hieroglyphs] to stink 104. 13; [hieroglyphs] 1

ḳau     [hieroglyphs] calamities 458. 15

ḳau     [hieroglyphs] caverns (?) 506. 11

ḳaui (?)     [hieroglyphs] name of a place or lake 255. 11;
[hieroglyphs] , [hieroglyphs]

ḳai     [hieroglyphs] lake 89. 6

ḳab     [hieroglyphs] to depart from 90. 13

ḳabti     [hieroglyphs] eyelashes 446. 7

ḳafu     [hieroglyphs] ape 296. 7, 16; plur. [hieroglyphs]
297. 14

ḳaṣt     [hieroglyphs] . . . . . . 325. 9

ḳat     [hieroglyphs] claw 417. 6

ḳata     [hieroglyphs] thoughts, meditations 92. 6

**ḳuat** to surround 397. 5

**Ḳeb** name of a god 205. 1

**ḳeb** great deep 359. 14

**ḳeba** to cast an evil glance at (?) 372. 14

**ḳeba** chamber 400. 15

**ḳen**
**ḳenen** } weak, feeble 29. 9, 11

**ḳenu** cattle 154. 14

**Ḳen-ur** a proper name 35. 2; var. ,

**ḳennut** decrees 92. 12

**Ḳenḳen-ur** name of a god 126. 6; 127. 11

**ḳent** slit 103. 11

**ḳer** . . . . . . 178. 15

**ḳer** moreover 243. 6

**ḳer** to be silent 114. 5; 225. 15; 244. 10; 265. 14; 373. 11; 166. 3; 293. 1

**ḳer** , lie, falsehood 15. 14; 17. 6; 70. 3; plur. 39. 4, 10; 67. 4; 96. 9; 253. 13; 260. 8; 269. 11; 467. 13; craft, fraud 488. 8; 490. 5; 90. 11

**ḳer** to possess, to have, to hold 140. 10; 327. 1; 457. 3; 459. 16; 460. 4; 481. 1; 486. 3; 488. 14; possessor 39. 7; 513. 1

**ḳer** possessions 97. 15

**Ḳert** name of a city 507. 12

**ḳerḥ**, **ḳerḥu**, **ḳerḥu**, **ḳerḥet** night, darkness 42. 5; 53. 8; 59. 11; 60. 12; 61. 4, 15; 62. 1; 71. 7; 72. 1, 10, 13; 73. 10; 74. 8; 75. 11; 76. 4; 78. 3; 79. 2; 81. 8; 82. 2; 83. 4, 5, 6, 7, 8, 9, 10; 84. 3, 4, 5, 6, 7, 8, 9; 85. 9; 88. 11; 128. 4; 158. 6; 192. 8; 228. 11; 236. 4; 262. 14; 286. 7; 304. 2; 315. 8; 330. 4; 338. 7; 343. 6; 356. 4; 366. 1; 391. 15; 439. 14; 441. 12; 456. 12; 466. 6; 467. 14; 492. 4; 497. 2; 506. 1; 508. 11; plur. 159. 1 *(bis)*

**Ḳerśer, Keräśer** a proper name 508. 4, 8, 12; 509. 4, 13; 510. 15; 511. 15; 512. 3, 10, 15; 513. 12; 514. 2, 5, 15; 515. 2, 4, 6, 8, 11, 13, 15; 516. 1

**ḳert** but, moreover 55. 2, 6, 11; 56. 12; 58. 15; 59. 2, 14; 60. 6; 61. 2, 4, 15; 141. 3; 143. 5; 145. 11; 280. 8; 421. 13; 457. 15; 458. 8, 11, 14; 459. 1, 2, 3, 6, 12, 16; 137. 5

**ḳeḥ** weak, helpless, humble, pained 215. 3; 359. 6; 106. 1

**ḳes** place, side, footprint of, half 7. 11; 15. 15;

**60.** 12; **61.** 2; **86.** 15; **98.** 8; **103.** 14; **219.** 16; **287.** 10; **334.** 16; **368.** 4; **369.** 5; **402.** 9; **404.** 7; **455.** 15; **503.** 6, 14; **507.** 10; , , both sides **106.** 13; **246.** 16; **439.** 2; **440.** 6; **486.** 8; plur. **287.** 11; left side **88.** 13; **89.** 6; **284.** 14; **395.** 14; **397.** 8; right side **284.** 14; **395.** 13; for (18. 9) *q. v.*

**ḳeś** pool, lake **144.** 8

## T.

*t* thy 136. 16; 334. 10, 11; 336. 4; 337. 10; 385. 3

*ta* the 326. 7; 409. 9; 410. 8; 411. 7, 9; 412. 8, 15; 413. 5; 414. 4; 416. 14; his 411. 12

*ta*, *taa*, *tau* to burn, flame, fire, hot, angry 256. 2; 305. 12, 14; 306. 2; 313. 1; 345. 3; 430. 6

*Ta-reṭ* one of the forty-two assessors 256. 10, 15

*tȧt* emanation, part of 416. 13; plur. 413. 3

*ta* the earth, world, land, country 1. 13; 61. 6; 63. 10; 67. 9, 10; 334. 2; 375. 6; 388. 8, 14; 389. 11; 436. 13; 440. 16; 461. 10; 474. 3; 488. 10; 489. 16; 517. 3; 324. 6; union with earth, *i. e.* burial 23. 14; beings of earth 114. 14

*taui* the two lands of Egypt, the world 6. 15; 65. 7, 10; 78. 1; 122. 15; 314. 3; 319. 1; 369. 14; 438. 14; 442. 15; 461. 2; 481. 1; 485. 3; [illegible] 506. 13

*taiu* — the world, all countries 2. 11; 9. 1, 12; 10. 6; 155. 7; 263. 6; 323. 7; 325. 1; 453. 9

*taiu Āḳert* — the regions of the underworld 14. 6

*ta āb* — the holy land, *i. e.*, the underworld 456. 9

*ta ānχtet* — the land of life, *i. e.*, the grave 323. 10

*Ta-ur* — name of a city 109. 1

*ta en Manu* — land of the setting sun 2. 12

*ta en Maāt* — land of law 413. 8

*ta en maātχeru* — land of triumph 3. 10

*Ta-merá* — land of the inundation, *i. e.*, Egypt 247. 1; 260. 5

*Ta meḥt* — land of the north, *i. e.*, Delta 321. 12; 324. 5; 326. 14; 453. 6

*Ta-mes-fetta* — "land which bringeth forth eternity" 315. 14

*ta nefer* — . . . . . . 315. 8

*tanenet* — name of place or region 25. 9

*ta neḥeḥ* — land of everlasting 41. 5; 399. 7

*taiu nu neteru* — lands of the gods 41. 14

*Ta-remu*  land of fish 234. 3, 6

*taui Reχti* / *taiu Reχti* 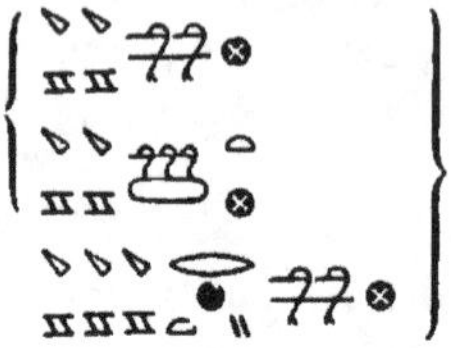 the lands of the Rekhti 19. 9; 73. 10, 13; 79. 12; 81. 12; 83. 9

*ta χaru*  land of Kharu birds 221. 5

*ta-Sekri*  land of Seker, *i. e.*, the tomb 322. 9

*Ta-śe*  land of the lake, *i. e.*, Fayyûm 234. 4; 254. 4; 432. 2

*ta-śeta* 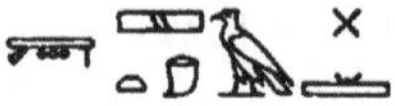 the hidden land 85. 14

*Ta-kenset*  Nubia 412. 15; 416. 3

*ta-qebḥ*  land of coolness 131. 8

*ta qemā* 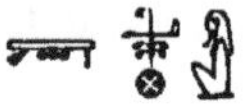 land of the south 324. 4; 326. 14

*ta ṭuat* 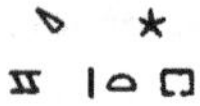 land of the underworld 434. 2

*Ta-ṭesert*  the holy land 14. 8; 22. 15; 39. 4; 44. 3; 348. 16; 365. 14; 383. 16; 428. 11; 431. 12; 452. 2; 476. 3; 479. 14; 482. 4; 484. 8, 14; 488. 7; 490. 10; 512. 14

*ta en ṭetta*  land of everlasting, *i. e.*, the grave 41. 6

*tau* 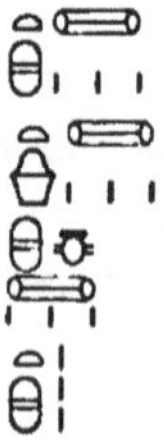 bread, cakes 14. 12; 21. 1, 2; 70. 4, 9; 124. 4, 5; 151. 7; 154. 13; 179. 7; 214. 14; 231. 3; 244. 3; 245. 3; 307. 13; 312. 6; 363. 9, 11, 16; 364. 7; 365. 1; 366. 6; 424. 2; 426. 2; 436. 5; 449. 3; 454. 7; 455. 16; 463. 16; 464. 6; 465. 2; 466. 8;

477. 15; 493. 4; 494. 10; 495. 6; 510. 3; 514. 13; 516. 6; cakes of fine flour 317. 5; white bread 333. 9; celestial bread 437. 6; cakes of Ȧnnu 439. 13; cakes of 439. 13; 437. 7; 439. 12; 494. 11, 13; 495. 6; 492. 15; 495. 5

***Tau-enenet*** name of a place 66. 16; 67. 7, 8, 11; 322. 4

***tau-atutu*** (?) a kind of wood 337. 5

***Tai***, ***Taiti*** } Osiris 322. 2; 325. 1

***tait*** sail, awning 206. 5

***Tait*** name of a goddess 180. 4; 449. 3

***tar*** a fiend 418. 1

***taḥenen*** to dip in water 229. 6

***Ta-ḥer-sta-nef*** a proper name 13. 16

***Tatunen***, ***Taθunen*** } name of a god 1. 13; 47. 1; 183. 4; 472. 9

***tu*** thee, thou 1. 8, 9; 2. 4; 5. 6; 7. 8; 23. 16; 30. 15; 40. 11; 129. 14; 192. 8; 266. 4, 6; 439. 6; 448. 10; 478. 16; 479. 4; 487. 4, 9; and see *passim*.

***tua*** to adore 406. 5

***tuȧ*** I 63. 5, 12; 98. 9; 160. 5; 394. 4

*tui* that 26. 2; 63. 6; 64. 5; 77. 12; 86. 13; 100. 3; 105. 7; 124. 4; 130. 15; 131. 1; 154. 11; 261. 15; 297. 1; 301. 2; 315. 7; 367. 14; 437. 5, 14; 508. 9

*tui* . . . . . . 408. 11

*tui* . . . . . . 106. 8

*tuf* his 20. 10; and see *passim*.

*tuni* ye, you (?) 496. 3

*turá* / *tur*(?) to cleanse, to purify, to be pure, clean 67. 13; 141. 15; 145. 16; 182. 17; 201. 10; 262. 9; 267. 14; 309. 11; 312. 4; 337. 3; 436. 16; 465. 9, 10; to celebrate in a pure manner 480. 4; 508. 6; 399. 16

*tuk* thou 248. 15; 508. 10; and see *passim*.

*tuk̦* apparel 440. 4

*tut* type, form, image, statue, similitude 57. 8; 63. 16; 64. 1; 77. 2; 112. 1; 178. 12; 196. 6; 226. 5; 239. 9; 245. 13; 284. 12; 289. 8; 291. 4, 6; 294. 6; 298. 4; 299. 15; 309. 2; 312. 1; 314. 17; 333. 3; 338. 7; 339. 12; 395. 12; 413. 15; 414. 1; 420. 3, 6, 9; 438. 10; 444. 10; 468. 4; plur. 420. 10; arranged 513. 1; 470. 15; as, like 380. 12; 478. 8

*tut ás* behold 128. 11; 272. 13; 275. 13; 289. 8; 367. 6; 372. 3; 461. 15; 464. 5

*tiu* (?) adorers 422. 4

***tini*** = you 114. 14; 231. 4; 394. 9; 396. 2, 5, 6, 8, 10, 12, 14, 16; 397. 2, 4, 6

***tit*** time (?) 180. 15

***tebu*** to be shod with 262. 15

***teb***
***tebi***
***tebt*** } sandals 123. 10; 214. 14; 244. 3; 438. 1; 448. 8; 494. 4; 495. 3

***Tebu***
***Tebti*** } name of a city 185. 10; 258. 3

***tebu*** . . . . . . 198. 7

***tebteb*** to walk 138. 11

***Tepa*** name of a cow 336. 15

***tepȧ*** to snuff the air 37. 1; 38. 1

***tepḥet*** cavern, den, dwelling 39. 6; 49. 14; 119. 9; 148. 16; 149. 2; 168. 6; 256. 8, 14; 258. 16; 259. 1; 357. 10; 433. 3; 489. 4; plur. 19. 13; 92. 13; 149. 13, 14; 171. 12; 172. 2; 210. 10

***tef*** father 65. 9; 77. 11, 14; 98. 10; 119. 15; 276. 15; 277. 3; 285. 8; 291. 10; 317. 15; 347. 3, 4; 405. 12; 437. 4, 5; 461. 10; 485. 10; 503. 10, 11

***tefa*** that 186. 5

***Tefnut*** a goddess 15. 5; 60. 10; 71. 12; 237. 15; 279. 3; 294. 4; 302. 2; 318. 8; 437. 3; 443. 9

*temam* to be complete **25.** 4; **245.** 9

*temamu* stations **478.** 3

*temaāu* (?) wind **44.** 13

*tem*, *temt*, *temem* not, without **5.** 10; **28.** 3; **29.** 11; **90.** 8; **91.** 13; **93.** 3, 12; **94.** 17; **95.** 15; **101.** 3, 10; **116.** 17; **119.** 8; **120.** 5, 13; **124.** 17; **132.** 3; **133.** 5; **145.** 6; **147.** 11; **148.** 2; **183.** 16; **192.** 11, 12; **193.** 15; **197.** 11; **198.** 15; **236.** 14; **365.** 5; **373.** 10; **374.** 9, 11; **378.** 7, 12; **399.** 2; **400.** 7; **410.** 16; **418.** 7; **438.** 1; **457.** 9; **460.** 13; **482.** 16; **492.** 7, 8; **501.** 3, 14; **505.** 16; **506.** 1

*temem* to be whole, complete, entire **5.** 11; **6.** 16; **485.** 6

*tem* to end **30.** 9; **135.** 16; wholly **113.** 5; **150.** 16; **242.** 7; **399.** 16; **400.** 3; **419.** 5; **420.** 1; wholly and entirely **78.** 2; **88.** 14; all **419.** 7

*Tem*, *Temu* the god Tem or Temu **4.** 1; **5.** 15; **8.** 14; **15.** 5; **27.** 4; **29.** 11; **32.** 12; **45.** 11; **51.** 5, 16; **53.** 16; **54.** 4; **55.** 8, 14; **56.** 5; **67.** 12, 16; **71.** 11; **77.** 11; **86.** 11; **92.** 12; **99.** 12; **103.** 1; **104.** 7, 11; **107.** 6; **110.** 12; **128.** 13; **145.** 3; **154.** 3; **160.** 15; **167.** 9; **173.** 8; **174.** 4; **180.** 6, 8; **192.** 7; **197.**

8; 198. 14; 207. 14; 220. 13; 238. 14; 242. 15; 287. 7; 294. 4; 302. 4; 314. 15; 318. 6; 325. 13; 347. 6; 367. 9; 382. 13; 391. 11; 399. 8; 406. 11; 413. 6; 443. 8; 455. 12; 456. 2; 457. 16; 458. 7, 14; 459. 1, 4; 471. 6; 472. 6; 477. 5; 484. 13; 485. 8; 496. 14; 509. 8; 442. 1

***Temu-Ḥeru-χuti*** Tem-Harmachis 4. 14; 11. 4; 35. 11; 49. 1; 315. 2

***Tem-Xeperȧ*** Tem-Kheperȧ 87. 6

***tememu*** parts of a net 393. 10

***temu*** / ***tememu*** mortals 2. 1; 6. 3; 8. 8; 33. 11; 176. 1; 350. 9; 369. 14; 438. 14; 482. 13

***Temem-reu*** .... .... a proper name 392. 15

***Tem-sep*** one of the forty-two assessors 258. 1

***temt*** sledge 38. 14; 210. 12

***ten*** this 23. 5; 155. 11, 14; 225. 7; 346. 14; 410. 6; 414. 10; 461. 15; 503. 17; 504. 15

***ten*** , ye, you 2. 3; 15. 17; 20. 13; 47. 15; 55. 16; 56. 1; 58. 1; 69. 12, 13, 15; 70. 7, 8; 82. 7; 90. 10, 11, 12; 107. 7, 9, 10; 108. 16; 119. 12; 128. 13; 151. 6; 303. 4; 315. 4; 316. 1; 335. 5; 336. 12; 338. 15; 339. 10; 342. 13; 344. 3; 345. 1; 346. 7; 360. 8; 364. 14; 377. 14, 15; 389. 6, 7, 9; 426. 2; 443. 16, 17; 444. 2; 462. 5; 465. 12, 15; 466. 8; 494. 4; 501. 10; 503. 17; 516. 2

***Teni*** This 74. 3; 215. 2

***Tenait*** god of light (?) **174**. 11

***ten***, ***teni***, ***tennu***, ***tennut*** what manner of? **124**. 6; **129**. 14; to distinguish, to discern, to declare **74**. 2; **84**. 3; **88**. 11; **109**. 3; **114**. 12; **172**. 1; **241**. 19; **309**. 2; **350**. 9; **399**. 5; **476**. 13, 14; **492**. 16; **494**. 14, 16; **495**. 9

***ten***, ***teni***, ***tennu*** to be or become great, great, to magnify, to increase, to enlarge, manifold **9**. 12; **115**. 5; **161**. 1; **167**. 11; **168**. 1; **203**. 4; **338**. 6; **352**. 7; **459**. 11; **460**. 1

***tentu*** (?) those who cry, to cry out **341**. 4; **354**. 4

***tenem*** to turn back **439**. 15

***Tenemit*** a proper name **437**. 2

***trå*** then **129**. 14; **138**. 15; **143**. 15; **241**. 18; **495**. 12; **503**. 9; **506**. 3; **507**. 5

***trå*** time, season **11**. 16; **56**. 13; **109**. 8; **114**. 6, 7; **115**. 4; **116**. 3; **234**. 1; **251**. 10; **288**. 4; **437**. 11; plur. **23**. 1; 11. 6

***trå-ui*** the two seasons, *i. e.*, morn and eve **1**. 9; **9**. 5; **21**. 2; **36**. 2, 6

***teriti*** the northern and southern heavens **4**. 5

***teh***, ***teha*** to advance against, to attack **251**. 12, 15, 16; **254**. 4; **255**. 12; **257**. 7, 13; **342**. 7; **411**. 5; **414**. 11

**tehenen** to adore 5. 11

**Teḥuti** Thoth 2. 5; 3. 3; 15. 16; 16. 7; 17. 1; 18. 8; 19. 3; 30. 4; 32. 12; 40. 14; 48. 3; 56. 12, 16; 57. 3; 58. 7; 62. 10; 71. 3, 14; 72. 12; 73. 7; 74. 11; 75. 8; 76. 10; 81. 3; 83. 2; 84. 1; 86. 9; 108. 12; 113. 4; 124. 5; 151. 13; 154. 12; 155. 1; 156. 14; 163. 11; 177. 3; 181. 10; 199. 8, 10, 12; 211. 12; 213. 16; 236. 5; 238. 13; 242. 16; 266. 9 *(bis)*, 16; 267. 1; 274. 14; 277. 1; 280. 8; 281. 1; 282. 6; 283. 5; 286. 6; 292. 16; 295. 11; 315. 12; 319. 8; 326. 3; 330. 3; 331. 3; 338. 9; 345. 12; 357. 8; 359. 6; 371. 11; 382. 10; 387. 14; 406. 4, 15; 421. 11, 13; 439. 7; 441. 10; 448. 2; 451. 3; 457. 10, 16; 458. 4; 465. 3, 4, 11; 466. 3; 467. 15; 475. 2; 479. 12; 480. 11, 13, 14; 481. 11, 15, 16; 483. 5, 9, 10, 14; 484. 11; 488. 11, 15; 492. 16; 510. 9; 511. 9; 514. 10

**Teḥuti-Ḥāpi** Thoth-Ḥapi 132. 11

**Teḥutit** the Thoth festival 497. 1

**tiḥṭut** offerings 495. 1

**teχ** pointer of the scales 251. 4; 264. 5; 264. 5

**teχni** hidden 418. 7

**teχteχ** to shake out the hair 68. 5; 69. 6

**teś** to depart, way, passage 27. 16; 248. 3; 348. 5, 11; 486. 13

**Teśteś** a name of Osiris 19. 12

**tekem** to approach 165. 15

**Tekem** name of a god 160. 8

***tekau*** 
***teka*** 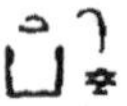
***tekat*** 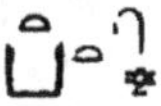
to burn, blaze, fire, spark, flame 303. 10, 13, 14, 15; 304. 2; 307. 9, 11; 308. 3, 9; 309. 1; 311. 5; 312. 13; 313. 1; 383. 13; 438. 16

***teken*** 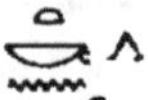 to enter, to go in 130. 1; 141. 16; 146. 1; 211. 9; 246. 12; 312. 5; 373. 10; 374. 12; 378. 12; 438. 5; 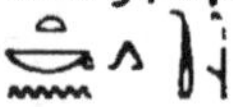 109. 14

***tekennu***  those who go in 135. 13; 171. 3

***tektek***  to pass by 233. 14

***teḳas***  to march on 108. 6

***tetbu***  to smear 311. 9

# Ṭ.

*ṭa* to pass away 120. 8

*ṭa* emission 106. 10

*ṭaṭa* to pollute oneself 250. 14; 255. 8, 15

*ṭaȧu* name of a garment 180. 4

*ṭaȧr* restraint 94. 2

*Ṭaśenȧtiṭ* mother of Ḳerāsher 508. 4, 8; 509. 1, 4, 14; 510. 15; 511. 16; 512. 4, 10, 16; 513. 12; 514. 3, 6, 15; 515. 2, 5, 7, 9, 11, 13, 16; 516. 2

*ṭā*, *ṭāṭā*, *ṭāṭāu* to give, to grant, to allow, to set, to place, to ascribe 1. 9; 21. 2; 33. 7; 41. 11; 43. 3; 61. 10; 62. 2; 65. 12; 80. 14; 69. 1; 97. 12; 108. 1; 130. 16; 131. 10; 134. 12; 142. 10; 184. 11; 191. 8; 192. 15, 16; 194. 1; 213. 10; 222. 15; 223. 1; 292. 6; 307. 8; 336. 1; 364. 6; 365. 1; 374. 5; 379. 8; 392. 8; 402. 14; 424. 14; 437. 9; 452. 7; 474. 1; 475. 5; 481. 6, 7, 489. 15; placing 147. 4; giving, a gift 379. 14; 380. 1; given 3. 7; 4. 9; 14. 12; 93. 6; 337. 10; 477. 15; as an auxiliary verb see *passim.*

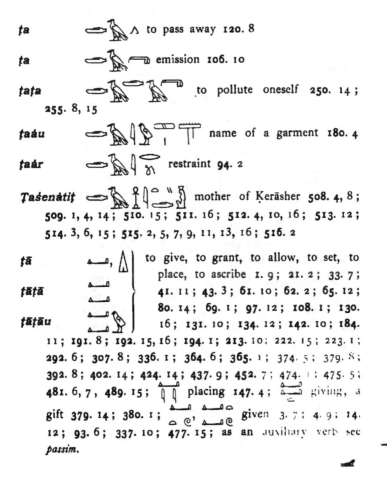

*ṭāṭāiu* givers 1. 13; 21. 1; 47. 13; 57. 15; 58. 10; 66. 9; 217. 16; 231. 15; 269. 8; 272. 5; 320. 4, 5, 6; 310. 10; 311. 3, 11; 363. 9, 16

*ṭāt àb*
*ṭāṭā ab* heart's desire 23. 3; 77. 2; 82. 17; 182. 4; 517. 1

*ṭā* to turn the face 43. 1; to put in fear 389. 6; 511. 7; 424. 5; 409. 6, 8, 11

*ṭā ḥef* white loaf or cake 317. 5, 6

*Ṭaṭāu* the city of Ṭaṭṭu 101. 12; 129. 1; 165. 11; 167. 5; 172. 7; 210. 9; 379. 14

*ṭu ā* to put forth the hand 429. 8

*ṭu*
*ṭut* evil, evil thing, sin, fault, wickedness, to do evil, sinner 34. 15; 38. 14; 107. 3; 114. 9; 115. 7; 153. 3, 5; 182. 8; 197. 2, 11; 198. 16; 216. 13, 14; 300. 5; 359. 15; 365. 8; 401. 1; 404. 7; 437. 3; 506. 9; 516. 2; plur. 44. 1; 50. 6; 54. 5, 8; 58. 1, 15; 76. 15; 91. 1; 116. 4; 175. 3; 185. 14; 187. 3, 4; 196. 1, 2; 198. 5; 203. 3; 249. 12; 260. 13; 269. 12, 13; 270. 4, 6; 271. 10; 273. 11; 274. 9; 365. 9, 10; 426. 7; 432. 9; 443. 17; 444. 2; 453. 1; 468. 3; 477. 1, 2, 14; 478. 9; 483. 8; 484. 16; 252. 7

*Ṭu* the evil one 44. 11

*Ṭuṭu*
*Ṭu-ṭut-f* one of the forty-two assessors 255. 3, 14

***Ṭu-s*** name of a rudder 242. 2

***ṭuȧu*** ale (?) 367. 5; 382. 5

***ṭu*** mountain 7. 15; 164. 13; 218. 12; 219. 1, 2, 5; 285. 7; 310. 12; 466. 16; plur. , 9. 4; 36. 14; 485. 12; 497. 4; 369. 15; 370. 2; 381. 6

***Ṭu-en-baχa*** mountain of the sunrise 496. 7

***Ṭu-en-Neter-χert*** mountain in the underworld 370. 3; 430. 13

***Ṭu-tef*** . . . . . . 98. 1

***Ṭu-menχ-rerek*** a proper name 372. 7

***ṭua*** five 221. 15; 317. 6, 7; 464. 6; 487. 4; fifth 337. 7; 351. 10; 360. 12

***ṭuau*** ,

***ṭuait***

***ṭuat***

— dawn, daybreak, morning, to-day, to-morrow morning 4. 3; 5. 5; 10. 15; 40. 3; 41. 11; 42. 10; 52. 3, 4; 57. 8; 80. 15; 134. 11; 284. 5; 440. 3; 481. 16; 486. 15

***ṭua*** , , , ,

***ṭuaui***

***ṭua ṭuau***

***ṭua***

— to praise, to worship, to adore 1. 3; 3. 3, 13; 6. 13; 11. 3; 34. 1; 35. 9, 12; 36. 12; 37. 10; 39. 14; 107. 15; 140. 1; 147. 6; 177. 10; 193. 16; 210. 13; 222. 12; 242. 11; 246. 6; 270. 13; 273. 16; 274. 8; 281. 1; 294. 9; 348. 16; 358. 8; 384. 2; 409. 3;

425. 9; 442. 3; 447. 15; 448. 2; 452. 4; 470. 9; 476. 1; 479. 4; 486. 15; 295. 11; 240. 13; praises 7. 13; praisers 430. 2; with 33. 12; 242. 9

*Ṭua-mut-f*
*Ṭua-māut-f* one of the four children of Horus 57. 13; 58. 8; 59. 3; 206. 16; 232. 9; 235. 4; 319. 5; 326. 9; 385. 5; 505. 4

*Ṭuat*
*Ṭuaut* the underworld 11. 12; 14. 12; 23. 13; 31. 14; 37. 13; 45. 9; 70. 14; 85. 16; 94. 10; 109. 2; 135. 13; 138. 2; 165. 14; 166. 8, 16; 167. 7; 168. 4; 170. 5; 171. 2, 15; 178. 16; 190. 5; 259. 16; 271. 2; 275. 10; 285. 5; 308. 14; 310. 1 *(bis)*; 315. 2; 317. 15; 333. 3; 365. 4, 13, 15; 414. 7; 420. 11; 424. 6; 425. 14; 427. 2; 429. 13; 430. 10; 432. 14; 433. 1; 455. 9; 471. 10; 472. 5; 473. 10; 474. 9, 13; 475. 1; 477. 6; 497. 3; 502. 10; 509. 5; 510. 9; 511. 3; 513. 15; 514. 5, 7; 516. 10; 517. 1; 419. 5; 416. 7; 447. 16; the god of Ṭuat 275. 11; beings of the Ṭuat 22. 9; 134. 13; 319. 16; 320. 1, 3; 470. 10

*ṭuatu* (?) decision, sentence 261. 12

*ṭun* to lift up or stretch out the legs 32. 7; 89. 13, 14; 195. 3; 436. 3

*Ṭun-peḥti* porter of the second Ārit 327. 15

*ṭurt* . . . . . . 507. 14

***ṭit*** gifts 214. 16

***ṭeb*** horn 197. 6; , the two horns 143. 10; 198. 12

***ṭeb*** tomb (?) 383. 12

***ṭeb*** to be furnished or equipped with 169. 2, 4; 225. 7; 226. 2; 227. 1; 279. 5; 284. 3; 286. 12; 301. 13; 386. 2; 451. 8

***ṭeb*** to wall up, to box in 310. 9; 311. 3, 11

***ṭebt*** box, coffer, coffin, chest, tomb 50. 5; 311. 4; 407. 3; 416. 5; plur. 163. 3; 511. 7

***ṭebu*** frame, part of the woodwork of a net 390. 13; 391. 8; 394. 5

***Ṭeb-ḥrȧ-keha-at*** the herald of the fifth Ārit 328. 11; 360. 15

***ṭeben*** to revolve 63. 8; 132. 15; 220. 9; 241. 1, 2; 318. 16; 330. 2; 353. 13; 364. 10; 370. 16; 371. 10; 466. 2

***ṭebḥ***, ***ṭebḥu*** to pray for, to make supplication 92. 4; 101. 15; 166. 15; 199. 6; 419. 1; 468. 15

***ṭebḥu*** prayers, supplications 22. 11; 337. 10; 351. 13

***ṭebḥ*** grain measure 251. 2; 253. 7

*ṭebḥu*, *ṭebḥet* offerings 208. 12; 289. 15; 347. 10; 463. 9; 487. 10

*ṭebt* block, slab 97. 1; 140. 14; 141. 6; 310. 6, 16; 311. 7, 16; 485. 9

*ṭep* unguent 502. 3

*ṭep* birds 441. 14

*ṭep* head, tip, top of any thing, chief 4. 10; 8. 6; 30. 4; 38. 11; 53. 12, 13, 14, 15; 54. 1; 62. 5; 99. 12; 106. 13, 14; 116. 17; 119. 1, 2, 3; 283. 8; 289. 16; 315. 10; 367. 9; 373. 3; 375. 11; 383. 3; 401. 15; 408. 5; 409. 5; 421. 1, 5, 6; 445. 14; 446. 12; 454. 16; 462. 16; 463. 1; 487. 5; 503. 16; plur. , 80. 7; 120. 18; 153. 7; 191. 7; 192. 16; 282. 11; 292. 11; 316. 7; 357. 3; 362. 11; 438. 3; 62. 7

*ṭep* upon 2. 14; 7. 13; 51. 4; 68. 8; 140. 11, 12; 142. 16; 145. 10; 147. 7; 313. 3; 371. 1; one upon 219. 5; 136. 6

*ṭep, ṭepi* , first 24. 5; 34. 11; 122. 1; 150. 7; 315. 10; 327. 11; 334. 9; 349. 14; 358. 3, 7; 367. 3; original state 483. 3

*ṭep-ā* straightway 105. 16; 139. 3; 201. 15; 282. 1

*ṭep* , the first, finest, or best of any thing 230. 9; 449. 1; 367. 16; 13. 8; 133. 9; 250. 4; ,

* 4. 3; 6. 2; 486. 15; 175. 14; 9. 1; 487. 14; 505. 15; 402. 15; 380. 5, 7

***ṭep-ā***, ***ṭept-ā*** ancestor 393. 1; 466. 7; plur. 85. 7; 391. 13; 393. 1, 10; 475. 6; of Rā 245. 1; 393. 9; 468. 5; of Seb 393. 10; of the year 244. 15; of Khu 245. 2

***ṭep re***, ***ṭep-retui*** utterance, speech, decree, ordinance 109. 15; 119. 13; 158. 14; 176. 11; 312. 16; 449. 13; 485. 1; plur. 482. 3; 504. 9

***Ṭep-ṭu***, ***Ṭepṭu-f*** he who is on his hill, a name of Anubis 247. 14; 310. 12; 348. 3; 383. 15; 466. 16

***ṭept*** uraeus crown 100. 6

***Ṭep***, ***Ṭepu***, ***Ṭept*** one part of the city of Buto 73. 1, 4; 79. 6; 81. 10; 83. 7; 109. 13; 160. 14; 163. 12; 209. 5; 322. 6; 439. 7; 442. 5; 454. 9; 483. 10; 323. 12

***ṭept*** taste 298. 5; to devour 411. 16; sting 106. 8

***ṭepu*** oar, paddle 296. 12; 297. 8

***ṭept*** boat 18. 10; 207. 9; 218. 5; 221. 8; 368. 10; 404. 7; 504. 15

**ṭem** — to cut, to gash 109. 11, 13; 414. 12; with — to speak in a shrill voice 446. 13

**ṭem**, **ṭemt** — knife, sword 12. 11; 36. 9; 346. 9; 357. 14; plur. 365. 10; double knife 44. 12

***Ṭem-re-χut-pet*** (?) . . . . . . . . 299. 5; 331. 8

***Ṭem-ur*** (?) a name of Osiris 321. 14

**ṭemamet** a hairy covering 169. 6

**ṭemam** to put an end to 301. 3

**ṭemam** to unite 453. 5

**ṭemȧ**, **ṭemȧi** — to unite, be united 189. 3, 11; 404. 7; 492. 12

**ṭemȧ** city 247. 1; plur. 214. 16

**ṭemṭ** — to collect, to assemble, to gather together 87. 8, 13; 146. 7; 164. 4, 16; 166. 11; 172. 3; 180. 6; 302. 7; 361. 1; 370. 9; 385. 10; 456. 16; 478. 11; 482. 11; 504. 4; all 78. 5; united 464. 11; 313. 11; 137. 11; 143. 10; 65. 10

***Ṭemṭiu*** a class of divine beings 87. 2

**ṭemṭ** to collect 457. 2

**ṭen** to cut **106.** 12

**ṭen** to place **456.** 11

**Ṭenȧ** name of a god **136.** 9

**ṭenȧ** to separate, be separated **211.** 3, 4; to breach a canal **251.** 10

**ṭenȧt** bank of a canal **251.** 10

**ṭenȧt** name of a festival **20.** 4

**ṭenȧ** name of a chamber (?) **10.** 3

**ṭenȧ**
**ṭenȧt** } basket **317.** 7 *(bis)*; **451.** 12

**ṭenȧu** lot, part **85.** 7

**ṭeni** vessel **130.** 8

**ṭenb** to gnaw, to separate **102.** 5

**Ṭenpu** a proper name **101.** 6

**ṭenem** worms **411.** 4

**ṭenḥui** pair of wings **164.** 11; **413.** 14; **417.** 6; **461.** 11; **505.** 7

**ṭens** weights **390.** 13; **391.** 8; **396.** 15; with **394.** 5

**ṭent** abode **114.** 3

**ṭenṭ** slaughterer **62.** 3

*ṭenṭen* might, valour, mighty one 21. 9; 181. 14; 343. 13; 355. 16

*ṭer* to destroy, to put away 20. 1; 27. 17; 54. 4; 58. 1; 65. 12; 76. 15 *(bis)*; 80. 7; 154. 7; 160. 11; 175. 1; 187. 2; 191. 5; 201. 6; 225. 2; 242. 16; 270. 4; 280. 12, 13; 286. 9; 306. 7, 15; 312. 16; 314. 1; 316. 6, 7; 332. 2; 354. 6; 359. 15; 401. 15; 443. 17; 444. 2; 453. 1; 463. 12; 478. 9; 480. 15; 481. 14; 484. 16; 485. 2; 488. 12; 497. 6; 190. 8; 269. 12; , 147. 8; 209. 3

*ṭerp* to offer up 437. 3; 449. 7; 450. 7

*ṭeref* wisdom, skill, cunning, understanding 386. 13; 446. 3, 4; 447. 12; 488. 14; 481. 1 (with )

*ṭehanti* brow 412. 15

*ṭehen* to meet with the head, to do homage 12. 1; 52. 8; to do homage to the earth 484. 8

*Ṭehent* name of a place 424. 4

*Ṭeḥuti* Thoth 44. 16

*ṭeḥer* hair, skin 504. 11

*ṭes*, *ṭesi* vase 80. 15; 209. 13; 242. 6; 268. 9; 270. 2, 8; 392. 4

*ṭes* to cut 66. 11; 106. 13; smiter 346. 9

*ṭes* flint knife 97. 16; 200. 10 *(bis)*; 219. 4; 253. 8; 263. 12; 341. 16; 376. 8; plur. , 63. 3; 105. 9; 182. 13; 280. 6; 336. 13; 351. 5; 448. 12; 469. 12; slaughters 354. 11

*ṭeser* sacred, holy 369. 11

*Ṭesert* a proper name 432. 12, 14

*ṭeśer* red, ruddy 151. 9; 318. 12; red 454. 8; gore 293. 4; red (of grain) 124. 11; 244. 4; of unguent 341. 11; of hair 343. 5; of feathered fowl 154. 15; of wing 505. 7; of eyes 462. 6; of bone 341. 11; red ones, ruddy ones, bloody ones 183. 4; 201. 2; 205. 3; 319. 4; 343. 14; 355. 16; 356. 4; 364. 13; 469. 12; 483. 7; red faces 115. 3

*Ṭeśer* name of a city and person 324. 10; 469. 5

*ṭeśer* blood 344. 12

*Ṭeśer* the red land, Arabia 486. 1

*Ṭeśert* the red lands between the Nile and the Red Sea 313. 14

*ṭeśert* red flame (?) 99. 7

*Ṭeśert* the red crown 369. 13

*ṭeq*, *ṭeqer* grain, germs (?) 211. 7; 317. 7; 181. 7

*ṭeḳa* to see, sight of 41. 3; 171. 6; 191. 12; 193. 4; 231. 10; 231. 11

*ṭeḳai* seeing, to see 3. 16; 5. 8; 44. 7

*ṭeḳeḳ* sight 3. 4; 70. 6

**ṭeka** to hide 140. 5

**ṭeka** plants 317. 6

**ṭekas** to run towards 22. 12

**ṭet**
**ṭet** hand 8. 3; 43. 7; 115. 15; 234. 5; 275. 14; 316. 1; 353. 5; 412. 6; 414. 9; 502. 14; 503. 16; the two hands 113. 7; 234. 8; , 153. 4; 272. 15; 390. 15

***Ṭet*** . . . . . . . . name of the *mātchabet* 206. 11

***Ṭet-ent-Àuset*** a proper name 391. 5; 393. 4; 394. 14

***ṭetrit*** . . . . . . 504. 11

***ṭeṭṭeṭ***
***ṭeṭṭeṭu*** to stablish, to be stablished 36. 2; 213. 7; 399. 5; 483. 3, 4; 512. 13; 509. 14; 480. 10; 486. 11

***ṭeṭ*** the *ṭeṭ* amulet 211. 15; 212. 2; 310. 4, 6; 383. 9, 10; 402. 6, 9, 11

***ṭeṭ*** , the divine image which was set up in Ṭeṭṭeṭu 72. 2, 5; 79. 1; 19. 6 *(bis)*

***Ṭeṭṭeṭu*** (see *Ṭāṭāu*) a name of the cities of Mendes and Busiris 13. 13; 14. 10; 19. 7 *(bis)*; 20. 5, 8; 23. 3; 24. 12; 38. 10; 60. 2, 11; 72. 1, 2, 3, 5; 74. 16; 75. 4, 8; 79. 1, 8; 81. 8; 83. 5 *(bis)*; 104. 16; 155. 7; 170. 11; 243. 11; 245. 14; 247. 6, 13; 258. 1; 276. 14, 15; 323. 8; 325. 9; 349. 7; 477. 7; 490. 2; 493. 3; 512. 8; 513. 9, 16

# TH.

*θ* thee, thou, thy 37. 14; 138. 4; 143. 2; 202. 11, 12; 205. 7; 207. 4, 6; 264. 8; 342. 2; 349. 15; 350. 3; 351. 4; 403. 4, 5

*θ* with verbs 486. 11; 10. 3; 38. 10; 486. 11; 37. 14; 487. 6; 9. 14; 486. 11

*θ* . . . . . . 10. 8

*θà* with verbs 138. 14; 85. 6; 299. 16; 436. 15; 36. 2; 458. 10; 467. 1; 189. 9; 190. 3; 312. 15; 406. 8; 8. 5; 483. 1; 483. 4; the beam of the scales being exactly level 467. 8; 11. 6; 36. 2; 49. 10; 406. 16; 300. 1; 47. 2; 447. 1, 4; 448. 7; 264. 3; 265. 11; 467. 2; 483. 4; 447. 7; 447. 4; 439. 3; 447. 16; 11. 4; 85. 6; 479. 5; 479. 5; 47. 2;

7. 10; 310. 12; 458. 10; 447. 1; 291. 3; 12. 8; 479. 5; 504. 4; 21. 15; 482. 11; 288. 15; 299. 16; 7. 1; 458. 10; 458. 9

**θånasa** name of a god 419. 13

**θåθå** thighs 436. 1

**θu** thou 164. 1; 249. 9; 266. 14; 267. 5, 9; 363. 7

**θut ås** behold 474. 4; 475. 8

**θui** that 26. 12; 33. 5; 124. 7; 126. 5; 127. 10; 163. 10; 181. 11; 187. 2; 199. 12; 202. 9; 221. 14; 262. 13; 281. 12; 284. 7; 289. 16; 297. 15; 304. 5; 367. 4; 368. 16; 369. 7, 10; 371. 14; 372. 1; 373. 5; 374. 3; 375. 2; 376. 1, 9, 13; 377. 6, 10; 378. 4; 379. 13; 380. 4; 389. 4; 390. 10, 12; 391. 6; 392. 2; 396. 3; 397. 5; 493. 1

**θeb** sandals 382. 15

**θepḥet** storehouse, cave, cavern 457. 6; 481. 8

**θemesu** decrees 110. 2; 111. 9; 262. 5

**θen** this 129. 4; 134. 6; 152. 10; 218. 13; 220. 9; 232. 12; 249. 3; 259. 9; 260. 7; 264. 2; 265. 13; 267. 13; 286. 12; 309. 10; 334. 1; 350. 7; 351. 5; 366. 2; 370. 16; 439. 5; 496. 16; 497. 12

**θen** ye, you, your 34. 15; 63. 11; 90. 18; 95. 8, 9, 10; 102. 11, 12; 107. 6, 9, 10; 115. 1, 2; 126. 12; 136. 10; 166. 3; 171. 2, 6; 174. 8; 175. 7; 206. 8, 10, 13; 207. 2; 222. 13; 231. 5; 259. 9, 10; 260. 1, 3; 269. 14; 280. 5; 292. 8; 301. 15; 302. 5; 303. 5; 306. 5, 14; 307. 5; 313. 12; 329. 8, 9; 332. 12, 13; 363. 10, 11, 12; 364. 1; 365. 1; 367. 6, 7; 369. 11; 371. 6, 7; 372. 2, 3, 4; 375. 7 *(ter)*, 13; 377. 15; 378. 1; 380. 8, 11, 13; 390. 8, 9, 10, 11, 12; 465. 11; 472. 12; 480. 1; 491. 3; 494. 8; 496. 6; 157. 16

**θen** a kind of tree 466. 11

**θen** . . . . . . 505. 12

**θena** a proper name 28. 12; 110. 11; 222. 11; 223. 12; 386. 1; 387. 7; 444. 11; 452. 6

**θennu** worthy 187. 1

**θenemi** one of the forty-two assessors 254. 11

**θent** to distinguish 81. 14

**θenθ** to be great, great 96. 10

**θenfat** throne chamber 471. 7

**θerem** to make to weep 256. 7, 13

**θert** a kind of tree 128. 14

**θeḥennu** unguent 336. 8

**θeḥennu** name of a country 308. 4

**θeḥent** / **θeḥenθ** crystal (?) 66. 15; 67. 7, 8, 11; 135. 6; 177. 5; 226. 7, 11; 263. 8, 14; 310. 6; 447. 13

*θeḥeḥ* to supplicate 175. 10

*θesu* to be firm 89. 14

*θes*, *θesu*, *θest* to lift up, to support, to rise up 46. 16; 56. 13, 16; 111. 5, 11; 152. 5; 176. 12; 204. 15; 230. 11; 277. 3, 6; 288. 13; 301. 12; 353. 13; 376. 10; 380. 11; 402. 7; 412. 11; 445. 8; 449. 14; 455. 14; 456. 2; 241. 1; 411. 2; 421. 2; 445. 7; 450. 4, 11; 476. 11; 482. 16; 445. 8, 11; 463. 10

*θeset* supports, props 308. 5

*θesu* word, speech, law-makers 158. 5; 192. 3; 193. 9; 216. 13

*θes*, *θesu* to bind, to tie up, to twine, to be tied, to coil up ropes 43. 9; 77. 11; 107. 6; 112. 5, 7; 115. 15; 119. 4; 121. 15, 18; 122. 9, 12; 136. 5; 142. 15; 204. 5, 10, 13; 210. 16; 215. 6; 228. 8; 229. 3; 230. 1, 10; 235. 3; 367. 7; 377. 1; 385. 3; 386. 4; 387. 9; 437. 4; 478. 10; 483. 15; bound, tied, coiled up 173. 2; 436. 9

*θes*, *θest* knot 115. 14; 121. 15, 16, 18

*θes*, *θest* back, backbone, joint of the back 29. 6; 204. 5, 10; 220. 5; 406. 7

**θest** / **θesu** vertebrae, joints of the neck **12.** 11; **36.** 9; **44.** 12; **402.** 8; **447.** 3

**θes rer** conversely **57.** 6; **67.** 14; **101.** 12; **109.** 12; **135.** 5; **146.** 10; **192.** 9, 10; **211.** 3; **373.** 2; **406.** 6; **412.** 12; **476.** 14

**θes-ur** a proper name **274.** 10

**θesθes** a garment **338.** 12

**θesem** dog, greyhound (?) **64.** 4; **136.** 11; plur. **33.** 14; **87.** 10, 15; **88.** 3; **341.** 11

**θekem** a proper name **208.** 15

**θet** the buckle amulet **163.** 6; **211.** 15; **212.** 2; **403.** 3, 7

**θet** / **θetet** to take possession of, to seize, to carry off **14.** 5; **24.** 15; **25.** 5; **29.** 8; **56.** 11; **67.** 15; **90.** 8, 11; **93.** 6, 12, 14; **94.** 3; **97.** 7; **98.** 6; **103.** 9; **110.** 1, 4, 5; **122.** 15; **146.** 10; **168.** 4, 9; **170.** 4; **188.** 12; **224.** 4; **225.** 16; **228.** 2; **280.** 3; **305.** 11; **313.** 1; **314.** 3; **331.** 6; **375.** 3; **388.** 4; **405.** 12; **411.** 16; **450.** 1; **482.** 9; **515.** 9; **91.** 14; **92.** 7; **121.** 3; **197.** 1; **198.** 4; **283.** 13; **373.** 15; **375.** 8; **401.** 15; **414.** 13; **495.** 11

**θetiu** seizers, robbers **90.** 10; **158.** 8;

avisher of hearts 346. 3; 357. 12;

ter of women 427. 14

name of a plank

destroyer 415. 10

# TCH.

*ťa* what is sent forth 99. 11

*ťa*, *ťau*, *ťat* safe, sound, in good case 5. 11; 182. 6; 407. 2; 438. 15

*ťa* to split, to cut through 132. 15

*ťa* to grasp 449. 4

*ťa* to set out, to go out 80. 5; 170. 14; 244. 14

*ťa* , to go forth by water, to sail 3. 9; 6. 8; 9. 16; 10. 9; 12. 7; 41. 9; 107. 12; 130. 1; 135. 11; 196. 11; 210. 8; 247. 11; 290. 12; 330. 4; 347. 13; 395. 1; 412. 16; 479. 11; 490. 14; 503. 14; 507. 10, 11; 242. 4; carried by boat 196. 16; 197. 15; 198. 3; 199. 1; one who sails 44. 5; 185. 6; 219. 16; 197. 9; 198. 15

*Ťa āat* "Great Boat" 281. 6

*ťa* to set out, to go forth 22. 8; 441. 12; 442. 4, 15

**taau**     hair (?) **155.** 8

**tau**     birds **394.** 10

**ta**     to carry     "wing-carrier" (Sekhet-Bast-Rā) **415.** 4

**tat**     ...... **338.** 10

**ta**     male **60.** 14

**tai**     phallus, male, husband **204.** 9; **219.** 1; **237.** 2; **255.** 6, 16; **318.** 15; **370.** 9

**ta**

**tau**     to lay hold upon violently, to seize, to rob, to ravish **5.** 2; **65.** 16; **253.** 3, 10; **494.** 7;

**tai**     a plundering **162.** 14

**taut**     twenty **357.** 10; XXth **345.** 16; twenty-one **357.** 14; XXIst **346.** 7

**taui**     the two birds, *i. e.,* Isis and Nephthys **417.** 1

**tafu**     flames **353.** 4

**Tafi**     the souls of Horus and Rá **60.** 1, 4, 6, 8; **157.** 10, 11

**tai**     fiend **37.** 14

**tau**     fiend **292.** 13; **298.** 11

**tait**     fiend **292.** 13

**ṭaiti**     slaughters 372. 6

**ṭamā**     papyrus 409. 15

**ṭamet**     coverings, garments 262. 6

**ṭat**     strong place (?) 256. 8, 14

**ṭat**     strong 236. 15

**ṭat**     measure 464. 16

**ṭatā**     knife 207. 10

**ṭatu**     foul or horrible things 144. 3

**ṭaṭa**     "Head", name of the upper post 206. 3

**ṭaṭa**     head, the crown of the head 136. 6; 142. 16; 197. 4; 198. 10; 450. 14

**ṭaṭat**     the chiefs, or principal divine beings of the gods 15. 11; 18. 11; 22. 16; 48. 4; 59. 12; 63. 1; 86. 1; 87. 8; 92. 15; 96. 3; 107. 7; 110. 3; 147. 10; 174. 3; 271. 16; 273. 5, 15; 275. 1, 3; 276. 5, 6; 277. 9, 16; 282. 3; 291. 2; 294. 1; 313. 10; 323. 11; 332. 15; 346. 13; 380. 5, 7; 438. 11; 445. 12; 469. 10; 470. 2; 471. 9; 501. 7; 502. 12; of Osiris 243. 16; 57. 14; 58. 8; and see 84. 7; 475. 13; 476. 1; the of 111. 18; 246. 15; 59. 13; 70. 8, 11; 71. 11; 72. 12; 74. 8; 272. 2;

76. 13; 81. 5; 82. 6; 84. 9

**ťaťat** the divine chiefs of 71. 11; 78. 11; 81. 6; 83. 4; of 74. 1, 4; 78. 13; 81. 13; 84. 3; of or 75. 11, 13; 79. 10; 82. 1; 83. 8; of 73. 1, 4; 79. 6; 81. 10; 83. 7; of 78. 15; of 72. 10, 11; 79. 4; 81. 8; 83. 6; of 73. 10, 13; 79. 12; 81. 12; 83. 9; of 72. 1, 3; 79. 1; 81. 7; 83. 5; of 76. 3, 7; 79. 14; 82. 1; 83. 10; of 74. 10; 79. 2; 81. 15; 84. 4; of 74. 16; 75. 3; 79. 8; of 84. 8

**ťaťat** funeral mountain 13. 12; 311. 5; 459. 12; plur. 11. 12; 320. 5; 446. 15

**ťaťat** city boundaries 291. 2

**ťāāu** staves 189. 15

**ťābet** burning coals 358. 15

**ťām** sceptre 473; 2; plur. 501. 11; 95. 9

**ťār** to go about in search of, to pry into 266. 6; 289. 14; 404. 5; 516. 3

**ṭārȧ** fortress 467. 6

**ṭebā** to count, to describe 10. 6

**ṭebā** finger 312. 1; 392. 15; two fingers 116. 5; plur. 56. 12; 62. 14; 90. 12; 118. 20; 206. 9; 233. 14; 382. 9; 386. 11; 387. 14; 391. 1; 401. 3; 448. 11; 492. 12; 510. 11; 392. 16

**Ṭebā-en-Sekri** a proper name 394. 13; a proper name 391. 2

**Ṭebā-en-Nemu** a proper name 396. 9

**Ṭebāu-en-Ḥeru-semsu** name of the paddles of the boat 206. 9

**Ṭebāui-en-ṭepu-ā-Rā** a proper name 393. 1

**ṭefau** food upon which the gods and the blessed dead live 1. 13; 22. 10; 55. 10; 126. 11; 160. 7; 208. 15; 217. 2, 15; 222. 15; 223. 9; 365. 2; 366. 6; 376. 15; 380. 11; 428. 4; 466. 11; 487. 16; 507. 2; 512. 3; 514. 14; 424. 14; 434. 14; 43. 12; give ye *tchefa* food 364. 7

**Ṭefet** a place in the Elysian Fields 229. 2; 257. 5

*ṭefeṭ* pupil of the eye **212.** 13; **413.** 2, 15; **414.** 1; **412.** 13

*ṭefṭef* to shed **466.** 9

*Ṭen* a proper name **346.** 14

*ṭenḥu* beam **207.** 8

*ṭenṭen* crushed **106.** 13

*Ṭenṭen* a proper name **472.** 1

*ṭer* to break **34.** 15

*ṭer* since, whilst, when **16.** 5; **59.** 1; **170.** 3; **197.** 8, 9 *(bis)*, 10; **207.** 13; **208.** 5; **306.** 7, 9, 14; **307.** 2; **338.** 6

*ṭer ā* straightway **288.** 13

*ṭer* to the limit of, all, the whole **61.** 7; **169.** 1; **414.** 12, 16; **450.** 5; **485.** 7; **497.** 11

*ṭerenti* since, because **458.** 2

*ṭerentet* since, because **189.** 14; **281.** 7, 14; **285.** 8; **286.** 8; **308.** 14; **334.** 3

*ṭerȧu* constrain **341.** 6; fettered **418.** 2

*ṭerȧ* fort, stronghold, place of restraint **147.** 8; **219.** 13, 15; **280.** 11; **370.** 7; **406.** 11

*ṭerȧu* a part of the body, heel (?) **347.** 11

*ṭerru* hoof **333.** 7

*Ṭeruu* name of a god **75.** 16

**feru** a bird with a plaintive cry 446. 13

**feru** the remotest parts or ends of anything, borders, boundaries, limits, edges, confines, ends of the earth 127. 1, 2 *(bis)*; 153. 9; 185. 4; 247. 6; 412. 9; 474. 9; 168. 6, 9; 168. 14; 286. 14; 163. 1; 188. 6; limitless 132. 16; 408. 8

**feri**
**ferit** ancestress 301. 15; 360. 7

**Fertetuu** the two ancestresses, *i. e.*, Isis and Nephthys 53. 14

**feres** abode, chamber (?) 136. 13

**Feḥes** name of a serpent 373. 2

**fes** self *fes-à* myself 154. 6; 184. 7; 215. 3; 394. 8; 398. 1; *fes-f* himself 8. 3; 9. 11; 11. 11; 40. 9; 49. 2; 51. 12; 53. 1; 55. 3; 56. 3, 12; 60. 14; 65. 13; 67. 1; 87. 6; 91. 7; 92. 4; 100. 7; 109. 8; 119. 14; 167. 9; 285. 9; 291. 9; 306. 10; 309. 14; 345. 12; 357. 8; 441. 10; 464. 2; 480. 13; 505. 4; with his own fingers 510. 11; the god himself 97. 2; *fes-s* herself 346. 3; 449. 4; with her own mouth 416. 16; *fes-sen* themselves 93. 9; 449. 12; *fes-k* thyself 156. 6, 11; 157. 1, 6; 166. 6; 291. 10; 308. 12; 366. 10; 408. 1; *fes-t* thyself 157. 16; 353. 15

***ṭesfu*** bond, restraint **134.** 5; to snare **392.** 13; **394.** 10; cordage **390.** 5; **393.** 14; fowler **391.** 1

***ṭeser*** to make clear or plain (the ways) **165.** 11; **288.** 12; cleared **375.** 11; to arrange in good order **290.** 7

***ṭeser***, ***ṭesert*** to sanctify, holy **48.** 9; **119.** 10; **163.** 11; **171.** 1; **300.** 5; **301.** 5, 7; **312.** 8; **371.** 14; **415.** 6; **433.** 1, 4; **481.** 9; **501.** 10

***Ṭesert*** a name of the funeral mountain **179.** 2; **426.** [illegible]; **490.** 11

***ṭeseru***, ***ṭesert*** holy, holy things, glories, splendours **46.** 4; **163.** 5; **169.** 15, 16; **171.** 4; **172.** 5; [illegible]; with 29. 14; **272.** 6; **426.** [illegible]; 95. 9

***Ṭesert*** a proper name **55.** 11

***Ṭesert*** a proper name **229.** 7, 13

***Ṭeser-tep*** one of the forty-two assessors **259.** 1

[illegible] body **24.** 6; **66.** 5; **146.** 13; **161.** 2; [illegible]; **185.** 1; **190.** 14; **314.** 8; **379.** 11; **388.** 10; **416.** [illegible] 4; **472.** 1, 2; **492.** 2; **503.** 7; **511.** 12; **512.** 13; my own body **154.** 6

[illegible] eternity, everlastingness **9.** 13; **10.** 14; **12.** 3; [illegible] 13; **37.** 10; **39.** 1; **53.** 7 *(bis)*; **70.** 6, 11; **77.** [illegible] 11; **106.** 10; **111.** 10; **113.** 13; **133.** 2; [illegible] **147.** 3; **185.** 2 *(bis)*; **190.** 14; **225.** 16; [illegible] **309.** 5; **315.** 13; **321.** 15; **322.** 1; **324.** [illegible] 14; **364.** 15; **369.** 12; **375.** 14; **376.**

9; 378. 1; 379. 11; 380. 14; 383. 2; 385. 5, 6; 386. 6; 401. 8; 412. 7; 424. 7; 427. 2; 428. 1; 431. 11, 14; 432. 9; 433. 2; 442. 2; 444. 2; 452. 5, 12; 468. 8; 471. 2; 478. 12; 479. 4, 15; 482. 5, 12; 484. 4, 10; 486. 4; 509. 13; 514. 4; 515. 1; 517. 4; 78. 4, 5; 477. 2; 504. 1

*ṭeṭ* to say 1. 5; 3. 14; 4. 13; 5. 14; 111. 5; 115. 11; 442. 15; 446. 13; 456. 7; 488. 3; 489. 11; 494. 8, 14; 495. 7, 13, 16; 503. 14; 507. 10; speech, things said 17. 1; 140. 9

*ṭeṭu*, *ṭeṭ-tu* to declare, to pronounce, spoken, said 60. 14; 77. 1; 80. 10; 261. 8, 10; 310. 5, 15; 408. 16; 462. 9

*ṭeṭet* words, orders 259. 14, 16; 260. 16; 406. 7; 420. 2; 514. 1, 4; 511. 10; 15. 8

*ṭeṭ* see under 52. 1, 7, 16, etc.

*ṭeṭ neḥes* negro speech 416. 2

*ṭeṭfet* reptiles 399. 13; 400. 6, 11, 13

*ṭeṭḥut* a place of restraint 411. 2; 414. 14

*ṭeṭḥu* to be imprisoned 418. 2; 437. 13

*ṭeṭ* an instrument or standard 457. 3

WORDS OF UNCERTAI

w to say 16. 7; 19. 10, 1

11; 457. 16; 458. 14; 459.

224. 7; 218. 14

2; 7. 1; 456. 6;

12; 437. 8;

14; 495. 14

P. 62, l. 16,

p. 245, l. 14, fo

p. 262, l. 1, fo

CPSIA information can be obtained
at www.ICGtesting.com
Printed in the USA
LVHW010620070121
675887LV00004B/142

9 781377 461076